The Way We Listen Now

Bayan Northcott in 2006 (Oliver Northcott)

Poetics of Music
General Editor: Christopher Wintle

The Way We Listen Now
and Other Writings on Music

Bayan Northcott

edited by
Christopher Wintle

drawings by
Milein Cosman and Michael Daley

published in association with
The Cosman Keller Art and Music Trust

Plumbago Books

2009

Plumbago Books and Arts
PO Box 55462
London sw4 0eg

plumbago@btinternet.com
www. plumbago.co.uk

Distribution and Sales:
Boydell & Brewer Ltd.
PO Box 9
Woodbridge
Suffolk IP12 3DF

trading@boydell.co.uk
tel. 01394 610 600
www.boydellandbrewer.com

Boydell and Brewer Inc.
668 Mount Hope Avenue
Rochester
NY 14620, USA

Bayan Northcott, *The Way We Listen Now and Other Writings on Music*
Poetics of Music, General Editor: Christopher Wintle

First published 2009
Supported financially by the Cosman Keller Art and Music Trust

ISBN: 978-0-9556087-2-8 (hardback), 978-0-9556087-3-5 (softback)

Typeset in Adobe Minion Pro

Printed by the MPG Books Group in the UK

Contents

Author's Preface   vii

Editor's Preface   xi

Notes on the Artists   xv

Part One: The Sense of Sound

  1   The Music that Remains   3

  2   Compose Yourself   6

  3   The Way We Listen Now   10

  4   The Time of Music   13

  5   The Music of Time   17

  6   'Could I But Express …'   22

  7   The Expressionist Moment   26

  8   Sight and Sound   29

  9   'Fain Would I Change That Note'   32

 10   New Notes for Old Instruments   37

 11   Survival of the Soundest   41

 12   But is it Mozart? (I)   45

Part Two: The Music of Words

  1   Setting Words to Rights   51

  2   Cross-talk   55

  3   The Librettist's Lament   60

  4   Notes on Auden   65

Part Three: Composing Mortals

  1   After Bach   79

  2   Haydn Alone   84

  3   But is it Mozart? (II)   87

4	Wagner Takes the Stage	90
5	Brahms and Antipathy	95
6	Poulenc *en collage*	99
7	The Case of Ruth Crawford Seeger	104
8	In Search of Walton	108
9	The Once and Future Tippett	116
10	The Britten Aesthetic	121
11	Stravinsky's Britten	127
12	Carter's Relativity Rag	134
13	The 'Found Sounds' of Judith Weir	141

Part Four: The States of Music

1	Earlier Than Thou	147
2	Style or Idea?	150
3	Down with Classical Music	153
4	Behind Closed Doors	156
5	Hollywood and Bust	159
6	Blueprints for an Expanding Universe	163
7	Less Means Less	166
8	Reverberations of 1968	169
9	Fear and Loathing of Modern Music	173
10	Voices of the World, Unite!	176
11	Green and Prescient Land	179
12	Deteriorating Reception on the Third	182
13	It's a Cultural Revolution	185
14	Last Waltz?	188

Envoi: In Search of an Ending

1	In Search of an Ending	193
2	It Tolls for Thee	198
3	Echoes from Selborne	201
4	The Rest is Silence	204

Bibliographical Note	211
Index	215

Author's Preface

To be invited – actually invited – to put together a collection of critical writings in an era when most publishers run for cover at the very suggestion, seemed at first amazing. Then apprehension set in. Even if the heaps of brief reviews and other musical ephemera that had accumulated over forty years of musical journalism were swept aside, there remained a daunting pile of longer texts to reread. How could a modest collection transcend the state of a mere miscellany?

Gradually, however, the material shuffled itself into three possible projects. The first, I had actually been considering for some time. This was to order chronologically the many composer-articles I had written to outline a kind of 'virtual' history of Western music from Perotin to the present day. The second was to compile, from my critical pieces and short reviews, perhaps with linking commentary, an ear-witness record of the last half-century of British music and music making. The third was to bring together, the many articles on the composition, dissemination, criticism and socio-economics of music that could be categorized under the unlovely term 'think-pieces'. This third option seemed most appropriate to a compact volume in a series entitled 'Poetics of Music'. Whether the first two projects will ever get published remains to be seen.

Once the likely writings had been sifted, the book's five-part arrangement emerged quite quickly, though from this stage, the Editor's unerring eye for what to pull and replace was also a strong shaping factor. *Part One* moves from aspects of musical perception to considerations of compositional structure, expression, instrumentation, and so on. *Part Two* examines the word-music relation from the different angles of song setting, speech and music, the librettist's art and the musical engagements of a great poet. *Part Three*, surveying composers from J. S. Bach to Judith Weir, might seem to belong more to my 'virtual' history project; but each of its essays has been included because it embodies a more general issue or historical process. *Part Four* considers the various plights of music amidst the pressures of history, ideology and commerce, though its articles are also broadly arranged in historical order. The pieces on Endings, Bells, Echoes and Silence comprising the *Envoi* might seem to belong more with the musical concerns of *Part One*.

But we agreed their grouping as a recessional made at least more literary sense.

For it was clear by now that, rather than comprising a strictly categorized selection of the texts as first printed, it was better if the book could be read, as nearly as possible, as a coherent whole. Beyond correcting errors and restoring cuts, I have accordingly rewritten here and there to clarify meaning or amplify implication – mostly towards the end of pieces which originally heralded now long-gone musical events. On a few occasions, I have combined separate articles that overlapped in subject into a single piece. Only once have I substantially rewritten an earlier text.

The choice is limited in other ways, too. Although I wrote copiously for *Music and Musicians, The New Statesman*, and the *Sunday Telegraph* throughout the 1970s, *The Way We Listen Now* contains no article earlier than 1980. This is not because I repudiate my previous efforts, but because they mostly seem to belong to the 'virtual' history or ear-witness projects. If, on the other hand, I seem to have drawn disproportionately upon *The Independent*, this is because, between 1988 and 2004, and particularly intensively in the early 1990s, I was granted the unique opportunity to work out an aesthetic position for myself in a regular series of c. 1,200-word lead pieces for the Arts Page.

A first collection of articles is liable to be a moment of truth for any working journalist, not only showing up habitual carelessnesses and repetitions in the writing, but more serious limitations of scope. Yet if much attention is paid in these pages to such composers as Mozart, Beethoven, Stravinsky and Britten, while, say, Handel, Schubert, Verdi and Bartók go little scrutinized, it is not because I love the latter less, but that my responses to them belong in a less dialectical context. And while such thinkers as Tovey, Schenker, Adorno, Hans Keller and Charles Rosen are variously cited as sources of ideas, the names of other authorities, colleagues, friends and acquaintances from whom I am all too conscious of having 'borrowed' notions and insights would stretch for pages.

A handful, however, I have long wished to acknowledge. It was Tom Sutcliffe back in 1968 who initially persuaded – no, goaded – me into writing for *Music and Musicians* and became the first in a succession of music editors, including the late Stanley Sadie at *The Musical Times*, Fiona Maddox and Mark Pappenheim at *The Independent* and Helen Wallace at the *BBC Music Magazine*, who made me feel my articles were genuinely welcome. Then, too, friendships with Alexander Goehr and Elliott Carter have proved lastingly stimulating for their ideas both in, and about music; while with three dear personal friends in particular – Robin Holloway, Oliver Knussen and Julian Anderson – I seem to have been engaged in a vastly suggestive musical discussion that has now lasted for decades.

Bayan Northcott with Elliott Carter at The Maltings, Snape in 1990
(Nigel Luckhurst)

Three names remain to be cited in the present context. The first is Milein Cosman, not only for her material support of this book and the contribution of her inimitable drawings, but also for her ever-inspiring buoyancy of spirit. The second is Christopher Wintle, for the illumination of his own writings, the incredible care he has brought to the presentation of mine, and because his music-book venture seems to me one of the most hopeful developments in recent publishing. And the third is the late Hans Keller, not only for his influence, which, often though I disagreed with him, will be evident throughout the following text, but for his priceless encouragement, both of my writing and my first efforts in composition. I would like to dedicate this book: to Milein and Christopher, and to the memory of Hans.

Bayan Northcott
Chiswick, 2009

Bayan Northcott in 1957 (Roger Bridgman)

Editor's Preface

It is elementary psychology to treat the advice someone gives others as a sign, however unwitting, of the advice they are trying to give themselves. For years Bayan Northcott has been telling certain of his friends to put out their writings in book form: so 'what about a volume of Northcott?' has been the no less elementary reaction. But what about it? After all, Northcott has been at the hub of London 'classical' music for the last 40 years, moving with enviable ease across the chasm that separates critics from the criticized, never pulling his punches, and standing by core musical values when others have happily settled for less. Who, indeed, could be *more* deserving? When a recent promise of funding opened the way, I suggested that the author make a selection of his own. However, I set one condition: that he concentrated on those texts that most clearly distilled their topics – whatever, in fact, would justify the book's inclusion in a 'Poetics of Music' series. Why so? Because his writings convey the sense, not just of an intensely articulate, enviably informed musical intelligence, but also of a composer in his own right (albeit a shy one): for 'on the side' Northcott has a burgeoning musical oeuvre of his own, one that reflects in a personable way the very standards he sets for others. What has duly emerged as *The Way We Listen Now* is a characteristic mix of poetics, aesthetics and actualité.

Like Keller before him, Northcott develops his ideas through an agglomeration of occasional pieces – features, reviews, talks, programme notes and so forth. There are thus many sources to draw upon and many agreements to reach. Of the 47 essays reprinted here, 35 first appeared in *The Independent*, 5 in the *BBC Music Magazine*, 3 in *The Musical Times* and 1 apiece in *The Royal Opera House Programme Book*, the *Times Literary Supplement*, *The New York Review of Books* and *The Aldeburgh Festival Programme Book* for 1994. There is also a thoroughly reworked transcription of a talk for the BBC Radio 3 programme, *Music Weekly*. I am especially grateful to *Independent News and Media Limited* for allowing us to reproduce the 35 essays gratis, though the paper still retains reproduction rights of the original material; and I also thank Oliver Condy of BBC Music Magazines (Bristol), Antony Bye of *The Musical Times* and Kate Hopkins of the Royal Opera House for their co-operation. As a matter of courtesy, I have contacted the other outlets, whether or not they have contracts with the author.

Bayan Northcott, Miriam Quick, Kate Hopkins and I shared the typing and proofing; Julian Littlewood was once more our indefatigable typesetter; Milein Cosman and Michael Daley readily offered their atmospheric drawings; Arnold Whittall and Hugh Wood were the supportive referees; the Department of Music at King's College London happily recognized the project as part of its ongoing research into Hans Keller and his circle; and, most importantly, Julian Hogg and the Cosman Keller Art and Music Trust met the printing costs. My warmest gratitude to them all.

Every edition of a collection of texts is a quest for its own house-style, and *The Way We Listen Now* is no exception. In co-ordinating these writings, I have had to make three main decisions: first, to have works dated according to the year of their completion or the period of their composition if protracted, but not according to the date of their first performance; second, to have composers cited mainly by their surname unless they are still alive or to avoid confusion (Bach, Strauss and so forth); and third, to agree to some modest revisions and updating to justify the 'now' of the title. From this last point of view, the book is a new one, and not just a retrospective selection of the old.

Christopher Wintle
King's College London, 2009

*Top: Bayan Northcott (left) at Dartington Summer School in 1980,
with Mary Thomas, Peter Maxwell Davies, Phillippa Davies,
Alexander Baillie and Ronald Caltabiano*

*Bottom: Bayan Northcott (centre) with Harrison Birtwistle (left)
and Oliver Knussen (right) at The Maltings, Snape in 1991* (Nigel Luckhurst)

Top left: Bayan Northcott (right) with Oliver and Celia Northcott in 1951

Top right: Bayan Northcott in a train from Dieppe to Paris in 1966

Bottom: Bayan Northcott (standing, left) in 1960 as stroke of a coxed four during the Christ Church Regatta in Oxford; the cox was Stephen Hawking (bottom right)

Notes on the Artists

Born in 1921 in Gotha, MILEIN COSMAN was educated in Düsseldorf and Geneva, and, from 1939, at the Slade School of Art in London. During the war she worked for the American Broadcasting Station in Europe, and after it settled in London where she worked as a freelance artist. In 1947 she met and subsequently married the Viennese-born writer, broadcaster and musician, Hans Keller. Her first solo exhibition was held in London in 1949, and was followed by other exhibitions in Europe and America. Her work has been taken into several leading British collections: the National Portrait Gallery in London, the Ashmolean in Oxford, the Fitzwilliam in Cambridge, and the Hunterian in Glasgow. Permanent collections of her drawings of musicians may be seen in the Wigmore Hall in London and the Palais des Beaux-Arts in Brussels. As a specialist in portraiture, she has formed a voluminous and astonishing record of the figures that have shaped music, letters and the arts for the last 60 years.

Born in 1944, MICHAEL DALEY trained in fine art (chiefly sculpture and etching) at Hull Regional College of Art (1960-65) and the Royal Academy Schools in London (1965-68). For fifteen years from 1968 to 1982, he taught art in Brighton, London and Kingston. Since 1983, he has worked principally as an illustrator for newspapers, magazines and children's books, including *The Independent* (for which he received a British Press award in 1987), *The Independent on Sunday*, *The Times Educational Supplements*, *The Financial Times*, *The Daily and Sunday Telegraphs*, *The Spectator* and *Standpoint*. He has also illustrated books for Viking Kestrel, Blackwell's, Methuen and Chatto and Windus. He has been a broadcaster and reviewer for a variety of papers and magazines, and in 1993 was co-author with James Beck of *Art Restoration – The Culture, The Business, The Scandal* for John Murray. The illustrations of his included here accompanied Bayan Northcott's articles when they first appeared in *The Independent*, with the exception of the picture of Elliott Carter, which is drawn from a different source.

Part One

Hans Keller, Milein Cosman

The Sense of Sound

1 The Music that Remains

Rattling homewards on the tube, your vacant mind is suddenly invaded by the development section of the first movement of Beethoven's *Pastoral Symphony* (1808) – and not just a phrase of it, revolving obsessively like a much-plugged pop song, but the whole luminous length, with its key shifts, twin climaxes and circuitous working-round to the recapitulation. At which point, you realize you failed to notice the last station and that the person opposite is eyeing you curiously, as though your inner absorption had somehow become visible. Granted, you have known the *Pastoral* for years, but it is some time since you last heard it either live or on disc. So why should Beethoven's alfresco jubilation overtake you in a stuffy Piccadilly-line carriage right now? A simple association such as the clatter of the train wheels with the music's recurrent tum-tiddle-um-tum rhythm? Or intimations of some deeper process whereby the voluntary or involuntary recall of musical states and structures helps to 'make sense' of our lives – a latter-day manifestation, even, of the mnemonic function music has apparently played in more 'primitive' societies since the dawn of time?

But then, according to the testimony of some of its greatest practitioners, composition itself is often an effort of memory: an attempt to recapture and develop an inspiration that may have flashed through the consciousness months, even years, before the work is begun, and that might have constituted anything from a fugitive melody to a compressed image of an entire form. The complication is that the themes and processes by which such inspirations are pinned down may soon begin to interact and lead lives of their own, so that, by the time a work is completed, its relation to the initial idea can seem pretty indirect, even to its own composer. After all, thematicism is a mnemonic process in itself, a reminder of how previous composers may have handled comparable materials or, in the later stages of a new composition, of how its own earlier stages were handled. We think of the interplay of leitmotifs in *The Ring* (1853-74) as a consummate musical device for commenting upon dramatic motivation. But for Wagner, its primary purpose must surely have been methodological: the best way he could devise to fill out those vast time-spans. By remembering previous appearances of his leitmotifs, he could always come up with appropriate options for what to do next.

Performers obviously cannot afford the luxury of their listeners, recalling just the 'best bits' of a work in any old sequence – even if the purpose of memorizing a score note-perfect may be, paradoxically, to recapture something of the supposed spontaneity of the composer's initial conception. For many players and singers, the actual process of memorizing seems to be intensely physical. Pianists often speak of getting a work 'under' or 'into' the fingers; and maybe the ability to encode a long and elaborate composition as a complex succession of conditioned reflexes ultimately depends upon the most ancient associations of music and physical movement. Yet there are some pianists who appear to rely as much, if not more, upon a visual memory of the actual score. Before launching into some large-scale recital piece such as Schumann's *Fantasy* in C major (1838), Charles Rosen has been known to plead with his listeners not to follow the performance from copies of the music in case they have different editions from the one he knows. Evidently, the subliminal sight or sound of a page being turned at a different bar from the page in his mind's eye is enough to play havoc with his memory.[1]

No less than in composing or performing, memory is bound to be a factor in listening if the work in progress is of any length or variety. Even the most casual listener – one, perhaps, who pays attention to the tunes but drifts away during the more developmental bits – is likely to become aware, not only that the opening idea of the *Pastoral*'s second movement comes back several times, but also that its accompaniment is more richly figured on each reappearance. The cognitive ear seems to distinguish between foregrounds and backgrounds, to group sonorous similarities and contrasts in time, in much the same way as Gestalt psychology tells us the eye distinguishes figures and grounds, and relates shapes in space.

Indeed, it might seem rather difficult to compose music so complex or undifferentiated as entirely to confound sorting out by the aural memory, though certain twentieth-century composers have had a good try. The post-war avant-garderies of such figures as Karlheinz Stockhausen and Brian Ferneyhough, father of the so-called New Complexity, have been reviled often enough for their dissonance. But the real problem is surely those composers' doctrinaire avoidance of exact or even approximate repetition – denying the ear any centre of stability amid the perpetual welter of variation. On the other hand, the minimalist processes of Steve Reich and Philip Glass, by inducing a kind of present-centred trance, have tended to suppress the functions of recollection and anticipation essential to traditional large-scale forms. Such musics seem to linger in the memory as little more than generalized sound; a turbid flux in the one case, a monotonous trundle in the other.

Not, of course, that all traditionally composed music is equally memorable. The degree of memorability often seems to depend upon the extent to which the composer has 'meaningfully contradicted' – to borrow Hans Keller's phrase

– the expectations set up by the conventions of his chosen genre or style.[2] Where the contradictions are minimal, in a more routine Vivaldi concerto, say, or one of Donizetti's lesser operas, it is possible to come out of a performance with the mind happily composing Vivaldi or Donizetti of its own – until one suddenly realizes that, of the actual work just heard, one can recall scarcely a note. Yet, perhaps the most salient cases are those composers who push the contradictions *almost* too far. It is unlikely that Arnold Schoenberg's later music will ever be widely loved. But, on the other hand, and despite decades of opposition, it has not gone away. This resilience seems to turn upon the propensity of passages even in his densest, fiercest works – the *Variations for Orchestra* Op. 31 (1926-28), say, or the opera *Moses und Aron* (1930-32) – somehow to clarify, to grow more tractable, even haunting in the memory. Maybe more perceptive nineteenth-century listeners had a similar experience with the unprecedented complexity of Beethoven's *Grosse Fuge* (1825-26). It is an aspect of musical memory that demands further investigation.

"I'm fond of classical music, but I don't really understand it," lay listeners are forever telling professional musicians – usually meaning that they unable to read notation, play an instrument or bandy about the correct technical terms. Yet, to be able to recall and savour long passages of favourite works, as many ordinary music-lovers surely can, *is* arguably to understand. And all the refinements of musical analysis and historical background are, or should be, simply ways of explaining that understanding. It was, in fact, Schoenberg of all people who asserted – and given the reception of his own music, one can imagine with what wistfulness – that 'music is only understood when one goes away singing it, and only loved when one falls asleep with it in one's head and finds it still there on waking up next morning.'[3]

NOTES

Source: 'The Melody Lingers On', *The Independent*, 8 December 1995.

1   Charles Rosen, *Piano Notes*, London, Allen Lane, 2003, pp. 130-31.
2   Hans Keller, 'Music 1975', *1974 (1984 minus 9)*, London, Dobson, 1977, pp. 135-37.
3   Arnold Schoenberg, 'Why No Great American Music?', *Style and Idea*, ed. Leonard Stein, tr. Leo Black, London, Faber, 1975, p. 180.

2   *Compose Yourself*

So, you have been teaching more or less willing children the piano over the last few years, and composing the odd pieces on the side – piano studies, bits of incidental music for school plays, nothing ambitious. But now a college chum has asked for an item or two to include in a piano album for Grade V he's compiling. You strum the keyboard a bit in search of an idea and, nothing much emerging, lapse almost absent-mindedly into a long-familiar Bach prelude. Then suddenly a mistake, and the way the fingers follow it through jerks at your attention. You play it over again – just a handful of notes, but with a shape, a charge and attractiveness of their own. Start there.

Instantly, the old music-college training snaps into action. Adding a little rhythmic kick to the note-shapes, you try this harmony and that by way of accompaniment, selecting a couple of chords that work and spreading them in figuration to add movement. In no time, there's a complete two-bar chunk. What next? Repeat for another two bars with a twist at the end to lead onwards? Or balance it with an 'answering' two-bar phrase – the same shape sort of reversed? Fiddling with the initial shape, you find it goes quite nicely with itself in canon at the fifth – but that this leads the harmony away from the home key too quickly to come so early in the piece. Save till later.

At which point you realize, with a sinking heart, that your starting idea bears a suspicious resemblance to a woodwind phrase in your favourite Sibelius symphony. No more than a suppressed memory, then? But it's not quite the same: two of your pitches are in reverse order to Sibelius and, of course, the two contexts are quite different. Would anyone else notice? And aren't the classics full of moments that remind us of other classics, anyway? So keep going. How about two bars plus answering two bars, then repeat the four-bar unit with the odd harmonic change and a new twist at the end, leading to …?

Well, after an opening paragraph, all good classical pieces are supposed to move from the tonic to the dominant – C major to G, say. But how about making it the dominant minor – much less usual in a major-key piece? By the end of a couple of hours, you've drafted 16 plausible bars – halfway there! And if the little canon is used to open the second half, it will simply be a matter of finding your way back to the home key and restating your opening material to finish it off. Tomorrow, though; for now, some urgent shopping. Before closing the piano, you repeat over that unexpected initial idea. Yes, it still has its specialness. So was its emergence an accident or a discovery, a gift, or even, in its utterly modest way, a bit of an inspiration?

Diving into the local bookshop 20 minutes later, you notice in the tiny music section a newly published paperback entitled – talk about synchronicity – *Music and Inspiration* by Jonathan Harvey (presumably the rather modernistic composer you've occasionally heard on Radio 3, though there was that rather striking electronic piece with bells …). Accordingly, you purchase and bear the book home, opening its introduction to read:

> Most composers would readily admit that inspiration, at some stage of the compositional process, is a necessary component of a fully satisfying work … it is the persistence of a particular experience of inspiration – transcending differences of period, nationality, social class, gender, religious and philosophical beliefs, and musical style – that I am concerned above all to show in this book.[1]

Rather flattered by the implication that the beginning of your own little piece was the same kind of experience as the inspirations of Beethoven, Wagner et al, you continue sampling the book for some time, noting that the first three of its four chapters are entitled 'The Conscious and the Unconscious', 'The Composer and Experience' and 'The Composer and the Audience'. Evidently, the idea is to work from inspiration as an innate mental experience 'outwards' to its cultivation by the composer's personal experience and training, and beyond these to its reception by his or her listeners – which seems an obvious way of going about it. But then, there's that final chapter, 'The Composer and the Ideal', plus the author's personal Postscript about Buddhist meditation and spiritual 'liberation from the fear of death' which suggest that a book you took to be an enquiry has somehow turned more into a religious tract.

Has this bias affected the choice of composer-testimonies that comprise the book's 'evidence', you wonder? Some of the quotes chime nicely with your own simple experience. Aaron Copland, for instance, writes: 'These germinal ideas … seem to be begging for their life, asking their creator, the composer, to find the ideal envelope, to evolve a shape and a colour and content that will most fully exploit their creative potential.'[2] But what exactly does Harvey think the atheistic Brahms really meant when he allegedly remarked: 'A good theme is a gift from God'? And why does the book not cite that other Brahms statement that

> There is no real creating without hard work. That which you would call invention, that is to say, a thought, an idea, is simply an inspiration from above, for which I am not responsible, which is no merit of mine. Yes, it is a present, a gift, which I ought even to despise until I have made it my own by right of hard work …

– suggesting that inspiration is only what you make of it, and what you make of it can be learned as craft or acquired by experience?[3]

For that matter, wasn't the donnée of your little piano piece itself largely preordained by the kind of thing you were aiming at, by your keyboard training, and by the Bach prelude – not to mention the Sibelius memory? So was your pleasure in its discovery any different, say, from a lucky throw in darts, or suddenly stumbling on the solution to a problem?

Just then, your eyes light on a college textbook you've kept on your shelf ever since: *The Musical Mind: The Cognitive Psychology of Music* by John A. Sloboda.[4] Turning to its long chapter on 'Composition and Improvisation', with its careful distinctions between the conscious and unconscious elements in play and the author's blow-by-blow commentary upon composing his own little choral piece, you're reminded this is still the most convincing account of the experience you've come across (or, at any rate, the closest to your own). If only Harvey had been as comparably rigorous in defining the aspects of inspiration that are actually closer to skill, luck, problem-solving and so on, his contention that there remains a common core of numinosity might convince a bit more, you conclude as you lay his book aside.

Only then do you realize that the provisional ideas for the 16-bar second half of the piece have been working themselves out at the back of your mind all along, and that you can now virtually write it out straight out – which means that tomorrow morning you can have a go at another one. After all, didn't Brahms and Stravinsky swear by routine as the fount of inspiration? And didn't Tchaikovsky, of all people, write: 'I sit down to the piano regularly at nine o'clock in the morning and *Mesdames les Muses* have learned to be on time for the rendezvous'?[5]

NOTES

Source: 'So Where Does Music *Really* Come From?' *The Independent*, 29 October 1999; rev. 2008.

1   Jonathan Harvey, *Music and Inspiration*, London, Faber, 1999, pp. x and xv.
2   Aaron Copland, 'Music as an Aspect of the Human Spirit', *Copland on Music*, New York, Doubleday, 1960, p. 63.
3   G. Henschel, *Personal Recollections of Johannes Brahms*, Boston, 1907, p. 22, cited in: Imogen Fellinger, 'Brahms's Way: A Composer's Self-view' in: *Brahms 2: Biographical, Documentary and Analytical Studies*, ed. Michael Musgrave, Cambridge, CUP, 1987, p. 53.
4   John A. Sloboda, *The Musical Mind: The Cognitive Psychology of Music*, Oxford, OUP, 1985.
5   Quoted in: Murray Schafer, *British Composers in Interview*, London, Faber, 1963, p. 17.

[Ed.: In 'Notes in the Margin', *The Independent*, 24 February 1990, the author considers the increasing significance accorded to compositional sketches over the last century or so, noting that: '… as recently as one hundred years ago, a fascination with composers' working processes would still have been widely regarded as incidental to the aesthetic effect of finished pieces, if not an outright invasion of creative privacy. Two hundred years ago, it would scarcely have been understood at all … The fact that relatively few Mozart sketches have come down to us is traditionally taken as evidence of an instant ability to conceive his works entire before setting down a note. But it could equally be that he simply chucked most of such material away because he could see no reason to keep it once a final score had been roughed out. Even Beethoven's exceptional hoarding of sketches over his entire career may have been primarily as an *aide-mémoire* to the innumerable scraps of unused material scattered among them.

It was only with the rise of Romantic self-absorption that interest in the creative process itself began to burgeon – and perhaps only with the studies of Beethoven's sketchbooks which the German scholar, Gustav Nottebohm, began to publish in the 1860s, that this became a musical issue. Nottebohm had a terrific impact upon the academic and, ultimately, popular image of Beethoven because the laborious working methods he revealed seemed so exactly to confirm the sense of struggle listeners had always discerned in the finished pieces. Yet this very success also seemed to serve notice upon living composers that in future their sketches too might be considered scholarly fair game.

The most interesting reaction came from Nottebohm's close friend, Brahms. While avidly collecting manuscripts from Schütz to Wagner and encouraging the researches of a whole generation of musicologists, Brahms proceeded rather pointedly to cover his own traces: in fact the only major bunch of sketches he allowed to survive from his entire career was for the *Variations on a Theme of Haydn* – a work that seems to have been especially close to his heart. Nor was he the last composer to fight a rearguard action against intrusiveness. Perfectionist Ravel was similarly concerned that his working drafts should be tidied away, while a son-in-law of Sibelius recounted [to the author] how he was just in time to save from one of the bonfires of the Master's later years the entire sketches of the Fourth Symphony.'

Towards the end of this article, the author asks: 'Is our understanding of Beethoven enhanced or undermined by the revelation that at almost any point during their protracted gestation, many of his seemingly immutable masterpieces might easily have turned out quite differently? And if Stravinsky's habit of piecing his works together from separate patches seems to underline his originality, could not Elgar's use of the same method equally be seized upon by those who would criticize his structures for lack of organic unity?']

3   The Way We Listen Now

The hall quietens, the famous conductor flicks a silent downbeat and the orchestra rips into Beethoven's Fifth. But what is the audience actually listening to? As far as its sprinkling of professionals is concerned, probably something pretty specialized. In one row, perhaps, sits a rival conductor, mentally scoring points over tempi and balance; in another, a scholar marvelling yet again at how Beethoven conjured such a blaze from those unpromising early sketches. Somewhere else, maybe, a young academic is reliving his semiotic analysis of the work, while the critics dotted here and there are desperately hoping for the odd fresh perception to verbalize before the dreaded deadline.

Among the lay intelligentsia, there is possibly a historian who hears the Fifth as a document of the Age of Revolution, a literary lady who keeps remembering that passage about gnomes tramping over the universe in E. M. Forster's *Howards End*, or a TV producer wondering which bits to use in his forthcoming feature on the last days of Hitler. Then, of course, there are the gramophiles, bridling at the imperfections of live performance compared with the 30 immaculate recordings, from Herbert von Karajan to Roger Norrington, they obsessively revolve at home. But most numerous, doubtless, are those enthusiasts who have kept Beethoven live and the live concert more or less viable for the last 200 years – the 'ordinary' music lovers.

Some will be there simply for the tunes or the pictures the symphony stimulates in the mind. But others, whether or not they can play or sing a bit, may be more deeply musical in the sense of being able to give themselves entirely to the work's unfolding, and to recall in detail long stretches of it between performances. Yet, as they scan the programme note with its jargon of key changes and thematic derivations, these are just the hearers most likely to be visited by a doubt as to whether absorption is enough, whether they ought not to be consciously listening *out* for things. Pressed to articulate their experience, they will often take refuge in the regret that, while they love music, they are not sure whether they 'understand' it.

In 1940, there died a scholar, teacher and critic who took a more downright stand on behalf of what he called the 'naïve listener' than any other British musician of the twentieth century. Born in 1875, Donald Francis Tovey would probably have liked to be remembered as a composer; but it seems his substantial output – including an endless 'cello concerto for Pablo Casals – rarely escapes from his overpowering reverence for the great Austro-German tradition of Bach to Brahms. As a pianist, he had a greater success, regularly appearing for 20 years with the celebrated string quartet led by Brahms's friend, Joseph Joachim. Yet it is his for his writings, which he began to assemble during his later years as Professor and conductor of the Reid Orchestra in Edinburgh, that he is really remembered: notably, his music entries for the *Encyclopedia Britannica* and the seven volumes of programme notes published as *Essays in Musical Analysis*.[1] Tovey held that whatever residual mystery might inhere in any work of genius, it ought to be possible to analyse its technical means and aesthetic effect in terms ordinary listeners could understand from their own experience. His note on Beethoven's Fifth begins with a refutation of the notion that 'the whole movement is built up of the initial figure of four notes'. On the contrary, he argues, what is remarkable about the movement is 'the length of its sentences' – for which the ta-ta-ta-<u>ta</u> figure supplies the momentum as it does in many other Beethoven works of the period.[2]

Tovey's downgrading of the thematic aspect here is typical of his empirical English contempt for those nineteenth-century German analysts who wanted to turn thematicism into a system, just as his careful detailing of the uniqueness of Beethoven's second movement represents his opposition to what he called the 'jelly-mould' theory of form. Maybe the note for the *Fifth Symphony* (1808) is not Tovey at his best: for this, one has to go to the long Beethoven and Schubert articles posthumously collected in *Essays and Lectures on Music*,[3] which in truth are likely to stretch any 'naïve' reader to the limit. Yet in a mere seven, quirky but highly readable pages, a notion has been conveyed of musical form as a dynamic process, a kind of drama unfolding in time according to its own principles.

It was a liberating notion in Tovey's day, and it can seem so still. If his essays grew out of an essentially nineteenth-century tradition of descriptive aesthetics, his influence has continued to touch such accessible latter-day writing as Robert Simpson on Beethoven, Bruckner and Sibelius, or *The Classical Style* (1971) of Charles Rosen. Yet, by concentrating on what is actually heard in performance, Tovey's commentaries have been attacked by those who believe the real job of the analyst is to get to the deep structures, the hidden ideas that unify the surface contrasts of musical forms.[4] There is a paradox here. For while Beethoven's Fifth takes some 35 minutes to play, when we think about it, we may experience a composite entity of its salient characteristics in a matter of seconds – and that entity may be closer to Beethoven's own moment of conception, and reveal more unexpected connections, than an actual performance. Yet, only listeners who have passed through a modern university music department, or who have scanned Ian Bent's masterly survey of musical analysis in *The New Grove*, can have any idea of the frenzied controversy such paradoxes have inspired in the seemingly endless quest to explain how music actually works.[5]

Over the last couple of centuries or so, virtually every intellectual development has been brought to bear on its forms and processes: models derived from logic, mathematics, psychoanalysis, phenomenology, structuralism, information theory – it goes on and on. Writings have poured forth ranging from the avowed populism of a Tovey to prodigies of figures and graphs one suspects only three and a half other colleagues in the faculty could ever understand. Taken up with conferences, research projects and journals, it was for a time possible for a musician to pass his working life as a 'career analyst'.

Yet one gets the strong impression that less is being claimed for analysis these days than of yore; that most analysts would now agree it is impossible to encompass all aspects of a work in a single methodological approach. Many have also become more aware, as they scrutinize the notes on the page, of the claims of historians, sociologists and philosophers of music that works can only be fully understood in the context of their period, society or the history of ideas. Meanwhile, those who cleave to internal structure or external context alike may continue to suspect that the 'naïve', or as Tovey sometimes called him, the 'ideal' listener, who takes in a work instinctively without the conscious mediation of theories and commentaries, is getting a more 'whole' experience than any of them.

But does the 'naïve listener' really exist? Not any more, at any rate so Hans Keller argued: the constant demotion of great music to background stimulation and the infinite repeatability of recordings have weakened the powers of concentration of even the most musical listeners. The hall quietens, the conductor flicks a silent downbeat, the orchestra raps ta-ta-ta-ta, and the mystery of what each one of us is actually hearing deepens.

NOTES

Source: 'The Way We Hear Now', *The Independent*, 14 July 1990.

1   Donald Francis Tovey, *Musical Articles from the Encyclopedia Brittanica*, ed. Hubert Foss, London, OUP, 1944; *Essays in Musical Analysis* (1935-39), ed. Hubert Foss, London, OUP, 1944.
2   Donald Francis Tovey, *Essays in Musical Analysis: Symphonies*, ed. Hubert Foss, London, OUP, 1944, pp. 38-44.
3   Donald Francis Tovey, *Essays and Lectures on Music*, ed. Hubert Foss, London, OUP, 1949.
4   Hans Keller, 'The Unity of Contrasting Themes and Movements' (*The Music Review*, Vol. 17, 1956) in: *Mozart Piano Concerto in C major, K. 503*, ed. Joseph Kerman, New York, Norton, 1970, pp. 176-200.
5   See: Ian Bent, 'Analysis' in: *The New Grove Dictionary of Music and Musicians*, ed. Stanley Sadie, London, Macmillan, 1980, Vol. 1, pp. 340-88.

4 The Time of Music

For page after Olympian page, the scherzo of the Symphony No. 9 in D minor has been bounding along in its *molto vivace* triple time. Suddenly the score asks for an acceleration and the music tumbles into a duple-time trio section marked presto. Though tricky to bring off, the notation would present no doubt as to Beethoven's meaning … had he not taken steps a couple of years after the work's first performance in 1824 to add at this point an utterly bemusing metronome mark.

Which is a bit ironic, considering that the metronome was always supposed to be an 'objective' measure of tempo. Certainly, its introduction in the second decade of the nineteenth century was no mere historical accident. Up till then the vast bulk of music had been composed in standard genres for immediate performance under the control of the composer himself. Baroque scores often contain tempo indications only where something unusual is required, while the directions on scores of the age of Haydn and Mozart are generally confined to a handful of normative terms for tempi ranging from *largo* to *presto*. But by Beethoven's generation, the cult of originality was stimulating an expectation for the unusual; the internationalization of publishing was spreading performances beyond the composer's control, and with a standard repertoire beginning to accumulate, it was apparent that some music might long outlast its creator. Beethoven had openly begun to talk of composing 'for a future age'.

So when in 1813 his dubious entrepreneurial friend, Johann Nepomuk Maelzel, first developed a 'musical chronometer', predecessor of the metronome he was to patent four years later, Beethoven, not surprisingly, sanctioned an announcement to the effect that he looked upon this invention 'as a welcome means with which to secure the performance of his brilliant compositions in all places in the tempos conceived by him, which to his regret have often been misunderstood' – and in due course, published sets of metronome marks for his first eight symphonies.[1] Among his successors Berlioz was particularly meticulous in his metronomic indications, even experimenting at one stage with a primitive electric device for coordinating tempi. Some subsequent composers – Verdi possibly, Bartók certainly – began deploying the metronome, not just to fix the tempi of completed pieces, but also to govern the pacing and proportioning of works in progress. And since the Second World War, composers as different as Elliott Carter, Robert Simpson, Karlheinz Stockhausen and Harrison Birtwistle have used metronomically defined grids of tempo relationships as actual starting-points in the composition of complex structures.[2]

Yet a surprising number of major figures seem to have felt either indifferent to the metronome, like Bruckner, ambivalent, like Richard Strauss, or actually hostile, like Sibelius, who could only be induced to supply exact speeds for his later works under pressure. Even more saliently: after carefully marking their earlier works, both Wagner and Brahms turned polemically against the gadget, while Mahler scarcely supplemented the copious verbal tempo indications scattered through his scores with a singly metronome mark. Mahler's objection was that, in the real world of performance, tempi inevitably fluctuate all the time; Wagner and Sibelius considered the most metronomically exact performance pointless if the spirit was lacking, while Brahms simply wrote 'I never believed that my blood and a mechanical instrument go well together'.[3]

What they were all arguing in effect was that a convincing tempo is as much a matter of articulation and expression as of correct pulse – and, by implication, that these considerations are all, to a degree, variable according to context. Even before a piece reaches performance, composers frequently find themselves modifying the tempo of, especially, fast music as they work out invention and scoring in more detail. In some notorious cases they have gone on changing their minds about tempi for years after an initial launching: one has only to contrast the metronome marks in the two editions that Schumann published of his First Symphony (1841/53) or in Stravinsky's two versions of *Petrushka* (1911/47). Then, of course, there are the variables of the performing situation itself – the number and proficiency of performers, for instance, or the acoustics of the venue – which may necessitate a considerable adjustment of pulse between one reading and another to re-create the desired effect. Not least, there are those ineluctable, almost imperceptible changes of taste and pace that affect musical performance over generations, like gradual shifts in the pronunciation of common speech.

Little that Beethoven seems to have worried about any of these matters in his first enthusiasm for Maelzel's little clockwork pendulum. But the metronome marks he duly scribbled into his scores have worried plenty since. Many of these tempi appear – or have come to appear – so fast that some scholars have wondered whether Beethoven's increasing deafness had effectively cut him off from the practicalities of performing or his metronome was simply out of order. The trouble with such suspicions is that not all the marks seem unreasonable; and we also have to take into account the subsequent broadening in Beethoven interpretation initiated by Wagner in which the focus of attention passed from the dancing pulse to the singing phrase – a tradition that has been carried into our own time by such conductors as Wilhelm Furtwängler and Leonard Bernstein. Yet in their determination to counter this tradition and get back as far as possible to Beethoven's original intentions, not even the most determined of our authenticists have hitherto quite come to terms with the problems of the Ninth Symphony.

It is not just that the added markings for the opening movement and the Adagio seem so rapid for the grandeur of the one and the serenity of the other –

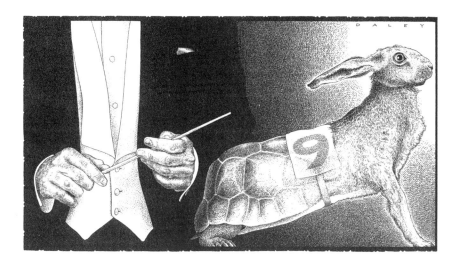

while that for the scherzo, by contrast, is acceptably moderate. There are also two junctures – the link from scherzo to trio, and the relation of the bouncy march-like tenor solo in the finale to the ensuing orchestral fugato – where the markings seem hopelessly ambiguous. Though scholars of the stature of Peter Stadlen have given years of their lives to investigating how the by-now stone deaf Beethoven, possibly with the help of his nephew Karl, might have arrived at, or even garbled the indications, these irrefutably seem to suggest tempi at both points that could be either far faster or slower than might be expected.[4] In his much praised 'authentic' recording with the London Classical Players on HMV, Roger Norrington still fell a bit short of the metronome speeds in the first and third movements, and opted for the slower solutions in the trio and march; but the trio comes out at an uninspiring plod, while the slow march necessitates an unmarked *accelerando* into the fugato.[5] Since then, however, the Anglo-American conductor Benjamin Zander and his semi-amateur, but professional-sounding Boston Philharmonic have brought out a reading that realizes the fast speeds and options throughout.[6]

   The first and third movements, though a bit stiff in execution, lose surprisingly little power at the metronomic speeds; and an interesting new set of proportions emerges, with the scherzo – all repeats observed – running only a little shorter than the opening movement and longer than the Adagio. Of the trouble spots, the quick-step march charging straight into the fugato convinces at least this pair of ears, not least because Schiller's text at this point comprises an injunction to 'haste ye, brothers, on your way'. But the incredibly fast trio is more of a shock, almost a new piece. Though Zander and his forces prove it possible to bring off at this speed, the suspicion must linger here, at least, that something came adrift in Beethoven's metronomic calculations, and that conductors who simply aim instinctively at a tempo somewhat short of the faster option may have been getting it right all along.

NOTES

Source: *The Independent*, 4 July 1992.

1   See: *Thayer's Life of Beethoven*, rev. and ed. Elliott Forbes, Princeton, Princeton UP, 1967, pp. 543-44 and 686-88.

2   See, for instance, the metronomic gearing of the 'metrical modulations' in most of Elliott Carter's works from his *Cello Sonata* (1948) onwards; the metronomic relation of contrasting tempi to a single pulse in Robert Simpson's *Symphony No. 9* (1985-86); the grid of metronome markings governing the cross-cutting of the three orchestras in Karlheinz Stockhausen's *Gruppen* (1955-57); and the 'pulse labyrinth' of graded tempi prefacing Harrison Birtwistle's *Silbury Air* (1977).

3   *Johannes Brahms: Life and Letters*, ed. Styra Avins, tr. Joseph Einsinger and Styra Avins, Oxford, OUP, 1997, p. 559.

4   See: Peter Stadlen, 'Beethoven and the Metronome', *Soundings*, No. VII, 1978, pp. 2-18, and No. IX, 1982, pp. 38-73.

5   London Classical Players, cond. Roger Norrington, EMI CDC 7 49221 2.

6   Boston Philharmonic Orchestra, cond. Benjamin Zander, Pickwick, NCD 40.

5   *The Music of Time*

How long is a piece of music? Surely, as long as it takes to perform. Or is it so simple? A work packed with forward-moving invention can leave a very different impression of length from a work filled with minimally varied repetition, even though their clock-timings are identical. And what of those pieces so boring they sound endless, or those moments so sublime that they seem to suspend all sense of time? W. H. Auden argued that music is actually about our 'experience of Time in its twofold aspect, natural or organic repetition, and historical novelty created by choice' – which might suggest at least a starting point for discussion.[1] Yet the mighty *New Grove Dictionary* (1980) itself contains no entry on the overall topic of 'Time'.

Why, with a few exceptions, have scholars, theorists and analysts been so reluctant to explore the time element in music – as distinct from matters of metre, tempo and so on? After all, the more dramatic genres such as opera or the symphony depend upon timing; many composers have expressed their individuality through a highly personal sense of time-scale – think only of Bruckner or Webern – while in our own era, Stravinsky, Messiaen, Elliott Carter, Stockhausen and Harrison Birtwistle have all had illuminating things to say about their own handling of time. And, working from these, it should not be so difficult to construct a few helpful distinctions.

It is generally agreed that Western music of the last four or five hundred years has been dominated to a degree unique among the musics of the world by a progressive, dynamic or goal-orientated sense of time. Such a notion, of course, implies a duality between stable and labile principles. When we listen to a Beethoven symphony, we do not lose touch with the background flow of ordinary, or 'real' time over the half-hour or so it takes to perform. But our foreground attention is engrossed by the way Beethoven seems to vary that flow, to push and pull at it through the interplay of statement and development, tension and release: Stravinsky has spoken of 'the leverage of Beethoven's timing'.[2]

The external analogy of the dynamic concept of time with Western traditions of rhetoric, narrative and drama is obvious enough; the internal analogy with the workings of collective or individual psychology more obvious still. And the 'time sweep' of the best music of such a contemporary composer as Carter suggests just how much potential for renewal the concept retains. True, there have always been elements in the Church to attack that dynamism, that individualism, as a betrayal of the essentially spiritual function of music, just as vulgar Marxism has sometimes sought to brand it as the aggressive expression of Western capitalism. But only in the present century have alternative time concepts gained ground in compositional practice itself.

There is no temporal duality in Nature: songs of birds, sounds of wave and thunderstorms last as long as they last. So do the 'abstract' sounds generated in electronic music, until deployed in some more recognizably traditional or 'human' context. For that matter, the simpler vernacular forms of many cultures, such as work songs – exactly fitting the daily actions they regulate – exist solely in ordinary or 'real' time. Not surprisingly, composers inspired by the explorations of the ethnomusicologists or striving to define a new electronic music – or just in love, like John Cage, with unstructured environmental noise – have increasingly asked whether 'real' time should not be restored as the basis of all music. But none has asked or acted so influentially as Messiaen.

Since Messiaen's world-view was entirely theocentric, since he viewed composing wholly as a matter of revealing the divine order and celebrating the mysteries of the Church, it follows that his music can countenance no real degree of argument or progression – the goal is already reached. Where rhythm in the dynamic Western tradition is conceived as a dialectic between pulse and phrasing, Messiaen simply thought of it as a measuring of durations. Where Western form characteristically puts its material through a process of becoming, Messiaen's forms are laid out in proportional sections, filled with birdsong, religious chants, exotic modes and rhythms gathered from around the globe. These huge, decorative frieze-like structures are sometimes mistakenly described as static. In fact, we are precisely located in the passing of 'real' time throughout the entire 75 minutes of the *Turangalîla-symphonie* (1946-48).[3]

Where a sense of stasis does sometimes become apparent is rather in the 'circular' time structures of a composer such as Birtwistle, who seems to have felt from the start that the revolving of the calendar or the life cycle offers a profounder model of time than any open-ended process of development or change. His music not only seeks to counter the dynamic tradition through the use of 'anti-developmental' material – repeat figures, harmonic drones, refrain-and-chorus structures – but even the passing of 'real' time through formal structures that seem to turn back on themselves. His opera *Gawain* (1991) revolves both in its music and text, and literally in its staging, around a masque of the four seasons. As in the ritualistic, pre-dynamic music of the Middle Ages from which Birtwistle has derived so many of his techniques, the ear is not carried forward in his structures, merely invited to listen through.

But at least they remain structures, dependent, even in their apparently timeless moments, upon a residual sense of anticipation or memory. The true timeless moments sought by mystics, mantra-murmurers and some minimalists – and, paradoxically, to be experienced at moments of transcendence in some of the most dynamic Western music, such as late Beethoven – apparently requires the obliteration of any before or after, a sense

of existing in an endless present. But perhaps only a Stockhausen would seek to turn such phenomena into a structural method. His concept of Moment Form, as realized in such gigantic works as *Momente* (1961/72), comprises successions of detached, homogenous sound-blocks or events – some of his 'moments' in fact last, by the clock, several minutes – between which all sense of connection has been suppressed. Theoretically, they could be performed in any order. Whether the result is actually more present-centred, whether the musical ear can ever be entirely prevented from seeking out longer-term connections is debatable.[4]

And maybe that is the analytical trouble. It is easy enough to find demonstration models of one time theory or another, but in most music, the reality is more complex, more mixed. Take even so notoriously 'primitive' a structure as Ravel's *Boléro* (1928). Does its seemingly endless repetition of the same long melody over an hypnotic accompaniment embody 'circular' time, or does the single harmonic side-slip right at the end that unexpectedly clinches a sense of climax and closure claim it for the goal-directed tradition? And does Schoenberg's intention to 'stretch an instant of maximum spiritual intensity to half an hour' in his monodrama *Erwartung* (1909) represent the apogee of dynamic time or a staggering anticipation of the Stockhausenesque moment?[5]

And what, beyond all, of Stravinsky, who declared that a 'piece of mine can survive almost anything but wrong or uncertain tempo' and yet whose own conducting tempi were often not only wide of his metronome marks but sometimes strikingly different from one reading to another of the same work?[6] The paradox is largely explained when we realize that the salient essential is not so much correct tempo as vital articulation: that utterly idiosyncratic way of projecting a note or a chord with a fierce attack and then instantaneously reining it back so that the sound seems to vibrate with a contained force.

And this sense of aggression instantly suppressed exemplifies Stravinsky's larger continuities, since such sharp attacks more often than not cut across his metres, or fall on weak beats: one has the constant feeling of forward momentum meeting equally strong resistance, of time reversed or time set against time, to create, as Hans Keller variously formulated it, a tense stasis of opposing dynamisms. It is this tense stasis, projected up to a structural level, that enables Stravinsky to grip together seemingly self-contained blocks of invention into a convincing form on the largest scale. No wonder Keller hailed it as 'an achievement as overpowering as the discovery of the diatonic scale or the tone row'.[7]

NOTES

Source: 'Notes on the Music of Time', *The Independent*, 25 May 1991; rev. 2008. Written before the premiere of Harrison Birtwistle's opera *Gawain*, 30 May 1991, at the Royal Opera House.

1   W. H. Auden. 'Notes on Music and Opera', *The Dyer's Hand*, London, Faber, 1963, p. 465.

2   Igor Stravinsky and Robert Craft, *Themes and Conclusions*, London, Faber, 1972, p. 135.

3   [Ed.: In his reflection on the death of Oliver Messiaen, 'When Time Stands Still,' *The Independent*, 2 May 1992, the author acknowledged the 'dazzling vividness and novelty' of the sonorous imagery Messiaen assembled in his works but suggested the legacy of their underlying time-concept was more equivocal: 'Entirely appropriate to his own vision, it has unexpectedly permeated the music of subsequent generations, and not only that of his direct pupils from Pierre Boulez to George Benjamin. Under his indirect influence, for instance, the music of Tippett seems to have gradually abandoned its earlier integration for a cruder formal approach of block juxtapositions, and it is now the upholders of the once-central ideal of symphonic momentum who seem the more embattled. There are doubtless those who argue that Messiaen's ultimate role in reaffirming the ritualistic – the state of being rather than becoming – may be to lead Western music back into harmony with the eternal patterns of World Music, from which its recent history represented a brief aberration. But it is also possible that the current popularity of Messiaen's essentially closed and unchanging world of musical thought reflects a wider retreat to this or that version of fundamentalism in the face of apparently insoluble problems and uncertainties. If so, then the reaffirming of the open world of symphonic thought becomes all the more urgent in its capacity to articulate the human need to speculate, to progress, to doubt.']

4   For a more detailed discussion of the concept of moment form, see 'Discontinuity and the Moment', chapter 8 of: Jonathan Kramer, *The Time of Music*, New York, Schirmer Books, 1988, pp. 201-20.

5   Arnold Schoenberg, 'New Music: My Music', *Style and Idea*, ed. Leonard Stein, tr. Leo Black, London, Faber, 1975, p. 105.

6   Igor Stravinsky and Robert Craft, *Conversations with Igor Stravinsky*, London, Faber, 1959, p. 119.

7   Hans Keller, 'Rhythm: Gershwin and Stravinsky', *Essays on Music*, ed. Christopher Wintle, Cambridge, CUP, 1994, p. 208. [Ed.: The author amplified his closing remarks in an essay on Stravinsky's recordings of his own music, 'In His Own Good Time' (*The Independent*, 1 June 1991): 'Many conductors have sought to emulate Stravinsky's characteristic way of attacking a note or chord with a smart tap or ping; fewer have possessed his knack of instantaneously reining it back so that the resulting sound seems to vibrate with a *contained* force. Fewer still have understood how to distribute such attacks, directly or glancingly, with sonorous lightness or weight, through entire passages, so that the dances of such a score as *Agon* (1953-57) seem to leap from the loudspeakers in their tensile precision, so that the monumental chords of the *Symphonies of Wind Instruments* (1920/47) seem to stand up with a multi-dimensionality one feels one could almost walk through.']

6 'Could I But Express ...'

In his curiously dry, not to say selective, chronicle of his life, published in English as *An Autobiography* (1935), Igor Stravinsky advanced one of the most notorious statements ever made by a composer about his art. 'I consider that music is, by its very nature, essentially powerless to *express* anything at all, whether a feeling, an attitude of mind, a psychological mood, a phenomenon of nature etc. ... If, as is nearly always the case, music appears to express something, this is only an illusion, not a reality. It is simply an additional attribute ... a convention – in short, an aspect unconsciously or by force of habit we have come to confuse with its essential being.'[1]

The uproar has scarcely ceased since. How could Stravinsky refute a view that had seemed obvious at least since Monteverdi? How could he deny the deep religious feeling of Bach, the sonorous ideology of Beethoven, the psychological insight of Wagner, or the evocative correspondences of Debussy – whatever he thought of their actual music? Come to that, how could he forget the magic of his own *Firebird* (1910), the pathos of his *Petrushka* (1911), the primitive excitement of his *Rite of Spring* (1913)? In fact, putting those achievements into perspective, if not actually denying them, was part of the subtext of Stravinsky's *Autobiography*. Still only 30 when the riotous reception of the *Rite* consummated his world fame, he had to face correspondingly early the choice of whether to go on exploiting a successful formula or whether to risk everything on new departures.

In the event, it took some years for Stravinsky's choice to become apparent, partly because of the disruptions of the First World War, and partly because the premiere of the culminating masterpiece of his Russian period, *Les noces*, was held up until 1923. But already in *The Soldier's Tale* (1918) and other, shorter pieces composed in his Swiss exile during the later war years, he was constructing little forms from Western vernacular sources – waltzes, tangos, ragtimes – rather than Russian folklore. Then, with the Communist takeover in the October Revolution, he was literally cut off from his homeland and language (not to mention his private income). When Serge Diaghilev flourished a bunch of Baroque pieces purporting to be by Pergolesi at him in 1919 and asked if he would like to arrange them as a ballet, Stravinsky seems to have leapt at the chance to re-make himself as a composer. Forty years later, he was to recall '*Pulcinella* was my rediscovery of the past ... but it was a look in the mirror too.'[2]

And so arose the dreaded notion of neo-Classicism, which ever since has been the standard explanation for Stravinsky's output over the following three decades up to *The Rake's Progress* of 1951 – after which, he is supposed to have belatedly salvaged his radical credentials by going over to a post-Schoenbergian serialism. Yet Stravinsky disliked the label, and even on the

most superficial level it hardly begins to account for the real variety of his middle years. If anything, his typical figures, rhythms and textures during the period owed more to the Baroque than to the Classical. While the Piano Sonata (1924) or *The Rake's Progress* may invoke Beethoven or Mozart, the *Piano Concerto* (1923), *Violin Concerto* (1931) and chamber concerto *Dumbarton Oaks* (1938) are all redolent of Bach. Yet Romantic elements are also to be found: Verdi behind the ostensibly Baroque façade of *Oedipus Rex* (1927), Delibes in the bland diaphony of *Apollo* (1928), Tchaikovsky all over the place after *The Fairy's Kiss* (1928). And later, Renaissance, even Medieval mannerisms were to inflect the shadowy elegance of *Orpheus* (1947) and the serenely hieratic *Mass* (1948).

Yet possibly the most intriguing fact about Stravinsky's middle-period music is that it has been understood quite differently by three successive generations. The musical intelligentsia between the wars seemed amused enough at first by what it heard as his almost annual changes of style, but tended to regard these as the smart moves of a *déraciné* creator who had left his soul in the Russian period. By contrast, critical listeners post-1945, prompted by such avant-garde ideologues as Pierre Boulez, revalued his early works, not for their Russianness but for their radicalism – writing off the so-called neo-Classical decades as a reactionary interregnum. Yet today it is difficult to hear the stylistic references of the middle-period output as less Stravinskian than those of before or after, so that the question arises whether all the allusions, the Russian and serial no less than the neo-Classical, were successively required and consciously invoked to realize afresh an essentially unchanging set of basic compositional procedures.

Which brings us back to the famous ruling about expression. Considered dispassionately, it is not so very startling. What Stravinsky was suggesting is that a sweeping phrase is not intrinsically romantic nor a minor key intrinsically sad, but that such devices have acquired their apparent expressivity by constant association, over the Western centuries, with certain texts, rituals or dramatic situations. Theorists who take an opposing, Expressionist, view might of course ask why those devices had been associated with those particular texts, rituals or dramatic situations in the first place. Yet Stravinsky was not denying that such associations should be deployed, nor is his music lacking in expressiveness – albeit an expressiveness of an idiosyncratic kind. Just as he evidently felt the need to oppose forward motion of rhythm, of time itself, by equally strong counter-rhythm, so he habitually confronted feeling by formality – achieving through 'suppressionism', as Hans Keller put it, an 'overwhelmingly expressive anti-espressivo', in order, it would seem, to sustain something more constant.[3]

What was that something? As the aesthetic controversies of Stravinsky's era recede, it has become clearer that an almost modular sense of proportion underlay his output from first to last: a concept of musical form as an architectonic balance of section lengths, quite opposed to nineteenth-century notions of organic evolution. In the Autobiography, Stravinsky proposes, almost theologically, that 'Music is the sole domain in which man realizes the present' – that is, the only means of apprehending stability and order amid the experiential flux of past and future.[4] Since the language of late-Romantic music and, in particular, Wagner's concept of music as the art of transition, depended precisely upon manipulation of that experiential flux, and since the young Stravinsky showed singularly little gift for such manipulation, his cleaving to a present-centred objectivity might be considered as merely compensatory. And, if music history itself is construed as an on-going process, evolving from past to future – as it has variously been seen by Wagner, Schoenberg and Boulez – then it is not surprising that Stravinsky's position, particularly in the middle years, could be mistaken as reactionary.

Yet, what his mature aesthetic enabled him to counter were, precisely, the apparent imperatives of historicism. It allowed him instead to vary and renew the surface of his proportional constants through the continual shuffling and cross-cutting of styles and procedures from different periods, whether archaic (Medieval canons, Renaissance polyphony), Baroque-Classical (fugal textures, ornate decoration) or Modernist-Futuristic (collage, serialism) for his present purposes. Indeed, when the young Alexander Goehr defied the historicist agenda in Darmstadt with the dictum, 'all art is new art and all art is conservative', he must surely have been thinking, not only of the traditional basis of Schoenberg's innovations, but also of the extra-historical integrity of Stravinsky's.[5]

Because Stravinsky's sustaining of a constant immediacy depends so much upon his denial of flux, there will always be lovers of the expressive surge who find his rigid, anti-developmental continuities frustrating. His own justification of ordered construction in the *Autobiography* as arousing 'a unique emotion having nothing in common with our ordinary sensations and our responses to the impressions of daily life' might seem defensively austere.[6] Yet almost the entire output of his middle years has now established itself, fitting equally harmoniously into programmes of early music, new music and core repertoire: such is the measure of how widely works once considered merely artificial, modish or reactionary have come to appeal – and, indeed, to move.

NOTES

Source: 'A Mover and a Shaker', *The Independent*, 5 December 1992; rev. 2008. Stravinsky was Composer of the Week on Radio 3.

1   Igor Stravinsky, *An Autobiography (Chroniques de ma vie, 1935)*, London, Calder, 1975, pp. 53-4.
2   Igor Stravinsky and Robert Craft, *Expositions and Developments*, London, Faber, 1962, p. 113.
3   In: Hans Keller and Milein Cosman, *Stravinsky Seen and Heard*, London, Toccata Press, 1982, p. 56.
4   Stravinsky, 1975, p. 54.
5   Alexander Goehr, 'Is There Only One Way?', *The Score*, No. 26, January 1960, reprinted in: *Finding the Key: Selected Writings of Alexander Goehr*, ed. Derrick Puffett, London, Faber, 1998, pp. 20-4.
6   Stravinsky, 1975, p. 54.

7 The Expressionist Moment

In January 1911, the Russian painter Wassily Kandinsky attended a concert of Arnold Schoenberg's music in Munich, including the fiercely atonal Three Piano Pieces, Op. 11 (1909), and sensed an immediate affinity with his own work. In an enthusiastic letter introducing himself to the composer, he wrote of his pursuit of a new pictorial harmony through anti-logical, 'dissonant' means, and his conviction that 'today's dissonance in painting and music is merely the consonance of tomorrow'.[1] Schoenberg responded with what amounted to a credo: 'Every formal procedure which aspires to traditional effects is not completely free from conscious motivation. But art belongs to the *unconscious*! One must express *oneself*! Express oneself *directly*! Not one's taste, or one's upbringing, or one's intelligence, knowledge or skill. Not all these *acquired* characteristics, but what is *inborn, instinctive*.'[2]

Such rampant subjectivity was unlikely to restrict itself to a single media, and it soon emerged that the pair had much more in common. While Kandinsky was an accomplished cellist and pianist, Schoenberg had been painting obsessively since 1907 – mainly hypnotic self-portraits and phantasmagoria entitled 'gazes', attempting to reveal the soul behind the visage. Both were currently involved in strange, proto-cinematic theatre projects exploiting synaesthesic correspondences between sound, colour, movement, lighting, and so on: Kandinsky with his scenario *Der gelbe Klang* ('The Yellow Sound', 1910-13) and Schoenberg in his symbolic one-acter, *Die glückliche Hand* (1913). And both were about to publish visionary treatises: Kandinsky's *On the Spiritual in Art* (1911) and Schoenberg's *Theory of Harmony* (1911). Their friendship rapidly deepened. Kandinsky included several of Schoenberg's paintings in the 1911 exhibition of the *Blaue Reiter* group. The following year, Schoenberg and his pupils Berg and Webern contributed scores to the *Blaue Reiter* 'Almanack', a manifesto ranging from primitive art, by way of Skryabin's sound-colour theories, to the latest in French painting – indeed, another *Blaue Reiter* painter, Franz Marc, had already drawn a parallel between Schoenberg's music and the pictures of Picasso.

Given such manifold cross-connections between all these figures, it might seem perverse to question whether we are now not in danger of seeing the Expressionist era as *too* much of a unity. For a start, it was essentially a Central European phenomenon with Scandinavian correlatives in the theatre of Strindberg and the painting of Munch, but comparatively little immediate influence in France or Italy, and virtually none in Britain. Again, for all the interconnection of personalities and their aspiration towards various forms of total art work, the Expressionist impulse actually ran its course rather unevenly between the different arts. Not till after the Great War, for instance, did it really take hold in the German cinema, whereas when Schoenberg wrote to Kandinsky of the need to express solely the inborn and instinctive – which we may now take as the classic formulation of musical Expressionism – he had already begun to react against it in his composing.

Of course, music may be, and has been, regarded as expressive in two quite distinct ways: either it has aimed to evoke certain feelings in its listeners, or to convey certain feelings of its composer. The first of these approaches dominated the Baroque period, but something of the sort survives in opera at least, to the extent that we are supposed to empathize with the characters rather than the composer himself. It is one of the queasier features of *Salome* (1905) and *Elektra* (1909) – which immediately anticipated the sound of Schoenbergian Expressionism – that Strauss seems so utterly detached from the emotional turmoil he is invoking. The second, self-expressive approach – whether exemplified in the confessional intimacy of a Schumann piano piece or the grandiose angst of a Mahler symphony – was essentially a development of nineteenth-century Romanticism. And Schoenberg's Expressionist doctrine, as outlined to Kandinsky, could be seen as the extreme and ultimate extension of this Romantic subjectivity; it seems to suggest that if an artist is authentically in touch with his deepest feelings then a whole new language of harmony and form should spontaneously emerge in their expression.

For a few astonishing months in 1909, when the general state of the musical language, the idiosyncratic evolution of Schoenberg's complex genius and a trauma in his private life somehow intersected, it seemed as though he was about to validate this revolutionary belief. In the inexhaustibly innovatory *Five Orchestral Pieces* (1909) and the monodrama *Erwartung* (1909) – a work of maximum spiritual intensity – Schoenberg entered a musical world in which a terrifying and hallucinatory strangeness of imagery is matched only by the mastery of technique with which it is mediated. But once the very special conditions that made for these masterpieces had passed, he rapidly came to feel that the promptings of the instinctive self were liable to remain on the level of brief, solipsistic outbursts, unless articulated by at least some conscious element of form-building. And once the need for a supervening coherence was readmitted, the shocks and frissons of Expressionism were bound to lose something of their force as emblems of an internal vision, and to settle into components of a received style. *Pierrot lunaire*, completed in 1912, not only invokes past forms; it already treats those shocks and frissons themselves with an ironic detachment.

Granted one can add to Schoenberg's tumultuous output of 1909 a number of subsequent Webern miniatures comprising tiny twitches of sensibility – Schoenberg praised him for 'compressing a novel into a sigh' – and the athematic Four Pieces for Clarinet and Piano, Op. 5 (1913), of Berg. But the corpus of pure musical Expressionism remains small. Unlike the fairly extended parallel developments in art or drama, one might think of the musical phenomenon as a period of ominous anticipation culminating in a single thunderburst, the echoes of which have been dying away ever since. After the spasmodic moment-forms of his Expressionist scores, for instance, Webern resorted to a period of text-setting to recapture longer continuities, while Berg was to harness the alienated quality of Expressionist material to the cause of social protest in his opera *Wozzeck* (1917-22).

By the end of the First World War, Expressionism had become a mere manner among many, to be taken up one week by a young composer such as Paul Hindemith and dropped the next in favour of a brisk neo-Baroque 'New Objectivity'. Yet to the extent that Weimar Germany still had its tortuous links with the pre-war past, it remained a living manner. Indeed, something of the Expressionist spirit was to flair up after the Second World War with the aspiration of the young Pierre Boulez towards an 'organized delirium' and in such Schoenbergian early works of Alexander Goehr as his cantata, *The Deluge* (1958). Only with Peter Maxwell Davies's self-consciously outrageous music-theatre pieces of the late-1960s, with their screaming nuns and full-frontal nudity, do we descend to a mere neo-Expressionism. By then, the unprecedented eruptions of the original Expressionist moment had long since been reduced to a set of standardized clichés by the horror film industry. Yet, in their radical authenticity, their intensity of colour and expression and corresponding audacity of harmony and formal process, the *Five Orchestral Pieces* will doubtless retain their impact as still, in certain ways, the most modern music ever written.

NOTES

Source: 'Sophisticated Instincts', *The Independent*, 29 February 1992. Written at the time of the Manchester Festival of Expressionism, 1992, which opened with a performance of Schoenberg's *Gurrelieder* (1900-11) in the Free Trade Hall.

1   *Arnold Schoenberg/Wassily Kandinsky: Letters, Picture, Documents*, ed. Jelena Hahl-Koch, tr. John C. Crawford, London, Faber, 1984, p. 21.
2   Ibid., p. 23.

8   *Sight and Sound*

Richard Strauss is reputed to have claimed once that he could depict anything in music – even a soup spoon. No doubt if he had got round to it, the utensil would have been immortalised as a shiny tinkling, not unlike the silver rose motif in *Der Rosenkavalier* (1911).   But how could listeners have known it was, precisely, a soup spoon? Unlike the sheep so realistically scored in *Don Quixote* (1897), soup spoons do not make a generic sound guaranteed to evoke a visual correspondence in the mind. For that matter, without its operatic context, the silver rose motif itself might as easily be construed as a fountain, a starry night sky or a musical snuffbox.

Yet we habitually, perhaps instinctively, tend to talk of music in visual terms. Pitches are described as high or low, sounds as dark or bright, textures as clear or blurred. We refer to the shape of phrases or the contours of form, while the unfolding of music through time is evoked in analogies of gesture, pattern, motion. Admittedly, these are all metaphors of a somewhat generalized kind – no soup spoons here. But there does seem to be a certain level of abstraction in the mind at which images of space and time can seem to interact meaningfully with one another. Consider the famous trio in Act One of *Così fan tutte* (1790), where Mozart's heroines wish their voyaging lovers a calm sea. This is accompanied almost throughout by a gentle undulation of parallel thirds from the muted violins. Of course, waves do not actually undulate in parallel thirds, even in the Bay of Naples. What Mozart is offering is an iconic figure, a kind of audio-visual emblem, of the way water ripples and flows – and an already conventional emblem at that. Such figures were as likely to turn up in Baroque cantatas evoking the waters of Babylon, say, as they were later in Romantic tone poems following the courses of great rivers.

Over the last few centuries, in fact, composers have built up quite a stock of musical emblems, beyond the merely onomatopaeic, for evoking storms, pastoral scenes, seascapes, night rides and sunrises, or whatever. And certain masters have been striking for their ability to add to that stock – we might think of the vast sense of space opened up in the '*Scène aux champs*' of Berlioz's *Symphonie fantastique* (1830) or the flickering patterns of the 'Forest Murmurs' in Wagner's *Siegfried* (1856-69). Yet up to the late nineteenth century, such iconic usages generally remained embedded in, and subservient to, essentially musical forms and procedures. Even Wagner ultimately dissolved his visual, poetic and symbolic connotations in an all-embracing symphonic flow.

Was this still true of Debussy, or did his music usher in a fundamentally new relationship between art and nature, sound and vision, essence and emblem? Though the 'Forest Murmurs' might be thought of as impressionistic, Wagner could never be labelled an Impressionist. Yet Debussy got called just that from early in his career by critics baffled over the radicalism of his music, which they took for vagueness – and the label has stuck. It serves up to a point. There is the common interest in evocations of light, watery reflections, effects of mist and cloud. Debussy's heightened sensitivity to sound in its own right, as distinct from musical substance, could be compared to the Impressionists' new responsiveness to paint as a medium, as distinct from their subject matter – and his methods of scoring in points of colour to their *plein-air* spots and dashes. Yet, on closer scrutiny, the connection proves less convincing – and not just because the French Impressionist painters came of age in the 1860s and '70s, whereas Debussy reached maturity in the very different ambience of the 1890s. It is, in fact, quite difficult to find specific references to their work in his music. Rather, the *Nocturnes* (1899) took their starting point from the more refined and stylised paintings of Whistler; and *La mer* (1905) was inspired, not by some stormy view of the English Channel from Etretat by Monet, but by Turner (whom Debussy emphatically distinguished from the Impressionists as a master of mystery), by the even more stylised *Great Wave* of Hokusai, and by observation of the English Channel itself.[1]

There is, to be sure, a recurrent insistence in Debussy's letters that the received procedures of music – all those fugal, operatic and symphonic formulae – need to be abandoned so that music can somehow be reborn freely from a direct interaction of nature and the psyche. He does indeed seem to have believed this might be achieved through an intensive focus on the iconic principle: that if the figures, rhythms and resonances most variously emblematic of visual, poetic, kinetic and psychic correspondences could be brought together, new forms would evolve from their interaction. The notion of the arabesque – a decorative linear figure – seems to have been particularly numinous to him. Like Wagner, Debussy evidently considered that the father of the arabesque in its primordial musicality was J. S. Bach – but that it had been accumulating sensory and expressive implications ever since.[2] In *Prélude à l'après-midi d'un faune* (1895), he achieved his first and, in a way, last emblematic masterpiece. The piece is conceived as an almost continuous, sinuously self-generating line – a nine-minute arabesque – winding through a succession of sensuously suggestive textures. Somehow, the musical processes, the symbolic aestheticism of Mallarmé's poem, and the warmth, sparkle and languor of its Mediterranean setting fuse in a new form, sound and feeling.

It would be misleading to suggest that Debussy's subsequent output, so utterly distinctive and influential as it was to prove, represented a falling away from this miracle. Yet there is curious sense that the more he strove to exploit the iconic principle, the more the old, purely musical forms he had sought to replace contrived to insinuate themselves back into his music – particularly the old dance types. Hence the waltz impulses that surface in *La mer* or *Jeux* (1913), or the habañera phrasing that underpins even so apparently hazy an evocation as '*Les parfums de la nuit*' in *Ibéria* from the three orchestral *Images*

(1905-12). Ironically, when Debussy finally achieved an even more radical development of the arabesque than in *L'après-midi* – in his late *Études* (1915) and Sonata for flute, viola and harp (1915) – it was by explicitly purging all emblematic correspondences and aspiring to 'pure' music again.

The orchestral *Images* comprise a particularly complex and ambiguous proposition. Not only do the veils and frissons of Debussy's impressionistic manner have to contend with a particularly resurgent and formalistic dance element, but also with touches of what he himself called 'reality' – by which he meant citations of actual music from various vernacular traditions. For the work is conceived as a tribute to three countries. In *Gigues*, his evocation of England, misty textures divulge lolloping variants of 'The Keel Row', while a favourite French folk song rides the vernal corybantics of *Rondes de Printemps*; and *Ibéria* in particular seems to refer back to a whole Franco-Russian tradition of Spanish local colour from Glinka to Rimsky-Korsakov, from Bizet to Chabrier. Maybe this uneasy, almost collage-like mix of soft-edged and hard-edged invention, of the impressionistic, realist and formulaic, helps to explain why the *Images* have never been so popular as the *Nocturnes* or *La mer*, or so prized by connoisseurs of the new as *L'après-midi* or *Jeux*. Yet every fastidious, vibrant bar proclaims the unique sensibility of Claude Debussy.

NOTES

Source: 'Watch This Sound?', *The Independent*, 28 March 1992. The essay preceded a tour of Debussy's *Images* for orchestra by Simon Rattle and the CBSO in their *Towards the Millennium* concert series.

1   See: *Debussy Letters*, ed. François Lesure and Roger Nichols, London, Faber, 1987, p. 188.
2   See: *Debussy on Music*, ed. François Lesure, tr. and ed. Richard Langham Smith, London, Secker & Warburg, 1977, pp. 27-8.

9 'Fain Would I Change That Note'

In 1953, Michael Tippett was approached by the Edinburgh Festival to write a piece for strings commemorating the tercentenary of the birth of Arcangelo Corelli. It was a rush commission, whereas he preferred to work slowly, and Corelli was not a composer he knew well. But Tippett did have some advantages: a proven record in writing for strings, most notably in his *Concerto for Double String Orchestra* (1939), and a grounding in Baroque techniques, especially fugue, from his counterpoint teacher R. O. Morris. He had also done something of the sort before, in his *Fantasia on a Theme of Handel* (1941), in which a Handelian harmonic sequence is put through a series of expanding variations culminating in a fugue and restatement.

So, throwing together a 'theme' from some C major chords and an A minor phrase-sequence from different parts of Corelli's Concerto Grosso, Op. 6, No. 2 (1714), and dividing his strings into two ensembles, with a concertante group of two violins and cello, he set to work. At first we hear the Corelli, just blurred a bit by added passing notes. Then the two violins run up a scale in parallel fourths instead of thirds and, step by step, we begin to pass over into Tippett's richly lyrical idiom of the 1950s. When he has worked through his expanding variations, Tippett takes advantage of his chance discovery that Bach wrote a Double Fugue on Themes of Corelli (BWV 579, n.d.) that bears motivic resemblances to his own Corellian theme, quoting the first 12 bars of the Bach before again beginning to extend and decorate it in his own manner. He then adds a pastoral Adagio with soaring solo violins by way of tribute to Corelli's 'Christmas' Concerto, before returning to Corelli pure. In description, the *Fantasia Concertante on a Theme of Corelli* sounds a mere allusive patchwork, a patently occasional piece. Yet it has come to be recognized as one of Tippett's most resolved and personal scores. So how does this square with our habitual notion that new music should be innovative and if possible, original?

Actually, it may not be so habitual as we assume. Most music up to 1800 and much thereafter was to a degree based upon music that already existed – broadly speaking, in one of three possible ways. The earliest of these was the technique of so called parody – parody in the serious sense – where a composer took an existing piece and made it anew by adding parts, pushing some of its notes into different positions or extending its material. Countless Medieval chants were built upon, and Renaissance masses generated, by these means. After all, in an age when most composers were in service to the church, royal courts, great houses or municipalities and the interrelation of such practical skills as improvisation, transcription, arrangement and composition remained fluid, ownership of specific pieces was scarcely critical. As late as the 1740s, Handel could still resort, when pushed for time, to seizing a set of keyboard pieces by a contemporary and turning them into the choruses of his next oratorio. And in his updating of *Messiah* in 1789, Mozart could yet turn the tables on Handel by filling up the bare paragraphs of 'The people that walked in darkness' with a vagrant drift of harmony in his own most advanced chromatic manner (incidentally setting hard-line period performers an exquisitely insoluble problem).

If such direct makeovers seemed less easy to justify by the nineteenth-century, this was doubtless partly because composers now found themselves released into an increasingly commercialized world of publishers, impresarios and virtuosi, competing for the favours of a ticket- and sheet-music-buying bourgeoisie seeking entertainment and cultural betterment. Hence the rise of the notion of the work as personal expression that remains the moral property of its composer. In a period before commercial copyright could be strictly enforced, plenty of 'parodying' still went on, of course; for instance, in the operatic potpourris of such composer-performers as Liszt. Nor did the twentieth century lack instances of recomposition (though generally based upon originals safely out of copyright). One thinks of Vaughan Williams's systematic exploration of the harmonies of his source in his *Fantasia on a Theme of Thomas Tallis* (1910), or Stravinsky's seamless fusion of his own manner with items of Tchaikovsky in *The Fairy's Kiss* (1928), or Robin Holloway's tone poem *Domination of Black* (1974) which gets 'inside' songs of Schumann and sends the notes in different directions. All three have been recognized as significant works in their respective oeuvres.

The second method of making music out of existing pieces is by taking them as models; where a composer analyses the materials, procedures or structure of an admired work and attempts to reconstitute some, or all of these aspects in his or her own terms. Of course, abstract models of simple song or dance forms, fugal procedures, and so on have an ancient history as teaching material. But the practice of turning specific pieces into models is particularly associated with the Classical Style, because the succession of Haydn, Mozart, Beethoven and Schubert seem so recurrently to have borrowed from one another in this way. Sometimes the connection is obvious – as when Beethoven models the canonic quartet in Act 1 of *Fidelio* (1805-14) on that in the finale of Mozart's *Così fan tutte* (1790). Sometimes the relation is more oblique. One may not hear much in common between the rondo themes of Beethoven's Piano Sonata Op. 31, No. 1 (1802), and those of Schubert's late A major Piano Sonata (1828). But Charles Rosen has shown how the textures, modulations and structure of the latter are quite closely modelled on the former – adding that, in this case, Schubert produced a movement that is unquestionably greater than its model.[1] In fact, composers of classicizing temperament – one thinks of Mendelssohn, Brahms and Stravinsky – continued to return to the method ever after. Tippett, Robert Simpson and Alexander Goehr have all, and recurrently, modelled pieces on Beethoven.[2]

The third music-from-music method, of course, is stylistic citation or pastiche; an approach one tends to think of as more modern, since it depends upon an awareness, whether critical or nostalgic, of musical history itself. In Brahms, historical self-consciousness already dictates that his (many) parodies of, or modellings upon, more recent composers such a Chopin, Mendelssohn, Schubert or Beethoven are hidden, or at least safeguarded by sarcasm ("Any fool can hear that!"). But he is quite prepared to appropriate the 'authority' of earlier music by citation. So a chorus – one of the *Fest- und ·Gedenksprüch*, Op. 109 (1889), say – may begin as a virtual pastiche of Schütz, which is then Brahmsified before our very ears as the piece unfolds. Indeed, the twentieth century has seen the phenomenon of composers who consciously project their sensibilities through the most eclectic array of parodies, modellings and allusions – Poulenc being the most flagrant example, but paralleled not so covertly by Ravel, Prokofiev, Walton, Tippett, even the young Britten.

Actually, Wagner was already accusing Brahms of just such eclecticism back in the 1870s, and the citation game goes back still further. In the Adagio grazioso of his Sonata Op. 31, No. 2 (1802), Beethoven seems to be harking back to the Mozartian-rococo style of twenty years before and gently sending up its clockwork accompaniments and frilly decorations. But that is not the end of it, for this movement apparently served as a model for the Adagietto of Stravinsky's Piano Sonata (1924) – which he himself described as 'Beethoven *frisé*'. Yet, instead of sending up the Beethoven in his turn,

Stravinsky superimposes its decorative turns upon a melodic line that has more in common with Bach than pastiche Mozart or Beethoven. Meanwhile, he plays a typical game with the conventional eighteenth-century harmony, nudging it into all sorts of ambiguities. So we have an interplay of parody, model and pastiche, deployed to wrest a complex of new meanings out of the past. And the music *is* new; not a bar of it could have been written this way in the eighteenth-century itself. So why have the practices of recomposition, and, in particular, the products of so-called neo-Classicism, had such a bad press in certain quarters? Why, in his notorious *Philosophy of New Music*, did Theodor Adorno feel driven so urgently to attack Stravinsky for evading the horrors of the age by composing merely 'Music about Music'?[3] Why are many composers to this day still liable to feel guilty about borrowing from existent music?

Doubtless fashion played its part in the evolution of genres at least as far back as the Renaissance. But the cult of originality really dates from the nineteenth century as composers, increasingly deprived of their old social functions, found themselves contending to lead the field in the high aesthetic stakes. Where the Classical Style had still largely been compounded from common material, even clichés, it was increasingly felt that every aspect of a work that aspired to the status of serious art – themes, accompaniments, processes, structures – ought to be drawn from an original idea of the composer's own. This was a development that led almost inevitably to such 'total' methods as serialism, and ultimately to the doctrine of the post-Second World War avant-garde, promulgated, at least for a time, by Pierre Boulez, that a work could only be relevant to the degree that it cut itself off from the past and virtually reinvented its musical language to meet the challenges of the present.

The trouble with this position is that it denies music's self-reflective power to convey new thought or feeling precisely to the degree that it departs from well-defined familiarity. A would-be reinventor of musical language may come up with the most striking succession of sounds, textures and gestures. But to avoid arbitrariness – the sense that any other succession might do as well – he will likely have to drag in all manner of extra-musical analogies, from the other arts, science, nature, landscape, whatever, to justify his choices. It remains questionable whether such a procedure could ever accumulate the equivalent richness to an inherited tradition that relies, in the first place, precisely upon music about music. In a way, the answer is obvious. If originality were the supreme criterion, we would value C. P. E. Bach above Haydn; Liszt above Wagner, Webern above Schoenberg – as, indeed, the post-war avant-garde did for a bit. In fact we still tend to think of these remarkable figures as special cases, catalysts to a more central tradition marked by the great synthesists such as Bach and Beethoven, Wagner and Brahms, and in the twentieth century Schoenberg – and Stravinsky, who perhaps turned the ultimate trick by recomposing Bach, Gesualdo, Machaut, and, indeed, Boulez, so idiosyncratically that, for many of us, it is difficult now not to hear those masters through *his* ears.

NOTES

Source: Script for *Music Weekly*, BBC Radio 3, March 1987; rev. 2008.

1   Charles Rosen, *The Classical Style* (1971), new ed., London, Faber, 1997, pp. 518-20.
2   The *Adagio cantabile* of Tippett's *Concerto for Double String Orchestra* is modelled upon the Allegretto ma non troppo of Beethoven's String Quartet in F minor, Op. 95. Simpson's String Quartets Nos. 4-6 are modelled on Beethoven's 'Razumovsky' Quartets, Op. 59, Nos. 1-3, and his Tenth Symphony upon the 'Hammerklavier' Sonata in B flat major, Op. 106. Goehr has, among other works, modelled his orchestral piece, *Metamorphosis/Dance*, Op. 36, on the Arietta from Beethoven's Sonata in C major, Op. 111, and the first movement of his String Quartet No. 3, Op. 37, on the first movement of the Piano Sonata in E minor, Op. 90. Other works of Goehr have been modelled on Bach, Handel, Mozart and Schumann. See Alexander Goehr, 'Using Models … for Making Original Music', *Common Knowledge*, Vol. 8, No. 1, Durham NC, Duke UP, 2002, pp. 108-23.
3   Theodor W. Adorno, *Philosophy of Modern Music*, tr. Anne G. Mitchell and Wesley V. Bloomster, London, Sheed & Ward, 1973, pp. 181-84.

10   New Notes for Old Instruments

Late one evening, towards the end of the 1960s, the BBC Third Programme broadcast a mysterious little feature entitled – if memory serves – *The Shagbutt, the Minikin and the Flemish Clackett*. These turned out to comprise a consort of exceedingly obsolete instruments from the fifteenth century. According to the announcer, the minikin had a keyboard action so slow that the performer – on this occasion, the redoubtable Tatiana Splod of the Schola Cantorum Neasdeniensis – was obliged to start playing fully 30 seconds ahead of the required sound, while the Flemish clackett was a monstrous Hieronymus Bosch kind of wind instrument that had to be played from *inside* – with constant danger to the performer of implosion. The Schola then embarked, in demonstration, upon a rondeau by Huckbald the One-Legged of Gröbhausen. But before the thing had honked and twangled its way through more than a few bars, there came a pop and a series of muffled cries. The Flemish clackett had imploded.

Though this naughty spoof was re-broadcast more than once in subsequent years, nobody ever seems to have admitted responsibility. Yet it encapsulated an attitude to the period instrument movement that was still surprisingly widespread at the time. Despite the earnest revivalism in the first decades of the twentieth century of Arnold Dolmetsch with his viols and spinets, Wanda Landowska with her harpsichords and Paul Hindemith with his early music studio at Yale; despite the arrival in the 1950s and 1960s of a new generation of scholar-showmen such as Noah Greenberg and his New York Pro Musica, Nikolaus Harnoncourt and his Vienna Concentus Musicus and David Munrow and his Early Music Consort of London, many listeners, not to say composers, continued to regard the cult of old instruments as an antiquarian fad or even a joke.

Behind this lay an evolutionary notion of musical history that dated back at least as far as the Enlightenment: an assumption that new musical developments inevitably went hand in glove with improvements in instrumental technology. So, following the great nineteenth-century drive to enhance the reliability and brilliance of all the standard instruments, the twentieth century could proceed to push their new possibilities to the limit and beyond, on the reasonable assumption that, by the time they were exhausted, a new world of electronic developments would be opening up for exploration. Earlier versions of the standard instruments, not to mention older instruments that had disappeared altogether, were self-evident failures in the evolutionary rat-race. Their latter-day revival could only be of 'museal' interest – to invoke Pierre Boulez's most witheringly dismissive adjective.

Which is not to say that composers were oblivious of their charms. Way back in the nineteenth century, Meyerbeer had deployed the antique tone of the viola d'amore in his grand opera *Les Huguenots* (1836); and, between the wars, Janáček developed a passion for the instrument – or at least for its name – while Hindemith actually mastered it, composing a plaintive little neo-Baroque chamber concerto for his own performance in 1927. Meanwhile, seeking a sweetly naïve timbre to characterize his infant son in his *Symphonia domestica* (1902-03), Richard Strauss hit upon the oboe d'amore. Nor was interest confined to single instruments: in 1971, Elisabeth Lutyens tried combining players from the Early Music Consort and the London Sinfonietta in her elegy *The Tears of Night* and the following year, Peter Maxwell Davies inserted whole sequences of what he called 'muzak behind the arras' for Munrow's period players into his first opera *Taverner*. Yet perhaps the most prophetic experiment of the post-war period was the extraordinary *Music for Renaissance Instruments* composed in 1966 by the Argentinian surrealist, Mauricio Kagel: a study in cultural 'alienation', the strange sounds of which were drawn from the old instruments by entirely unconventional, avant-garde playing techniques.

And on top of these still relatively isolated instances, there was the whole history of the revival of the harpsichord. Yet this tended to confound the 'museal' charge from the start. For the clangorous, steel-framed instruments that Wanda Landowska ordered for her use from Pleyel – the instruments for which Manuel de Falla wrote his Concerto of 1926 and Poulenc his *Concert champêtre* in 1928 – were far removed from Baroque models, almost amounting to new instruments and inaugurating a distinctively twentieth-century tradition of powerful concert harpsichords. Accordingly, when Elliott Carter embarked upon his vastly intricate *Double Concerto* for harpsichord, piano and two chamber orchestras (1961), he carefully adjusted his textures to the instrument his harpsichordist, Ralph Kirkpatrick, was using – a heavy model with all manner of stops and pedals by the New York maker, Challis. But such instruments, in turn, have tended to disappear in more recent decades with the reversion to lighter-toned 'authentic' harpsichords. As a result, putting on this most advanced piece already raises 'authenticity' problems of its own, which may be mitigated but not entirely solved by electronically amplifying a Baroque instrument – a peculiarly post-modern predicament.

Yet the real issue of the last 20-odd years is not merely post-modern but, by implication, post-historical. Despite the supreme vision and skill of the greatest pioneering period performers, from Hindemith to Harnoncourt, from Landowska to Thurston Dart, it used to be widely suspected that the early music movement harboured many a performer who was simply not good enough to make it on modern standard instruments. Whatever truth there might once have been in this, however, the intense cultivation of period performance in recent decades seems to have transformed the situation. London now teems with performers who not only play their Renaissance viols, Baroque oboes and classical horns technically as well as modern instruments, but as if to the manner born: raising the positively philosophical question as to how far these can any longer be regarded as specifically 'early' instruments at all.

Take George Benjamin's striking song *On Silence*, for mezzo-soprano and five viols, of 1990. His initial approach to the viol consort Fretwork seems to have arisen out of an enthusiasm for the Purcell viol fantasias. But he soon realized that the medium effectively constituted 'a new family of string instruments ... capable of an array of hitherto unexplored techniques and sonorities ... amongst these ... the almost complete absence of vibrato, the novel bowing technique, the potential for numerous natural harmonics, super-fast tremolo and resonant pizzicati'. The result was a setting of Yeats's 'Long-Legged Fly' of exquisite sensitivity and strangeness. Since then, Benjamin has skilfully transcribed his viol textures into an alternative version for 'ordinary' strings, though this cannot quite recapture the fine-spun aura of viol tone.[1]

Meanwhile, an increasing number of other composers have been rising to the opportunities of early music ensembles – from the 1991 Glyndebourne Serenades for period wind ensemble commissioned from Jonathan Dove and Nigel Osborne in celebration of the Mozart Bicentenary, to John Woolrich's deployment of the full Mozartian line-up of the Orchestra of the Age of Enlightenment in *The Theatre Represents a Garden – Night* (1991), by way of whole arrays of viol pieces commissioned by Fretwork in celebration of the 1995 Purcell Tercentenary, and more recently by Concordia to complement the pavan sequence of Dowland's *Lachrymae*. Not only have established British figures such as Alexander Goehr and rising young talents such as Tansy Davies tried their hands, but so too have composers as diverse as Gavin Bryers, Peter Sculthorpe, Paul Ruders, Tan Dun, even Elvis Costello ...

Not all of them have gone beyond revampings of the sort of thing they usually do anyway. But the more thoughtful have realized, with George Benjamin, that the unfamiliar constraints and possibilities of period instruments can offer as stimulating a challenge to compositional habits as the latest developments in computerized sound. Composers facing the Baroque harpsichord for the first time suddenly find that the sustained lines and fluctuating dynamics they have so heavily relied upon to characterize phrasing and maintain continuity are simply not available; can compensations, or equivalents be found by exploiting the instrument's exceptional precision of articulation or its propensity for fuller, denser textures to convey the illusion of louder volume? Or maybe such composers find their usual mode of dissonant harmony is reduced to percussive note-clusters by the harpsichord's complex overtones; can they find vertical combinations and progressions that turn those resonances to positive account?

Again, composers used to thinking primarily in terms of harmony, gesture or texture may feel compelled to renew their command of counterpoint if they are to make the most of the special clarity with which the viol consort reveals the interweaving of independent lines. Others, confronted by the pinched sounds of those notes in the ranges of pre-valve horns in the period classical orchestra that can only be produced by hand-stopping, may seek to gear harmony and phrasing to exploit such tones as expressive nuances – as a period performance of Beethoven's 'Eroica' Symphony reveals that he did in the trio of its scherzo. Maybe the timbral and textural discoveries some of these composers make in working with period instruments will, in turn, feed back into their music for modern forces – a potentially endless dialectic just at the point when history was supposed to be sweeping away such acoustic-instrumental concerns in a flux of electronic possibilities. Admittedly, the singular propensities of the Flemish clackett have yet to be explored. No doubt, it is merely a matter of time …

NOTES

Source: 'Old Before Their Time', *The Independent*, 3 March 1995; rev. 2008.

1   Both versions are recorded on Nimbus NI 5505.

11   *Survival of the Soundest*

Music, too, has its mad scientists, and in 1995 one of the more colourful of them died in Moscow at the age of 97. Leon Theremin attained a passing fame between the wars with his invention of an early electronic instrument, duly dubbed the Theremin. This generated a single continuous tone, the pitch and volume of which could be varied by the performer's hands hovering, respectively, around a vertical antenna and a horizontal loop. Patented and manufactured in the United States, its eerie glissandi found their way into a number of Hollywood film scores and even into Edgard Varèse's futuristic *Ecuatorial* (1934). But these were not enough to save the thing from ultimately declining into a mere music-hall stunt – and those who attended the British premiere of David Del Tredici's Lewis Carroll fantasy *Final Alice*, in 1982, are unlikely to forget the mystic passes of the aged performer the BBC had somehow found to render the Theremin effects the composer had naughtily demanded to suggest Alice's fluctuations in size.

In fact, the gadget was by no means the first attempt to break away from traditional acoustic instruments. Even before the invention of the amplifier, nineteenth-century American experiments in generating and transmitting musical tones over the telephone system had already culminated by 1900 in Thaddeus Cahill's so-called Telharmonium: a mammoth contraption played from organ consoles and weighing 200 tons. Nor was the Theremin by any means the last of its kind, being effectively replaced by the invention of the

more precise Ondes Martenot in 1928. Yet no sooner had the latter gained a toe-hold in the orchestra, through Messiaen's involvement of its celestial howlings in the *Turangalîla-symphonie* (1946-48), than younger composers were lured onwards by the successive post-war developments of the tape-recorder, synthesiser, sampler and computer-controlled sound.

And so it goes? Sibelius once remarked to a pupil that "orchestration is the discomfiture of absolute idealism," meaning that the free play of the sonorous imagination is constantly up against the limitations in range, volume and agility of actual instruments.[1] In one sense, the whole history of Western musical instruments, their evolution, standardization and refinement, could be interpreted as an endless quest to bridge the gap between the actual and the ideal. So the skirling medieval fiddle was amplified into the piercingly sweet Stradivarius violin, and the pungent, out-of-doors shawm mollified into the plaintive modern oboe; so the succession of the serpent, ophicleide and cimbasso has in turn been displaced (still not altogether satisfactorily) by the tuba in the search for an ever more sonorous orchestral bass.

It is striking, indeed, how many instruments of the modern symphony orchestra can still trace some sort of lineage back to ancient times; surprising, on the other hand, how comparatively few seem to have been invented from scratch in more recent times. No doubt the piano is the great exception. Its distinctive action was virtually devised in 1709 by a single maker, Bartolomeo Cristofori – little though he can have foreseen the instrument's ubiquitous acceptance by the beginning of the nineteenth century. That tinkling mini-piano, the celesta, patented in Paris by Mustel in 1886, has proved a useful orchestral extra. Then again, the twentieth-century percussion section has been steadily expanded by all manner of novelties of which the swivel-drum rototoms and John Cage's water gong are only two of the more enterprising examples.

All the same, the failure rate of would-be inventors seems to have been inordinately high. Among the myriad manufactures of the nineteenth-century Belgian, Adolphe Sax – including a project to suspend a giant pipe organ over Paris – only the saxophone and, in military bands, the saxhorns, have lasted. And *pace* James Wood's aspirations for his Centre for Microtonal Music at the Guildhall School of Music and Drama, earlier twentieth-century attempts to create fresh possibilities by cramming more pitches into an octave than the evenly spaced 12 semitones of conventional Western tuning have proved none too fertile. "That's the kind of experiment that is forever being made – and forgotten in next to no time," remarked Sibelius of the indeed little-remembered music that the Czech, Alois Haba (1893-1973), wrote for quarter-tone and even sixth-tone instruments.[2]

Yet the real puzzle is more fundamental. Why, after several decades now of ever-accelerating technological sophistication, are electronic instruments and

methods of sound manipulation not well on the way, as early prophets such
as Varèse hoped, to superseding traditional orchestral instruments, which, as
Boulez often complains, have developed little since the nineteenth century?
Part of the answer is that the orchestra has proved unexpectedly adaptable;
that, after toiling in their electronic laboratories to devise unprecedented
sounds, composers have found they could draw the same effects from complex
blendings of acoustic instruments – resulting in a whole new range of cloud
textures and sonic frissons in the orchestral works of such composers as Ligeti
and Berio. But part of the answer is surely artistic. Electro-acoustic music
has undoubtedly achieved a handful of classics since Varèse's interspersing
of taped *musique concrète* between the instrumental sections of his *Déserts*
(1954) or Stockhausen's interplay of choirboy voices and electronically
generated sounds in his *Gesang der Jünglinge* (1956). Yet it would be idle to
pretend that the yield to date anywhere near fulfils the kind of expectation
implied by Messiaen's dictum, even before the electro-acoustic age had really
got under way, that 'an abundance of technical means enables the heart to
expand freely'.[3]

And the explanation for this surely lies in Stravinsky's counter-assertion that
art proceeds not from possibilities but from choice. 'I shall go even further,'
he remarked in his 1939 *Poetics of Music*: 'My freedom will be so much the
greater and more meaningful the more narrowly I limit my field of action …
Whatever diminishes constraint diminishes strength. The more constraints
one imposes, the more one frees oneself from the chains that shackle the
spirit.'[4] In other words, far from inhibiting invention, the very limitations of
traditional instruments, their tuning and the compositional materials that
can be wrested from them constitute both a challenge to a composer to create
something new and a measure of the degree to which he succeeds. From
this point of view, the devising of instruments capable of ever more subtle
subdivisions of pitch, rhythm and dynamics, would tend to be retrograde,
subverting possibilities of strong contrast in ever smoother degrees of
transition. And the invention, perhaps no longer so far off, of some ultimate
electronic gadget wired to the brain, and capable of translating whatever the
free play of the sonorous imagination could come up with into instant reality,
would for Stravinsky have constituted the ultimate threat: by removing all
constraint, also removing any criterion for why one compositional choice is
better than another.

Actually, he was not so conservative as this might make him sound: believing
that the retuning of scales probably would open new expressive possibilities
for Western music, but selectively and in specific contexts, not through some
systematic all-or-nothing revolution.[5] In the end, new instrument-makers,
like everyone else, come up against the limits of perception and their artistic
consequences. The ear is able to follow the minute microtonal inflections of

line of an Indian sitar player precisely because these are thrown into relief against an unchanging drone; import those inflections into every level of a harmonic texture and one would be liable to end up with the aural equivalent of squeezing all the brightest coloured plasticines together – and producing an undifferentiated grey. Once again, it was Sibelius in old age, dutifully keeping up with broadcasts of the latest trends, who underlined the point, after some particularly complex and doubtless grey offering, when he asserted that "true personality can show itself in five notes".[6]

NOTES

Source: 'Smart, But Not So Sweet', *The Independent*, 27 November 1995.

1   Bengt de Törne, *Sibelius: A Close-up*, London, Faber, 1937, pp. 53-4.

2   Santeri Levas, *Sibelius: A Personal Portrait*, London, Dent, 1972, p. 74

3   Olivier Messiaen, 'The Emotion, the Sincerity of the Musical Work …' (c. 1935) in: Peter Hill and Nigel Simeone, *Messiaen*, New Haven, Yale UP, 2005, p. 59.

4   Igor Stravinsky, *Poetics of Music*, tr. Arthur Knodel and Ingolf Dahl, Cambridge, Harvard UP, 1947, p. 68.

5   Igor Stravinsky and Robert Craft, *Memories and Commentaries*, London, Faber, 1960, p. 121.

6   Levas, 1972, p. 76.

12   But is it Mozart?(I)

The image on the cover of the *New Scientist* for 9 August 1997 was lurid: a head with a great cello-shaped bulge on one side of its brain and bars of (upside down) music protruding from the other. The caption read: 'Watch out. This machine could steal your soul.' Admittedly, these offered a somewhat sensationalized gloss on the actual response of the eminent cognitive scientist Douglas Hofstadter (author of the once-cult brain-teaser *Gödel, Escher, Bach*) to the news that a computer had recently generated what its programmer was pleased to call Mozart's 42nd Symphony. Concerned that a machine which "has no model whatsoever of life experiences, has no sense of itself, has never heard a note of music" could imitate the creative process of a great composer to a degree that allegedly convinced at least some of the experts some of the time, Hofstadter wondered whether this meant that the composer's soul is irrelevant to the music, because "if that's the case – and I'm not saying it is – then I've been fooled by music all my life. I've been sucked in by a vast illusion. And that would be for me an absolute tragedy ..."

The source of these perturbations turned out to be the 56-year-old American composer and academic David Cope, whose student orchestra in the University of California at Santa Cruz had premiered the 'new' Mozart symphony the previous April. In fact, Cope began to develop his Experiments in Musical Intelligence programme – or (rather confusingly for British CD collectors) EMI for short – some 15 years earlier, not to fabricate Mozart but to help himself over a spot of composer's block. By analytically breaking down and programming the gamut of procedures in his previous works, Cope hoped he could generate a choice of logical continuations at any point where he got stuck. In a way, his initial motivation hints at what may be the fundamental limitation of artificial intelligence as applied to musical composition to date: its circularity. For other composers, by contrast, might well consider that such blocks constitute an invitation, even a sanction, to follow through with something new, unexpected, or positively illogical. As Stravinsky, who seems to have foreseen the whole issue four decades ago, once remarked: "I expect in my own case that when the computer has quantified my musical characteristics, I shall try to do something different."[1]

Actually, EMI represented only the latest stage in what, by now, is quite an extended history of efforts to fabricate music by machines, ranging from such programmes as Brian Eno's Koan for generating ambient music, back via the methods of mathematical patterning promoted between the wars by Joseph Schillinger (to the profit of sundry movie composers and even George Gershwin) all the way, as Cope acknowledged, to the musical dice game attributed to Mozart for composing endless waltzes 'without the least knowledge of music'. Nor should these recurrent attempts to construct such labour-saving mechanisms surprise any save the most incorrigibly romantic. For Western composition has traditionally rested upon teachable – and hence potentially programmable – skills, supplemented, or supplanted in more recent times by such constructivist systems as serialism or the musical exploration of probability and chance. One might, indeed, hazard the assertion that up to 90% of the musical fabric of some of the greatest masterpieces could have been generated by some putative programme drawn from the composer's previous works and the prevailing compositional practices of their time. The real challenge to the advance of artificial intelligence in music presumably lies in those 10% of idiosyncratic strokes and procedures, complexities of affect, and so on that distinguish a Mozart from a Salieri, and which duly evoke from performers, and for listeners, the soul that Professor Hofstadter so hankers for.

The matter is rather complicated by a phenomenon long familiar to music schools and university faculties: the periodic appearance of students with seemingly faultless talents for pastiche in the style of Bach, Mozart, or whoever. To suggest that such assimilative abilities often correlate rather precisely with the absence of strong individual creativity might seem tendentious; but it is difficult to think of a composer of any standing who, in attempting to write in the style of another, has been able to resist doing something of his or her own to it. It might have been easier to determine whether Cope's programme transcended such powers of pastiche, penetrating that last 10%, had his Mozart 42nd been available on disc. What led one to suspect that he had not got that far was his frank admission in the *New Scientist* that he cheats. For while his programme was evidently capable of throwing up any number of generic classical symphonies and then Mozartifying them through an input of sampled personal characteristics, Cope still relied upon his own composerly intuition to spot the likeliest version amid the incessant turn-over of hit-or-miss permutations, and to give it the finishing tweak. As he confessed: "It would horrify me personally to walk into a hall and hear someone else's EMI Mozart symphony and to hear it was as good as the one I produced."

Maybe that is why, for all EMI's simulations of other composers – including the production of a Chopin mazurka which almost convinced even Hofstadter – and Cope's declared ambition to try, no less, for a Mahler's 11th, he has so far apparently avoided what one might have thought would offer the most stringent, quantifiable type of test of his programme: the completion by computer of the sketches for Mahler's Tenth to set beside the human completion prepared with such musicianly care by Deryck Cooke, with the assistance of the late Berthold Goldschmidt and the Matthews brothers, David and Colin, or an EMI Elgar's Third to compare with the completion by Anthony Payne; or a Mozart Requiem to contrast with the many attempted fillings-out since Süssmayr – or, beyond that, any of the dozens of other works for which Mozart left only promising beginnings.[2]

In fact, Cope seemed to accept that his programme might ultimately benefit the present more than the past: "Since I've finished EMI, I have composed more works than I ever thought possible. Having an EMI around will, I hope, inspire more composition, not less."[3] Yet sociologically this would surely compound the problem already raised by the computer cloning of past masters. For if the manufacture of 'new' works by Mozart seems questionable when there are already enough of the real thing to keep most performers and listeners happy for life, the multiplying of today's already multifarious compositional activity in the face of a music industry and a public that seem less and less inclined to absorb the bulk of it will likely lead to some sort of crisis – at least for composers.

Which is not to say that if one were attempting to compose, say, a complex canon, involving many redraftings, much pulling and pushing of material to find the best fit, one might not welcome a programme that instantly presented all the possible solutions. Except that this could well raise the question of the extent to which the ultimate character of a piece of music is dependent upon the very gropings and doubts, the time-consuming process of trial and error that went into its making – a character that might well be lost were the salient choices too quickly presented, too facilely made. But whatever the future role of artificial intelligence in the art of musical composition, its recent developments at least raise the most searching questions about the nature of creativity, the traditional notions of personal style and the unified work, about function, reception and not least such dread philosophical conundrums as intentionality, which are quite enough for mere composers to be getting on with.

NOTES

Source: 'But is it Mozart ...?', *The Independent*, 5 September 1997; rev. 2008.

1   Igor Stravinsky and Robert Craft, *Dialogues and a Diary*, London, Faber, 1968, p. 69.
2   Shortly after this essay appeared, the BBC Radio 4 arts programme *Kaleidoscope* broadcast a discussion in which Anthony Payne – having heard the Cope symphony – diagnosed the main give-away as its unconvincing juxtaposition of elements from quite different periods of Mozart's music.
3   See: David Cope in discussion with Steven Poole, *The Guardian*, 29 August 1997.

Part Two

Pierrot, Milein Cosman

The Music of Words

1   Setting Words to Right

Among its teeming tenth-anniversary themes, the 1990 Almeida Festival featured something called *Music for Words*: a 'gradual enquiry' into the relationship of the two media, which ranged from an evening of melodrama – in the old sense of music-accompanied speech – devised by the producer Peter Sellars, via a presentation of music inspired by the late Samuel Beckett, to a concert of works by the then 80-year-old American composer-novelist, Paul Bowles.[1]

Since his extensive early output of stage pieces and songs includes at least some settings of his own words, Bowles at least could be plausibly placed in that old tradition of poet-songwriter ranging from the twelfth-century troubadours, by way of such Elizabethans as Thomas Campion to, if you will, Bob Dylan. Yet poets pure have often proved ambivalent about getting set – if not, like A. E. Housman, downright hostile. Goethe notoriously preferred the reverential treatment of his lyrics by such almost forgotten composers as J. F. Reichardt and C. F. Zelter to those of Schubert. W. B. Yeats – reputedly tone-deaf, though one could hardly guess it from the finesse of his recorded readings – guardedly entitled one of his most famous verse-sequences *Words for Music Perhaps*.

Not that the tradition of words for music is the real problem. Ever since the Middle Ages there have been music-conscious poets willing to channel their fancies into simple lyric moods, the most singable sequences of vowels and consonants and the verse forms most compatible with the cadence-structures of music. One thinks of the texts of Renaissance madrigals and lute songs, the bel canto verses of eighteenth- and nineteenth-century Italian opera librettists, the song lyrics of such moderns as Bertolt Brecht and W. H. Auden. It would be possible to compile a skeleton history of song over the last four centuries from Shakespeare settings alone – and not only by native composers but also by figures as diverse as Schubert, Mendelssohn, Sibelius, Stravinsky and Poulenc.

It is mainly through the reverse transaction – music for words – that the friction grows. The history of church music is full of ecclesiastical fulminations against composers for obscuring the Word with florid counterpoint or subverting its gravity in saucy tunes; opera remains as ever a perilous juggle between drama and song. As for song itself, commentators often point the paradox of how many of the profoundest songs of Purcell, Schubert or Brahms were inspired by second-rate verse. A talent such as Benjamin Britten's for serving the greatest poetry in a way that continually illuminates its literary qualities without sacrificing musical continuity seems rare indeed.

Of course, pre-existing texts vary vastly in their openness to music. A writer such as Beckett, who depends upon the exact placing and pacing of a minimum of words, not to mention the silences between them, suggests obvious musical affinities, especially with a composer such as Morton Feldman who handled notes so similarly. At the other extreme, a poet such as Gerard Manley Hopkins, whose diction may already involve elaborately 'sprung rhythms' against an implied metre, would seem to defy the power of music to add anything except further layers of complexity – though this did not stop Michael Tippett from having a typically exuberant go at *The Windhover* back in 1942.

Writers of Housman's defensiveness often complain that composers have thrust different moods upon their words than they imagined or have distorted their rhythmic values to suit some melody. But the deepest fear seems to be music's propensity for reducing texts to syllables, if not swallowing them whole. Auden recalled the Cambridge psychologist, P. E. Vernon, who 'once performed the experiment of having a Thomas Campion song sung with nonsense verses of equivalent syllabic value substituted for the original; only 6% of his test audience noticed that something was wrong'.[2]

According to Auden, the words-music friction is exclusive to Western culture and only emerged historically when sound and signification developed beyond the stage of mnemonic chant into autonomous arts.[3] A questionable proposition, no doubt. But anyone who has attempted to set a text will recall feelingly Auden's formulation that 'a verbal art like poetry is reflective; it stops to think. Music is immediate, it goes on to become'.[4] Charmed by Britten's *Serenade* (1943), perhaps, a composer seizes ambitiously upon Keats's 'last' sonnet, 'Bright star, would I were steadfast as thou art'. Unless he is too inspired to think of anything except dashing his song down, Schubert-like, on the back of a menu, he soon discovers he can wrest half a dozen distinct nuances of meaning from the line by re-reading with a different word emphasized each time. Yet his setting will have to plump for just one of these emphases before it moves on to the next line.

But what a variety of musical options he can draw upon by way of compensation! Shall he set the text according to its speech rhythms or open out certain syllables in expressive flourishes of notes? Shall he concentrate on a lieder-like intimacy of tone or a bel-canto beauty of tune? Shall he heighten emotion through a seismographic Schoenbergian line or contain it within an objective Stravinskian incantation? Shall he confirm the sonnet structure in his musical phrasing, or break out of it through verbal repetition? Shall he set up thematic connections with further Keats settings to make a song cycle, or project its musical atmosphere through some Britten-like anthology? Or shall he reject all of these as hopelessly old hat in favour of 'extended vocal techniques', phonetic deconstruction or the extravagances of 'performance art'?

Alas, poor Keats! Yet some of the most innovatory twentieth-century treatments of words and music have sprung from a yearning for new ways to draw the two elements more closely together. In Walton's *Façade* (1923), the method, admittedly, is severely reductive. The spoken inflections of Edith Sitwell's zany texts and the cliché allusions of the jazz band accompaniments are reduced to a common rhythmic stylization and re-assembled in a kind of cubist melodrama. Yet Schoenberg had already attempted a complete, if elusive, fusion of speech and song in *Pierrot lunaire* (1912), seeking a balance of the natural contours of the one with the lyric expansiveness of the other – the effect reinforced by 'casting' the singer as a protagonist living through the various emotions of the cycle.

In *Le marteau sans maître* (1955), Pierre Boulez seemed concerned rather to find deep-structural analogies between text and music, setting René Char's lines, sometimes more than once, in a labyrinth of instrumental 'commentaries' while lapping the mezzo-soprano in such closely-related timbres as alto flute, viola and vibraphone. And for Alexander Goehr's 40-minute Aldeburgh Festival commission in 1990, Frank Kermode came up with a further textural angle. It was not so much an anthology – though his choice ranged from Shakespeare to Larkin – as a cross-cutting of fragments, or cento, linked by certain keywords or phrases (as if they were leitmotifs) implying some sort of emotional trajectory behind the texts, and encompassed by periodic resurfacings of lines from Auden's lyric 'Sing Ariel', which gives the cycle its title. Goehr set this to an almost Stravinskian range of historical allusions and compositional methods – a reference to the 'quire of birds' in Spenser's *Faerie Queene*, Book II, for instance, touched off a fugue on a birdsong of Messiaen. His accompanying ensemble, again jazz-based, even harboured a close-harmony group of two extra sopranos who step out from time to time to join the mezzo-soprano protagonist in madrigalian ensembles – and so on. *Sing Ariel* offers a fascinating further twist to a long, if sometimes difficult relationship.[5]

NOTES

Source: 'Setting Words to Rights', *The Independent*, 16 June 1990. The Almeida Festival ran until 14 July.

1   Under the direction of Pierre Audi, this annual event, based at the restored Almeida Theatre in Islington, emerged in the 1980s as Britain's most idiosyncratic modern music festival, offering retrospectives of figures such as Stefan Wolpe, Hanns Eisler and Jean Barraqué, and attracting such rare visitors as Ernst Krenek, Lou Harrison, Conlon Nancarrow, Nicolas Slonimsky and Astor Piazzolla.

2   W. H. Auden, 'Notes on Music and Opera', *The Dyer's Hand*, London, Faber, 1963, p. 473.

3   Ibid., p. 466.

4   W. H. Auden, 'The Sea and the Mirror', *For the Time Being*, London, Faber, 1944.

5   *Sing Ariel* was performed at Snape Maltings on 23 June 1990, conducted by its dedicatee, Oliver Knussen. It was recorded on Unicorn-Kanchana, DKP 9128, and subsequently re-released on NMC D0296.

[Ed: In an essay on settings of John Milton, 'At a Solemn Musick', *The Independent*, 11 August 1990, the author wrote that

> W. H. Auden once proposed an affinity between Milton and Wagner – both tyrannical personalities, both creators of would-be national epics – on the grounds they were better at evoking evil than good: Milton (as William Blake said) being 'of the Devil's party without knowing it' and Wagner's heroic characters exhibiting 'all that is irrational, morbid, cranky, self-destructive'. But he might have extended the comparison to the medium of Milton's heroic verse itself, the fluid, sometimes almost dreamlike syntax of which allows for the surfacing and combining of keywords and images almost like leitmotifs. The very challenge of such syntax probably helps to explain why no general tradition of Milton setting has ever emerged and why such settings as there have been are often so exceptionally striking.

The works touched on in the essay include Thomas Arne's *Comus* (1738), the first two parts of Handel's *L'allegro, Il penseroso ed Il moderato* (1740) and his *Samson* (1743), Hubert Parry's *Blest Pair of Sirens* (1887) and, in modern times, Hugh Wood's *Scenes from Comus* (1965), the first of Alexander Goehr's *Two Choruses* (1962) and Goehr's extended scena, *Eve Dreams in Paradise* (1990).]

2   *Cross-talk*

There they go again, one thinks crossly, on attempting to take in the words of a BBC Radio 4 programme-trailer against some maddeningly obtrusive backing-track of musical noodlings. Surely the BBC should have learnt by now from the fated old *PM* news-programme signature tune? Every weekday throughout the 1980s, we had to endure its 40 seconds of inane clatter, with the implication that listeners could no longer take in headlines without excited B-feature vampings in the background. Then came the death of Princess Di, and the thing was hastily suppressed as inappropriately upbeat. And when, a few years later, an attempt was made to bring it back, listeners voted with a resounding 'no'. Yet, despite endless letters of protest to such listener-opinion programmes as *Feedback* about the obtrusiveness of background music in this radio drama or that investigative programme, the dubious device of 'voice-over' seems more established than ever. Evidently, some barrier was breached a while back when the presenter of the arts programme *Kaleidoscope* praised an ingenious new jazz track by one of our most versatile young concert pianists – and then proceeded to interview her over its entire length; and while trendy producers would doubtless justify blasting out snippets of the classics behind trailers for *Composer of the Week* or the Proms as 'signals' of works to be heard for themselves, some of these are getting perilously close to the pop-commercial manner of Classic FM …

   But then, one recalls, 'voice-over' has quite a history – for instance, in those arty drama features of the old BBC Home and Third programmes such as *The Rescue* (1943), in which verses of Edward Sackville-West were declaimed over a specially commissioned orchestral score by Benjamin Britten, or *The Shadow of Cain* (1951), in which Edith Sitwell's incantations had to contend with bilious outbursts of Humphrey Searle. And, of course, such concatenations long pre-date the BBC. Even if we leave aside the sporadic demands of dramatists such as Shakespeare for mood music, 'hautboys under the stage' and so on, there have been recurrent attempts by writers and composers to fuse speech and music since at least the mid-eighteenth century. The philosopher, Jean-Jacques Rousseau, was the earliest to devise, and indeed co-compose, an entire music-accompanied play with his *Pygmalion* in the 1760s – though the acknowledged master of the genre that came to be known as 'melodrama' was the Bohemian composer, Georg Benda. One enthusiast for Benda's *Medea* (1775) wrote, 'nothing has ever surprised me so much, for I have always imagined such a piece would be quite ineffective … I think most operatic recitatives should be treated this way – and only sung occasionally when the words can be perfectly expressed by the music.'[1] The writer was none other than Mozart; and though the Singspiel *Zaide* (1779), in which he made his most substantial attempt at melodrama, was left unfinished, accompanied speech was later taken up as an operatic device, especially for evoking frightening or uncanny goings-on: memorably in the dungeon scene in Beethoven's *Fidelio* (1805-14) or the Wolf's Glen horrors of Weber's *Der Freischütz* (1821).

Yet there seems to have been a general acceptance that, in through-composed opera at least, the impact of melodrama was inversely proportional to its frequency: Verdi gives the dying Violetta just a few spoken words of false hope before she expires in *La traviata* (1853); Britten marks the climax of *The Turn of the Screw* (1954) with a single shouted imprecation as Miles denounces Quint. A more frequent use of melodrama was to be found in the spoken theatre – at least, as long as drama companies could still afford pit orchestras and extensive incidental music. One thinks of Mendelssohn, Grieg and Sibelius, with Schumann's magnificent music for Byron's *Manfred* (1852) including perhaps the finest instance. Or there was the alternative tradition of recitation to music, ranging from Schubert's affecting *Abschied von der Erde* (1826) to Richard Strauss's extended treatment of Tennyson's *Enoch Arden* (1897), both with piano accompaniment. But none of the leading Romantics ever seems to have regarded melodrama as more than a special effect or side-line: perhaps they suspected that declamation would always tend to reduce music to a mere affective or onomatopoeic prop. Indeed, in that respect, the ultimate destination of the melodrama has proved to be the Hollywood sound-track.

Meanwhile, most twentieth-century composers evidently came to feel that simply shoving emotive music behind emotive words was too easy, too manipulative, and above all, too approximate – that it hardly began to exploit the potential range of parallels and analogies in sound and structure between speech and music. From the rhythmicised speech patterns of Walton's *Façade* (1923) to the de-semanticised conversations of Ligeti's *Aventures* (1962), from the expressionistic speech-song of Berg's *Wozzeck* (1922-25) to the split-second juggling of sung, spoken and approximately pitched words in Berio's *Circles* (1960), the age has been full of explorations. Yet, no composer worried away at the problem of integrating speech and music, and all the gradations between, more than Arnold Schoenberg. From the rhapsodic declamation of the notated speech-song of 'The Wild Hunt of the Summer Wind' in his early masterpiece, *Gurrelieder* (1900-12), to the hieratic utterances of his final, uncompleted *Modern Psalm* for speaker, chorus and orchestra (1950), Schoenberg strove to relate speech and music in some ten scores. These range in approach from his *Kol Nidre* (1938), which mostly only prescribes the speaker's rhythms, by way of *A Survivor from Warsaw* (1947), which, in addition, suggests the approximate rise and fall of the voice by notes above, on or below a single-line stave, to his stage works *Die glückliche Hand* (1913/24) and *Moses und Aron* (1932), which include whole choruses of exactly notated speech-song counterpoint.[2]

However, the locus classicus of the speech and music challenge – or, specifically, the speech-song problem – has remained *Pierrot lunaire* (1912). This came out of a request by the actress, Albertine Zehme, for some piano pieces to back her recitations of German translations of a series of decadent verses in rondeau form by the Belgian poet, Albert Giraud. But Schoenberg kept adding instruments, so that by the time his 'thrice seven' settings were completed, the voice was located amid an ensemble of five players and often treated, in terms of melodic contour and motivic cross-play, almost as if it were an equal, sixth part in the compositional fabric. Yet, although the vocal pitches were prescribed down to the last accidental, they came with the insistence that, a few specified notes aside, they were not to be sung but recited in a manner halfway between speech and song. Schoenberg called this '*Sprechstimme*', which George Perle defines as 'a type of declamation invented by Schoenberg, in which the vocal part is spoken in exact time, with the vowels momentarily touching the indicated pitch and at once rising or falling away from it.'[3] Since then, hundreds of performers have striven to achieve this elusive golden mean – with the recording Schoenberg conducted in 1942 with the vocalist Erika Stiedry-Wagner offering no more definitive a solution than any other. Meanwhile, scholars and critics have struggled with the questions of whether Schoenberg really knew what he wanted, and whether his fusion is theoretically or practically achievable. Indeed, the distinguished soprano, Jane Manning, who has maintained *Pierrot lunaire* at the heart of her repertoire for over four decades, has recently completed an entire book on the work's challenges and performing history.[4]

At least part of the problem seems to be that Schoenberg often sets vowel sounds to rhythmic durations that would be natural for singing but are too drawn-out for speech, so that the rises and falls Perle mentions are distended and can scarcely avoid emerging as pitched glissandi, turning the vocal line into a weird roller-coaster. Of course, it could be suggested that, whether or not this was Schoenberg's intention, the effect is wholly appropriate to the fantastical imagery of Giraud's verse. Hans Keller, indeed, has argued that the work's very discomfort is functional, arising from the primitive, pre-harmonic background of its atonality, and the pre-verbal emotion of its vocal inflections – a combination bound to disturb the cultivated ear, but eventually to be experienced as an extension of musical possibilities.[5] Certainly, some distinguished ears have found the whole thing hard to take. 'The audience was very quiet and attentive and I wanted Frau Zehme to be quiet too, so that I could hear the music,' recalled Stravinsky of an early performance, with a copy of Schoenberg's manuscript on his knee.[6] Fifty years later, Boulez was still asserting that Schoenberg's attempted fusion of speech and song in *Pierrot* was an 'error', because the part is 'both too high and too low' for the usual tessitura of the speaking voice and because the speaking voice is a 'kind of percussion instrument – hence the impossibility of any actually spoken sound having any long duration.'[7] Stravinsky naughtily suggested that the instrumental score should be released on disc alone (on the Music Minus One label, no doubt) so that listeners could add their own ululations.[8] The performance this writer would love to hear, in contravention of Schoenberg's wishes (if not his notation), is one that is purely sung throughout, without speech inflections – if only to establish whether this takes the sting out of the work or adds an extra dimension.[9]

In any case, Schoenberg himself seems implicitly to have acknowledged that his attempted middle way was a chimera when he exemplified the spiritual incompatibility of Aron and Moses in his opera by casting one as a lyric tenor and the other as a lumbering speaker, albeit a speaker with his part notated in speech-song (*Sprechstimme*). Whether this incompatibility has more to do with language and musical cognition arising from the opposite hemispheres of the brain or some complex disparity between degrees of their definition, it does seem well-nigh insurmountable. Even the apparent balance of lyric song is, at least arguably, an illusion, for melody deconstructs verbal syntax and phrasing, substituting its own. And it is one of the ironies of musical history that, when the intellectuals of the Florentine court attempted in the 1590s to reconstruct what they imagined was the authentic way with Ancient Greek drama, they came up instead with the entirely new formula of opera. None of which is to say that speech and music can never be combined; only that the most successful attempts have generally treated speech as a rare and exotic incursion into the musical flow or turned their very disparity to expressive effect – witness that terrifying film score manqué, Schoenberg's own *A Survivor from Warsaw*.

Yet, if setting up aesthetic dialectics, let alone achieving fusion, between the two media has taxed some of the subtlest minds among the great composers, what of the brightly indiscriminate proliferation of 'voice-over' on our broadcast wavelengths? The problem for the genuinely musical ear is that it cannot help but focus on the sonic background, no matter how trivial or empty – but still more if it happens to comprise music of any substance – rather than the verbal message. For the less-than-musical ear, inured to the use of music as mere background conditioner, or 'unmusic' as Keller once dubbed it (unnoticed unless it is not there), focussing on the words is no problem.[10] Must one presume a cynical assumption in the broadcasting media that the first category is so vastly outnumbered by the second that it can be disregarded? Ought a 'public service' body such as the BBC to be advancing 'unmusic' quite so unquestioningly?

NOTES

Source: 'Hearing Voices in the Air', *The Independent*, 9 February 1991, p. 44; rev. 2008.

1   W. A. Mozart, *The Letters of Mozart and His Family*, 2nd ed., tr. and ed. Emily Anderson, London, Macmillan, 1966, p. 631.

2   Other works by Schoenberg to include the speaking voice were *Die Jakobsleiter* (1917-22), *Von Heute auf Morgen* (1930) and the *Ode to Napoleon* (1942).

3   George Perle, liner note to the 1974 reissue on LP of the 1942 recording of *Pierrot lunaire* conducted by Arnold Schoenberg, CBS Classics, 61442.

4   Jane Manning, *Voicing Pierrot*, ed. Graham Hair, Glasgow, Southern Voices, forthcoming in 2009.

5   Hans Keller, 'Whose Fault is the Speaking Voice?', *Essays on Music*, ed. Christopher Wintle, Cambridge, CUP, 1994, pp. 192-97.

6   Igor Stravinsky and Robert Craft, *Dialogues and a Diary*, London, Faber, 1968, p. 104.

7   Pierre Boulez, 'Speaking, Playing, Singing', *Orientations*, ed. Jean-Jacques Nattiez, tr. Martin Cooper, London, Faber, 1986, pp. 330-43.

8   Igor Stravinsky and Robert Craft, *Expositions and Developments*, London, Faber, 1962, p. 78.

9   In Pierre Boulez's 1977 recording with the mezzo-soprano Yvonne Minton (Sony, SMK 48 466), virtually all the pitches *are* sung – but not the phrases, since Boulez retains the rhythmic durations of speech, resulting in an oddly detached, staccato effect.

10   Hans Keller, *1975 (1984 minus 9)*, London, Dobson, 1977, pp. 256-69.

3   The Librettist's Lament

Sir Harrison Birtwistle almost groaned. For, bearing down purposefully along the empty stalls of the rehearsal hall came his publisher with a large envelope and a wicked grin. Sure enough, it was yet another unsolicited libretto by some aspiring unknown. Decades ago, Benjamin Britten was already insisting, "I get lots of libretti in the post but I have never accepted one. A few of the ideas are attractive enough, but I have to be in on it from the beginning."[1] And Stephen Oliver claimed that many of the libretti he received were simply mad: "Curiously, enough, you can distinguish them immediately: the stage directions are invariably typed in red."[2]

Mad or not, such efforts surely represent a triumph of hope over experience, for it is difficult to think of a single opera in the standard repertoire that was directly inspired by a finished libretto arriving out of the blue. These days, it would be far more likely for a composer obsessed with a dramatic idea to contact a potential librettist out of the blue – as Birtwistle apparently approached David Harsent over *Gawain* (1991) – or to attempt a libretto of his or her own, such as Stephen Oliver's cogent reworking of Shakespeare's *Timon of Athens* (1991). Or, even if invited to co-operate 'from the beginning' *à la* Britten, a librettist may soon find he or she is required to compromise, rewrite and cut endlessly to serve the developing demands of the music.

The rehearsals are liable to bring further shocks, such as just how few words come over in the singing or just how many notions of his own the producer wants to put over in the staging. Come the first night, the applause will inevitably flow to the singers, the conductor and composer if the work is deemed successful – or the notoriety to the production team if it is all found 'controversial'. Yet, after anything less than a triumph, a librettist may find himself assailed for 'unsingable' words or dubious dramaturgy. Ronald Duncan was criticized for years over the poetic diction and pious ending of *The Rape of Lucretia* (1946), in which, as we now know, he was simply meeting Britten's exact demands.

Indeed, a history of opera could be written around the relative decline in power of the librettist in this ostensibly most collaborative of arts. Not that the libretto was ever totally supreme: even in that earliest of great operas, the *'favola per musica'*, *L'Orfeo* (1607), Monteverdi made significant changes to Alessandro Striggio's text. But a variety of factors tended to sustain, if not the pre-eminence, at least the parity of words with music over the next couple of centuries. In serious opera especially, the choice and treatment of subject were often imposed upon the poet and composer alike by their royal or aristocratic employers. The very form of high Baroque opera, with its regular alternation of lightly accompanied recitatives and florid arias, was calculated to switch the focus between verbal drama and musical expression. Moreover, in candle-lit auditoriums that were rarely dimmed, it was customary for eighteenth-century audiences to follow the text itself from tiny printed copies (*libretto* means 'little book'), something that opponents of surtitles might do well to remember.

Accordingly, a figure such as the Viennese court poet Metastasio was able to influence the entire course of *opera seria* through a stream of published libretti that composers went on re-setting for generations. Even in the first half of the nineteenth century, when opera was evolving into a more competitive phase, it was still possible for a librettist of the unspeakable fertility of Eugène Scribe to dominate the Parisian scene, so that composers seeking their fortune there, from Meyerbeer and Bellini to Verdi and Gounod, vied for his influential collaboration. Yet, already back in 1781 Mozart was writing to his father that 'the best thing of all is when a good composer, who understands the stage and is talented enough to make sound suggestions, meets an able poet, that true phoenix'.[3] And by the mid-nineteenth century, Verdi was regularly giving his librettists hell to get what he wanted out of them – a relationship that on a more civilized level was to continue through the famous correspondence between Richard Strauss and Hugo von Hofmannsthal. Doubtless, the same is true of Britten's dealings with the several librettists he subsequently discarded.

Meanwhile, other composers increasingly sought to dispense with librettists altogether. In *Pelléas et Mélisande* (1893-1902) Debussy set Maeterlinck's stage play verbatim save for a few cuts – a procedure followed by Strauss in *Salome* (1905), Alban Berg in *Wozzeck* (1914-22) and *Lulu* (1928/34), and with rather more cuts but only a single inserted line, by Britten and Peter Pears in *A Midsummer Night's Dream* (1960). With Wagner, of course, came the advent of the composer who did it all himself, initiating not only a succession of composer-librettists from Berlioz and Mussorgsky to Pfitzner and Tippett, but also the more fundamental notion that everything about an opera should emerge organically from its own musico-dramatic donnée. Since Wagner, it has certainly been more difficult for composers aspiring to anything beyond the spills or thrills of a Sullivan or a Menotti simply to take up the old standard genres of comedy, melodrama or whatever without loading them with the kind of mythological, psycho-symbolic or socio-political ballast deemed necessary to ensure 'depth' or 'relevance'.

Has this now gone too far – have such requirements merely become inhibiting and wearisome conventions in themselves? In this respect, the premieres of *Gawain* and *Timon* in 1991 were not unsuggestive – if paradoxically. Birtwistle's massive, wave-like score of slow-grinding textures seemed so exactly matched to the portentous repetitiousness of Harsent's libretto and to the grey ponderousness of the designs and production of Alison Chitty and Di Trevis, that *Gawain* was hailed in some critical quarters as a well-nigh Wagnerian achievement. Yet it hardly began to rival the flexibility of pacing with which Wagner actually managed to unfold his seemingly slow-

moving dramas. Nor was it easy to imagine what scope its indulgent, symbol-laden ritualism might offer for alternative interpretations. Stephen Oliver's opera, by contrast, was widely panned by those same critics, ostensibly on the periodic inaudibility of its text – though one heard more words than in Gawain. What ought to have been praised were the economy and variety of the handling of both words and music that, without pretentiousness, brought a fresh range of implications to Shakespeare's text – in a sense, indeed, 'completing' an incompletely realized play – through an eclectic but apt array of musical ideas. One could hardly claim that, as a composer, Oliver matched Birtwistle's uncompromising radicalism. Yet his musico-dramatic treatment suggested more ways forward.

What then of the aspiring librettist about to get down to work with the composer he or she has just teamed up with? Previous experience will doubtless be an advantage, if only to be prepared for the usual dismissal of opera by unmusical realists as artificial and absurd. In fact, all theatrical forms have their conventions, including realism: people do not actually live in houses with one wall missing or agonize around the kitchen sink in strictly consecutive dialogue. And whatever opera's peculiarities, it has evolved ways of varying the flow of dramatic time, heightening lyric expression and simultaneously conveying contrary feelings in concerted ensembles beyond the power of any other theatrical form. Admittedly there remains a perennial argument as to whether opera's conventions should be disguised as far as possible or openly flaunted as in Handel, Bellini or Strauss – the reformer who wants to rein in vocal writing and restore 'truth to diction' has been a recurrent figure, witness Gluck, Dargomïzhsky and Janáček. Doubtless it will help if our librettist is aware of all this and able, early on, to establish with the composer which line to follow.

Aware, too, of how, over time, musico-dramatic approaches have tended to swing between the poles of number opera and music drama. There is nothing like the Wagnerian continuum for conveying the oceanic depths of myth, symbolism and the collective unconscious, even if, lacking any formal principle distinct from the libretto, or 'dramatic poem' as Wagner called it, the music is rather obliged to go 'up and down' with the actions and emotions of the text. Sequences of set forms – arias, ensembles, choruses – may be shorter-winded, but they can nevertheless imply a critical counter-structure to the drama – as in those Mozartean moments of sublime detachment where the characters are all agitation yet the music goes its own sweet way. Of course, many composers, from the later Verdi to Britten have contrived various compromises between number opera and music drama, and these offer a further range of models. Or maybe our librettist and composer will attempt to jettison all such traditions for the hopeful freedoms of 'music-theatre': an acting space, a few singers and players, some props and lighting, a book of words – what could be more liberating? Yet they should know that they are likely to find themselves back at square one, having consciously to tackle the basic problems of form and expression that have already been solved over the 400 years of 'conventional' opera.

Not least, the librettist will need to be aware of the riskiness of the wager in which he or she is involved. A mere glance at that graveyard of past aspirations, Alfred Lowenberg's *Annals of Opera* 1597-1940, will reveal how tiny a proportion of operas staged over the centuries have meaningfully survived; nor, apart from the Britten canon and *The Rake's Progress* (1948-51) of Stravinsky, along with the honourable runner-up attainments of Tippett and Hans Werner Henze, has the second half of the twentieth century proved any more encouraging. Again, once text and score are submitted to the marmoreal grindings of the production process, there may be little more that librettist or composer – unless the latter is a Britten – can do to influence the result. Even before that, though, the librettist will need to recognize that, no matter how skilfully the prose sentences and verse forms, the line lengths and sequences of vowels and consonants have been devised to draw the best from the composer, the result is most likely to succeed or fail on the basis of the work's 'pacing' – that supreme instinct that Mozart, Wagner, Verdi and Britten shared for fusing music and drama in a way that transcends the static theatricality of masque on the one hand, and mere sung play with background music on the other, to attain a dramatic momentum all its own.

Above all, perhaps, the librettist must really feel that his or her own words are insufficient; that their meaning, emotion and poetry, can only be truly realized through opera. That highly literate composer, Robin Holloway – who has both written the libretto for his own *Clarissa* (1976) and worked with a gifted lyricist, the late Gavin Ewart, on his as-yet unperformed comedy, *Boys and Girls Come out to Play* (1991-95) – recalls that, long before either, he thought of turning Nathaniel West's dystopian novella, *Miss Lonelyhearts*, into an opera. With the assurance of youth, he wrote to W. H. Auden inviting a libretto. The poet's reply was kindly but firm: it was an interesting idea, but he couldn't do it because the characters in the story were all too miserable to sing.

NOTES

Source: 'Of Writer's Blocks', *The Independent*, 29 June 1991; rev. 2008.

1   Murray Schafer, *British Composers in Interview*, London, Faber, 1963, p. 115.
2   Paul Griffiths, *New Sounds, New Personalities: British Composers of the 1980s*, London, Faber, 1985, p. 147.
3   Letter of 13 October 1781 in: W. A. Mozart, *The Letters of Mozart and His Family*, 2nd ed., tr. and ed. Emily Anderson, London, Macmillan, 1966, p. 713.

4   Notes on Auden

In the winter of 1942-43, W. H. Auden was in Pennsylvania working hard at his latest long poem – a commentary upon *The Tempest* entitled *The Sea and the Mirror* – and waiting even more eagerly for news of the previous one. This was *For the Time Being*, the text of a full-length Christmas oratorio he had begun in October 1941 in the hope of tempting his fellow émigré, Benjamin Britten. Britten *was* interested, even though he had returned to England by the time he received the finished text, sometime in the early autumn of 1942. Yet in the end he only set a couple of brief extracts, and Auden was deeply hurt. Indeed, the debacle marked something of a turning point in Auden's development. Up till then, his texts for music had comprised individual lyrics and choruses, film and radio scripts and musical plays, culminating in the so-called operetta, *Paul Bunyan*, he and Britten had written in 1941. Thereafter, he would mainly be preoccupied with full-scale opera librettos – though never for Britten. What remained from first to last was his quite special devotion to music itself. With the arguable exception of Bertolt Brecht, Auden was ultimately to instigate or inspire a larger number of scores in a wider variety of forms than any other poet of the twentieth century.

It would, of course, be rash to suggest any simple correlation between the degree of a writer's musicality and the aptness of his work for setting. W. B. Yeats was reputedly tone-deaf: Ezra Pound affected musicality in his pronouncements and even composed (with help) a pair of primitive little operas of his own, while T. S. Eliot appears to have carried over certain deep intuitions of form and transformation from the music he listened to into his poetic process. Yet there are probably as many settings of Yeats as there are of Eliot, and more than of Pound. In his listening, Auden could be as partial or prejudiced as the next man: "Verdi and Mozart are the top composers, Alpha Plus," he might declare, or "If we were to make up our own *Index*, Brahms, Shelley and Sibelius would all go on in toto."[1] But, unlike most of his poetic peers, he was musically literate – brought up on J. S. Bach by a gifted mother with whom, rather more piquantly, he also learnt to sing the love-potion duet from *Tristan und Isolde*. By his teens, he had evidently laid the basis of a piano technique that, years later, would enable him to hold his own playing four-hands with Stravinsky – though those who praised his skill were likely to be deflected by his assertion, 'actually, Morgan Forster is the truly impressive keyboard amateur'.[2] As a schoolboy and young teacher, he also sang in the usual choral works, occasionally taking a solo. And, at least once, he composed tunes for his own verses, in the Christmas revue he devised in 1934 while teaching at the Downs School, Colwall. It was here, on 5 July

1935, that the 21-year-old Britten first visited him to discuss their forthcoming collaboration in the GPO Film Unit.

He was not the earliest composer to set Auden, who a couple of years before had apparently hoped the as-yet unknown Michael Tippett would provide music for his *Dance of Death*. In the event, the Group Theatre had used Herbert Murrill, who was also to supply the score ('Just clever & rather dull jazz,' Britten privately thought it)[3] for the Auden-Isherwood morality, *The Dog Beneath the Skin* in 1936. 'What immediately struck me,' Auden was to recall years later, 'was his extraordinary musical sensibility in relation to the English language. One had always been told that English was an impossible tongue to set or sing. Since I already knew the songs of the Elizabethans like Dowland (I don't think I knew Purcell then), I knew this to be false, but the influence of that great composer, Handel, on the setting of English had been unfortunate … Here at last was a composer who could both set the language without undue distortion of its rhythmical values, and at the same time write music to which it was a real pleasure to listen.'[4] And Britten, looking back in 1963, almost a decade after breaking off personal contact, was still prepared to concede Auden's primacy as his political and literary mentor: 'He also had some lively, slightly dotty ideas about music. He played the piano reasonably well and was a great one for singing unlikely words to Anglican chants.'[5] Nevertheless, Britten insisted he had only been influenced by Auden personally, never musically.[6]

In the strictest sense, this was doubtless true. Apart from such generalized encomia as his sonnet, *The Composer* (1938), and the *Anthem for St. Cecilia's Day* (1942), Auden's earlier ideas about music are less than easy to track down. Whether dotty or not, they were only to reach print in such later, marvellous collections of prose and aphorisms as *The Dyer's Hand* (1963) and in the memoirs of friends, and are rarely concerned with composition as such – tending rather to propositions about the nature and the social function of music or discussions of word-setting and operatic translation. All the same, his effect upon Britten's musical development was surely more specific than simply putting such poets as Rimbaud and Donne so fruitfully his way. Hans Keller argued that Britten's leaning towards vocal music 'was intimately bound up with his ability to create tensions between musical and verbal rhythm,' and that 'these tensions were of a magnitude that made it possible for him to create extended structures with comparative ease.'[7] From recently published diaries and letters of the 1930s, to say nothing of the works themselves, it seems clear that Britten's collaboration with Auden was crucial in mastering such musico-verbal tensions; that setting Auden stretched him more than working with any subsequent living writer (in the operas, librettists would be expected to adapt to his requirements), and that, at least up to *Paul Bunyan*, he mostly welcomed being so stretched.

Not all their projects between 1935 and 1942 were determined by Auden. Britten seems to have chosen freely from his recent lyrics for the song-set with piano, *On This Island* (1937) – though with an acute eye for the verses that would enable him, as it were, to vocalise the idiosyncratic mixture of sharp parody and simple lyricism in his concurrent instrumental pieces to create his first mature recital sequence. Other workings-together were more dictated by circumstance: the cross-cutting of speech with choral or instrumental effects required for the GPO documentaries, *Coal Face* (1935) and *Night Mail* (1936); the stagings of the last two Auden-Isherwood plays, *The Ascent of F6* (1937) and *On the Frontier* (1938), in which both composer and authors had often to submit to the Group Theatre's producer, Rupert Doone; the choral and orchestral *Ballad of Heroes* (1939), composed for a Festival of Music for the People, in which Britten set verses from an earlier 'farewell' poem by Auden to recycled scherzo material of his own. But the texts Auden selected and wrote specifically for Britten are so vastly varied in purpose, tone and technique – from the emblematic protest of *Our Hunting Fathers* (1936) to the glitzy insouciance of the *Cabaret Songs* (1938), from the moralizing populism of *Paul Bunyan* to the affirming litanies of the *Hymn to St. Cecilia* – that one wonders, after a certain point, whether they were not consciously conceived to test Britten to his limit as 'the white hope of music'. For so Auden hailed him in a now-famous admonitory letter written on the eve of Britten's return home from America in 1942.[8]

Already in 1936, Britten had risen with searing virtuosity to the challenge of Auden's central choice of texts for *Our Hunting Fathers*: the serio-comic rhetoric of the medieval exorcism of rats; the innocent excess of Messalina's lament for her pet monkey; the terrifying rampage of Ravenscroft's evocation of hawking. Auden's own Prologue and Epilogue have been criticized as unduly obscure, but he seems to have concluded quite early on that what composers responded to were not so much clear-cut sentences as rhythmically stressed syllables and carefully placed keywords. The final lines run:

> …
> And make it his mature ambition
> To think no thought but ours,
> To hunger, work illegally,
> And be anonymous?

Maybe Britten wondered privately what this had to do with a work concerning man's relation to the animals. But his setting shows no sign of strain; on the contrary, he meaningfully counterpoints Auden's rhythm and enriches his sense by emphases on the words 'his' and 'no' and a strangely yielding melisma on 'anonymous'. Indeed, when Britten recognised the cycle as 'my Op. 1 alright',[9] he must have been acutely aware of Auden's agency in releasing for the first time his full powers. Whether that awareness had begun to chafe by the time of *Paul Bunyan* is difficult to determine, since the attitude of both collaborators was evidently coloured by its apparent New York failure – for which Auden was generously prepared to take all the blame, but which its 1976 revival proved quite unwarranted. Donald Mitchell has suggested that some of Auden's proffered lyrics had by now attained such a teasing intricacy as to be virtually unsettable, and has even speculated whether

> Auden ever wholly comprehended that while words are words, words written for transformation into and by music – for consumption by music – are something entirely different. I think that it was in fact an increasing inability to see this that finally brought about the end of his creative association with Britten.[10]

But quite apart from Hans Keller's contention that Britten needed verbal tensions to work against, this does scant justice to Auden's willingness during the preparation of *Paul Bunyan* to scrap, rewrite and come up with fresh material to meet all exigencies: the exquisitely touching 'Tiny's Song' is only one instance of a number the collaborators happily conjured up at the last moment. And the imputation of Auden's 'increasing inability' does still less justice to his part in contriving the *Hymn to St. Cecilia* the following year – that well-nigh perfect marriage of voice and verse.

So what, apart from the interposing of the Atlantic Ocean, served to frustrate *For the Time Being*? In retrospect, both Britten and Peter Pears were inclined to blame the inordinate length of the text. But this does not seem to have been such a problem at the time; Auden was evidently prepared to accept cuts and Britten spent some time considering what might go.[11] More critical may have been their diverging concepts of the work as whole. Letters from Auden over the winter of 1942-43 shows he increasingly envisaged it as a modernist montage, matching the varied verse forms with contrasting musical styles including folk song and jazz, scored for small forces and perhaps best put out on radio. Britten's preliminary list of performers, including large-scale choral forces, suggests rather a more traditional, indeed monumental oratorio approach, and this, in turn, would seem to touch on wider, extra-musical divergences. Auden always claimed he preferred the exile and anonymity of New York because English cultural life was in the last resort a family life; and that, although he loved his family, he did not always want to live with them. Britten's return home, by contrast, was very much a re-embracing of that cultural family of which, in due course, he would establish himself as a father figure. Did the process require the psychological rejection of his own cultural father-figure – Auden himself – for its successful accomplishment?

In any case, Britten was never to set Auden again after including the lyric 'Out on the lawn I lie in bed' in the *Spring Symphony* of 1949. In selecting a text from Auden's Downs School period just before they met, Britten may have intended a nostalgic tribute. But the poem, with its allusions to violence in Poland and the dubious security of English life, was also about the last he was ever to tackle with specific contemporary political reference.[12] Unlike the quixotic Tippett, none of his operas were set in the present, and when he came to make his definitive pacifist protest in the *War Requiem* of 1962, it proved to hark back, not to the Second World War, but to the morally less complex First. In later years, Auden too would deny that art could exert any political leverage, but, whether following the speculations of science or reacting to the indignity of being frisked by the police, his verse would never quite lose touch with a sense of the contemporary. It may be that in freezing Auden out and ultimately cutting him off so cruelly, Britten was also cutting off some of his own potential. In any case, before he had composed a note of the Spring Symphony, Auden had already received Stravinsky's invitation to write the libretto for *The Rake's Progress* and replied, "I need hardly say that the chance of working with you is the greatest honour of my life."[13]

II

So it was in November 1947 that Auden flew to California to spend a week with Stravinsky working out a scenario for *The Rake*. He had just turned 40, and was a changed man from the charismatic young poet-teacher Britten had met back in July 1935. Not only had he formalized his self-imposed exile by taking American citizenship in 1946, but, after seeking salvation in psychoanalysis and political engagement, he had also returned to Christian worship in 1941: henceforth he would insist that the only serious matters in life were 'loving God and your neighbour'.[14] As Stravinsky recalled from their initial sessions, 'The making of poetry he seemed to regard as a game, albeit a game to be played in a magic circle … and any technical question, of versification, for example, put him in a passion; he was even eloquent about such matters.'[15] But if Auden had come to believe that all pursuits outside man's religious obligations were 'fundamentally frivolous' because voluntary, few interests engaged his passionate playfulness more intensely from the early 1940s than opera.

No doubt he exaggerated a bit when he blamed the apparent failure of *Paul Bunyan* in 1941 on the submission that 'I knew nothing whatever about opera or what is required of a librettist. In consequence, some very lovely music of Britten's went down the drain …'[16] The work was hardly conceived as an opera in the first place; more a moralistic pageant-cum-high-school musical.

And Auden had evidently known some of Mozart's and Wagner's operatic music since his youth, even if he claimed he only learned to love the latter after reading Nietzsche's arguments against it.[17] Nor, for that matter, were his interests entirely absorbed by opera in his later years. Despite such naughty aperçus as 'people who attend chamber music concerts are like Englishmen who go to church when abroad,'[18] his conversations and letters of the late 1940s and '50s are full of enthusiastic comments on choral, symphonic and chamber music works by Bach, Handel, Haydn, Berlioz, Liszt, Fauré, Wolf and Stravinsky.[19] Nevertheless, it is evident that his first encounter in New York in 1939 with Chester Kallman, who was to become the wayward companion of his remaining years, effected a conversion almost as decisive as his return to the Church. Though only 18 at the time of their meeting, Kallman was already a knowledgeable opera buff who soon had the sartorially careless Auden into evening dress and attending the Met once a week. The major revelation was apparently the Italian repertoire from Rossini to Verdi – at the time so critically *infra dig.* in the Britain Auden had just abandoned. But he also got deeper into Wagner, acquired a taste for Richard Strauss – not to mention Hugo von Hofmannsthal – and began accumulating a large collection of operatic recordings which he would play and hold forth upon by the hour.

Whatever the fancied shortcomings of *Paul Bunyan* – in much of which, words and music actually fit like a glove – Auden had reached some settled conclusions about the art of opera by the time he received Stravinsky's summons. Since it was 'the librettist's job to satisfy the composer, not the other way round,'[20] it followed that 'a good opera plot is one which provides as many and as varied situations in which it seems plausible that characters should sing. This means that no opera plot can be sensible, for in sensible situations, people do not sing.'[21] Anyway, 'in writing words to be set to music, one has to remember that, probably, only one word in three will be heard.'[22] Accordingly, 'the verses which the librettist writes are not addressed to the public but are really a private letter to the composer. They have their moment of glory, the moment in which they suggest to him a certain melody; once that is over … they must efface themselves and cease to care what happens to them.'[23] These might sound more like prescriptions for an eighteenth- or early nineteenth-century number-opera than for the, at least theoretical, fusion of words and music in Wagnerian music-drama – let alone the kind of text-led Brechtian or Broadway musical theatre that to some extent lay behind *Paul Bunyan*. But Stravinsky had already decided his eighteenth-century subject required a Mozartian operatic scheme and was primarily looking for 'a versifier with whom I could collaborate in writing songs … hoping that we could evolve the theatrical form together and that it would inspire Wystan to dramatic poetry.'[24]

To a poet of the skill of Auden – or, indeed, of Kallman, once he had been admitted to the collaboration under Auden's critical tutelage – providing appropriate verses was no problem at all. 'Wystan had a genius for operatic wording,' Stravinsky acknowledged later: 'His lines were always the right length for singing and his words the right ones to sustain musical emphasis.'[25] But the three collaborators found themselves having to impose upon the vestigial narrative of Hogarth's pictures both a fairy-tale scheme of three wishes and a Faustian pact with the Devil, in order to touch their essentially passive protagonist with that spirit of wilfulness, that insistence on having feelings at whatever cost, that Auden asserted was the essence of all great operatic roles.[26] No one, at least, could object that such functional interpolations as Baba the bearded lady and the magic bread-machine were too sensible to appear in an opera; on the contrary, Baba emerges as the most splendidly wilful character of the lot, while even the bread-machine will go down, as Stravinsky noted, 'if the stage director has not lost sight of the opera's "moral fable" proposition by overplaying the realism'.[27] But what is most striking is that neither the composer nor his librettists seem to have been remotely hung up on the question that exercised their subsequent critics for years: whether an opera apparently based upon long outmoded conventions and stylistic pastiche could possibly be considered authentic or relevant in the century of modernism. In addition to recognising instantly in one another 'a professional artist, concerned not for his personal glory, but solely for the thing-to-be-made,'[28] Stravinsky and Auden were both inveterate formalists, holding to the paradox that it requires the strictest means to convey the fullest message. The strict musical and literary forms of *The Rake* enabled its creators to mediate the most wide-ranging allusions and resonances – stylistic, historical, mythological, and so on. Where these are brought together, in the ultimate reunion of Tom Rakewell and Anne Trulove in Bedlam, the scene attains a timeless depth of pathos unique in twentieth-century opera.

With *The Rake* so rapidly establishing itself in the repertoire after its premiere in 1951, it seemed highly desirable that the collaboration should continue; and early in 1952 Auden and Kallman sent Stravinsky a new libretto for an evening-length one-act opera entitled *Delia* or *A Masque of Night*. Distantly based upon George Peele's play, *The Old Wives' Tale* (1595), it follows the trials of a knight, Orlando, to win Delia from the enchantments of Sacrapant, a magus. The action is cross-cut by the tribulations of Bungay ('an amateur sorcerer') and his shrewish wife, and suggests a sophisticated combination of mummers' play and *The Magic Flute*. With pastiche Elizabethan verses for arias and ensembles, it culminates in a dawn chorus that proves to be an early draft of the poem Auden was to publish as 'Lauds' in his 1955 verse sequence, *Horae canonicae*. By this time, however, Stravinsky was already moving towards the lapidary serial manner of his old age, making

it more and more unlikely he would ever again undertake so expansive a
project. After some hesitation he laid the text of *Delia* aside. It was eventually
published in a short-lived arts magazine, but has never been set to this day.[29]

Though Auden and Stravinsky remained convivial friends, they only
collaborated again once, when Stravinsky asked for some brief verses in
memory of President Kennedy in 1964. Responding with craftsmanly
enthusiasm, Auden came up with a set of four eloquent haiku, the last of
which could be used as a refrain:

> When a just man dies,
> Lamentation and praise,
> Sorrow and joy, are one.

Gratefully acknowledging that 'Mr. Auden knows my time-scale,'[30]
Stravinsky set them for medium voice and three clarinets as his *Elegy for JFK*,
a haunting little memorial lasting hardly more than a hundred seconds. Not
all of Auden's later projects-for-music proved so inspiring. 'Here at last is
the draft of that bloody anthem,'[31] he wrote to William Walton in December
1964 with verses for *The Twelve* which they had been jointly commissioned to
write by their old college, Christ Church, Oxford. Yet his recourse to a deft,
internally-rhymed prose seemed almost wickedly calculated to reanimate the
hustle of Sir William's old festive choral style. By contrast, the nursery-rhyme
rhythms of *Moralities*, three 'scenic cantatas' after Aesop commissioned for
school performance in 1967, drew a rather pallid response from Hans Werner
Henze, while Auden admitted that to come up with anything much in the
way of a *United Nations Hymn* for setting by the 94-year-old Pablo Casals in
1971, he had to fall back on self-quotation. But by a happy chance, his very
last musical text, which he worked on with Kallman in the summer of 1973,
was an interpolation to a masque – that emblematic form with its flourishes
and personifications that hovers in the background of so much of Auden's
poetry, dramatic and lyric – though by the time John Gardner's setting of *The
Entertainment of the Senses* reached performance, he was already four months
dead.[32]

Yet such commissions were by no means the only way in which Auden
impinged upon the musical world in his final three decades. Loathing opera in
translation, he and Kallman nevertheless concluded that, if it had to be done,
it had better be done by them.[33] In 1956, they published an English singing
version of *The Magic Flute*, to which Auden added a witty verse *Metalogue* in
celebration of the bicentenary of Mozart's birth. Their subsequent translations
included *Don Giovanni* as well as *The Seven Deadly Sins* and *The Rise and Fall
of the City of Mahagonny* of Brecht and Weill. Meanwhile, in 1955 they edited a
choice of lute songs as *An Elizabethan Song Book* with the director of the New

York Pro Musica, Noah Greenberg, who also induced Auden in 1957 to write and perform in monk's garb an alliterative verse-narrative for his pioneering production of the twelfth-century music drama, *The Play of Daniel*.

Indeed, by the time of Auden's death, quite a substantial song book could already have been compiled from diverse settings of his own verse. Already, in the wake of Britten, Elisabeth Lutyens and Lennox Berkeley had tackled individual lyrics back in the 1940s, and Berkeley's later treatment of 'Lauds' and 'O lurcher-loving collier' in his *Five Poems of W. H. Auden* (1958) remain among the most felicitous settings of the poet. That same year, the young Nicholas Maw took the lyric 'Make this night lovable' for the culminating song of his *Nocturne* for mezzo and chamber orchestra, while in 1960, Lukas Foss opened his *Time Cycle* with 'Clocks cannot tell the time of day'. Oliver Knussen's haunting setting of 'If I could tell you' in his *Requiem: Songs for Sue* (2006) is only the latest in a long line of Auden songs by such composers as Ned Rorem, Hans Werner Henze and Robin Holloway. Sometimes his work had wider repercussions. In 1949, Leonard Bernstein modelled an entire symphony, the Second, on the form of Auden's long 'baroque eclogue' of big city alienation, *The Age of Anxiety*, published two years before. And in 1954, Luciano Berio, despairing of his plan to set Auden's *Nones* as an oratorio, concentrated its sketches into an orchestral piece of the same name. Between 1979-84, he also took the plan of Auden's *The Sea and the Mirror* (1944), comprising Prospero's farewells to the various characters of *The Tempest*, as the framework for his most accomplished contribution to the musical theatre, *Un re in ascolto*, embedding a number of Auden's lines in his libretto.

Of course, Auden and Kallman themselves continued to explore alternative operatic genres in the two librettos they wrote for Henze. Where *The Rake* had been a moral fable based upon eighteenth-century material scored for Mozartian forces and structured in separate numbers, *Elegy for Young Lovers*, first staged in 1961, was a fin-de-siècle psychological drama on original material, scored for chamber forces and structured in a more continuous form of linked numbers. And *The Bassarids*, rapturously received in 1966, comprised a modern gloss on ancient material, scored for huge forces and structured as a through-composed music drama, at the opposite pole – one neo-classical intermezzo aside – from *The Rake*. If *Elegy* in particular has subsequently failed to establish itself in the repertoire, the fault may lie partly in the wordy texture of the libretto – in this instance comprising more Kallman than Auden – which the collaborators dedicated to the memory of Hugo von Hofmannsthal. Indeed, Auden later criticized one of his own scenes as far too literary and in need of complete rewriting.[34] Yet the Alpine setting, the vividly contrasted characters in circulation around the poet-protagonist and the librettists' idea that the greatness of his verse would better be symbolized in music than represented in words, offered Henze all the opportunities for 'tender, beautiful noises' he had requested in the first place.[35] Ultimately, it is his failure to complement his often exquisite textures with clear melodic lines and firmly directional harmonies that hampers dramatic pacing.

Such deficiencies may at first seem to matter less in *The Bassarids*. The terrible events derived from *The Bacchae* of Euripides would seem made for Henze's immediate gifts for violent gesture and sensuous elaboration. Moreover, Henze not only induced his librettists to cast their scenario in the semblance of a four-movement symphony, but also found the firmness to cut their still more elaborate text by pages. In such moments as the massive passacaglia-apotheosis near the end, he seems to come close to the fusion of frenzy and elevation suggested by the librettists in their generic subtitle, '*opera seria*'. But, on further acquaintance, too much of the score remains blurred and diffuse. Yet there was to be one subsequent libretto. Auden had long argued that the only Shakespeare play that could be turned into an English-language opera was *Love's Labours Lost*, and in 1969 he and Kallman prepared a simplified version, removing handfuls of minor characters, for Nicolas Nabokov – one of Sergei Diaghilev's last discoveries, an energetic organizer of cultural congresses and old friend of both Auden and Stravinsky. Though the opera was staged in Brussels in 1973, it has never reached Britain or been recorded, and it is difficult to know whether dismissals of the score as a mere sequence of parodies are just. Auden would probably not be surprised at its subsequent unsuccess, for he once described Nabokov as 'a composer who will never realize his talent, because he cannot bear to be long enough alone'.

Would Auden really have liked to be a composer himself? Composing was the one human activity he regarded as 'an absolute gift'; moreover, he evidently found the sensuous experience of music – 'O delight, cascading/The falls of the knee and the weirs of the spine'[36] – an essential counter-balance to his dialectical mentality. And beyond this, he also seems to have thought of the writing, performing and listening to music as a model of the Good Society. As he wrote in his very last collection, *Thank You, Fog*, published in 1974:

> When truly brothers,
> Men don't sing in unison
> But in harmony. [37]

But whether a mind so addicted to concepts of 'either-or' could ever have creatively engaged itself in music's special propensity, as Hans Keller often put it, for 'having it both ways' – of swimming against the rhythmic tide as in Stravinsky; of simultaneously conveying both joy and sadness as in Mozart – might be doubted. Maybe it is the very way that the antithetical propositions of his lyrics and song texts cry out for musical resolution that makes them such a gift *to* composers.

NOTES

Source: This essay was printed in two parts in *The Musical Times*, Vol. 124, Nos. 1799 and 1800, January and February 1993, pp. 6-8 and 68-72 respectively. The ending of the second part was revised in 2008.

I

1   Alan Ansen, *The Table Talk of W. H. Auden*, ed. Nicholas Jenkins, London, Faber, 1991, pp. 16 and 57.
2   Charles H. Miller, *Auden: An American Friendship*, New York, Paragon House, 1983, p. 73.
3   Donald Mitchell, *Britten & Auden in the Thirties*, London, Faber, 1981, p. 119.
4   Unpublished tribute for Britten's fiftieth birthday in: Mitchell, 1981, p. 119.
5   Murray Schafer, *British Composers in Interview*, London, Faber, 1963, pp. 114-15.
6   Interview with Charles Osborne (*London Magazine*, Vol. 3, No. 7, October 1963) in: Benjamin Britten, *Letters from a Life*, Vol. 1, ed. Donald Mitchell and Philip Reed, London, Faber, 1991, p. 384.
7   Hans Keller in: *Remembering Britten*, ed. Alan Blyth, London, Hutchinson, 1981, p. 90.
8   Quoted in: Mitchell, 1981, pp. 161-62.
9   Ibid., p. 19.
10 Ibid., p. 139.
11 Benjamin Britten, *Letters from a Life*, Vol. 2, ed. Donald Mitchell and Philip Reed, London, Faber, 1991, p. 1091-95. *For the Time Being* was eventually set as an oratorio by the American composer Marvin David Levy (b. 1932) and premiered in New York in 1959; but it failed to enter the repertory.
12 Unless one counts such late treatments of Second World War violence against the young in *The Children's Crusade* (1968) and *Who Are These Children?* (1969).
13 Igor Stravinsky and Robert Craft, *Memories and Commentaries*, London, Faber, 1960, p. 155.

II

14 Ansen, 1991, p. 37.
15 Stravinsky and Craft, 1960, p. 157.
16 Unpublished tribute for Britten's fiftieth birthday, cited in: Donald Mitchell, liner notes to *Paul Bunyan*, Virgin Classics, VCD 7, 90701-02, 1988.
17 Anselm, 1991, p. 44.
18 Robert Craft, *Stravinsky: The Chronicle of a Friendship* (1972), rev. ed., Nashville, Vanderbilt UP, 1994, p. 344.
19 See, for instance: Anselm, 1991, pp. 15-18, 212 and 26; and: Dorothy J. Farnon, *Auden in Love*, London, Faber, 1984, pp. 151-52.
20 Stravinsky and Craft, 1960, p. 155.
21 W. H. Auden, *Secondary Worlds*, London, Faber, 1968, p. 84.

22 Auden in interview with Michael Newman, 1972, in: George Plimpton (ed.), Poets at Work, London, Penguin, 1989, p. 300.

23 W. H. Auden, *The Dyer's Hand*, London, Faber, 1963, p. 473.

24 Interview with Stravinsky for a BBC Television documentary on Auden, 1965, in: Paul Griffiths, *The Rake's Progress*, Cambridge, CUP, 1982, p. 4.

25 Ibid., p. 4.

26 Auden, 1963, p. 470.

27 Stravinsky, programme note, 1964, in: Griffiths, 1982, p. 3.

28 Auden, note for Columbia Records, 1967, in: Vera Stravinsky and Robert Craft, *Stravinsky in Pictures and Documents*, London, Hutchinson, 1972, p. 397.

29 *Botteghe oscura*, Autumn, 1953. 'Delia' appears in: W. H. Auden and Chester Kallmann, *Libretti 1939-73*, the second published volume of *The Complete Works of W. H. Auden*, ed. Edward Mendelson, London, Faber, 1993, pp. 95-126.

30 Igor Stravinsky and Robert Craft, *Themes and Conclusions*, London, Faber, 1972, pp. 60-2.

31 Quoted in: Christopher Palmer, note to the 1990 recording of Sir William Walton's *The Twelve,* Chandos, CHAN 8824.

32 Auden died in September 1973, at the age of 66.

33 W. H. Auden and Chester Kallman, 'Translating Opera Libretti' in: Auden, 1963, pp. 483-99.

34 Auden, 1968, p. 95.

35 W. H. Auden and Chester Kallman, 'Genesis of a Libretto', published with the libretto of *Elegy for Young Lovers*, Mainz, Schott, 1961, p. 62.

36 W. H. Auden, sonnet: 'The Composer', *Another Time*, London, Faber, 1940.

37 W. H. Auden, *Thank You Fog*, London, Faber, 1974, p. 29.

Part Three

William Walton, Milein Cosman

Composing Mortals

1 After Bach

At just after 8.15 pm on the 27 July 1750, a stout, virtually blind 65-year-old Saxon organist, teacher and composer succumbed to the complications of a condition, possibly diabetes, that had been sapping his hitherto robust constitution over the last year – and a posthumous cult which, in time, would border on a secular religion, was born.

For the notion that the output and influence of Johann Sebastian Bach passed into more or less immediate obscurity after his death until the young Mendelssohn revived his *Passion according to St. Matthew* in 1829 was never substantially true. Granted, Bach had published only selectively and, of his massive output still in manuscript, something like two fifths was subsequently lost. Granted, his cantatas and passions did lapse into neglect for a time owing to changes in the Lutheran liturgy. Yet the motets evidently continued to be sung; for Mozart, visiting Leipzig in 1789, was regaled with a stirring performance of *Singet dem Herrn* (c. 1727), exclaiming "Now there's something from which one can learn!"[1]

Meanwhile, Bach's peerless reputation as a performer and teacher ensured that his practices and methods were widely disseminated through the writings of devoted pupils, not least in *The True Art of Playing Keyboard Instruments* (1753) by his second son Carl Philipp Emanuel Bach. Concurrently, manuscript copies of his keyboard works increasingly circulated as teaching material from which rising young talents such as Beethoven duly learnt their basic techniques as composers and performers. By the eighteen-hundreds, quite a lot of this material had found its way into print, though it was to take the centenary of Bach's death in 1850 to prompt the great Bach-Gesellschaft enterprise to collect, edit and publish his every note in a mighty sequence of volumes which enthusiasts such as Brahms took to anticipating like the instalments of a thriller.

As the nineteenth century unfolded and aspects of Bach insinuated their way into the techniques and aesthetics of composers as diverse as Schubert and Schumann, Chopin and Liszt, Wagner and Brahms, Mahler and Debussy, it became increasingly difficult to find major talents less than fundamentally beholden to him, though Berlioz remained sceptical almost to the end and Tchaikovsky denied him true genius. Nor was Bach's influence to wane in the ensuing age of Modernism. Long after he had devised his 12-note method, Schoenberg still cited Bach (together with Mozart) as his primary influence, singling out Bach's 'contrapuntal thinking; i.e. the art of inventing figures that can be used to accompany themselves', and his art 'of producing everything from one thing and of relating figures by transformation'.[2] Stravinsky, whose so-miscalled neo-Classicism owed far more to the contours and procedures of Bach, evidently began his every composing day by playing something out of *The Well-tempered Clavier* (1722-42) to get his own ideas going. Even the implacably future-orientated young Pierre Boulez conceded that Bach's chorale preludes constituted the all-time greatest models of musical forming by 'proliferation' from the simplest elements.[3]

No doubt the gradual revelation over decades of a compositional technique, a knowledge of the art of combination, so comprehensive, so all-knowing, was bound to generate extra-musical veneration. Beethoven was already hailing Bach as the father of harmony, while Mendelssohn's *St. Matthew* and the publication of cantata after cantata in successive Bach-Gesellschaft volumes powerfully boosted the image of Bach, not only as the supreme craftsman, but also the most all-embracingly communal, in his power to express collective feeling. And not least, the most German in spirit – and no matter that he had synthesized elements from such un-Germanic figures as Couperin and Vivaldi. For Wagner, Bach was the musical equivalent of Luther and Dürer; the source from which he proceeded, if somewhat anachronistically, to fabricate an entire musical style to evoke the Renaissance Nuremberg of his master-craftsman Hans Sachs in *Die Meistersinger* (1862-67). For obvious reasons, the Nationalistic-Germanic Bach tended in the twentieth century to be re-branded as Bach the Universal. But the communal master-craftsman ideal continued to drive the efforts of such composers as Hindemith and inspire the spirit in which such musicians as Mengelberg and Klemperer, Vaughan Williams and Britten, periodically conducted the Passions. Towards the end of his glittering career, even Stravinsky voiced the, not entirely convincing, wish to have been 'a small Bach' instead.[4]

Over and above all this, there early emerged a still more numinous view of Bach as a kind of musical demiurge. Goethe's comments in 1827 after hearing some of the organ music seem to have been the start of it: 'It is as though eternal harmony were conversing with itself, as may have happened in God's bosom shortly before He created the world.'[5] Cut to Wagner's Swiss lake-side refuge in 1871, with the young Hans Richter at the piano playing a Bach fugue. 'Bach's music is certainly a conception of the world,' Wagner exclaims, 'his figurations, devoid of feeling, are like unfeeling Nature itself – birth and death, winds, storms, sunshine – all these things take place like figurations …'[6] This, according to Cosima Wagner's *Diaries*, was a theme to which he often returned in later years when he was much pre-occupied with *The Well-*

tempered Clavier: that Bach represented the very fount and essence of music before the limiting agencies of sensibility, taste and style came into play.

We may smile now at such unhistorical Idealism and wonder whether it partly arose from the flowing look of Bach's notation on the page with its paucity of expression marks. We may even suspect that when Wagner likens the undulating C major Prelude in Book 1 to a river 'which one can go on watching forever', he is really talking about himself; about such evocations of nature through the play of sub-thematic figurations as the preludes to *Das Rheingold* (1854) and *Die Walküre* (1856).[7] Yet thirty years on, Mahler is still exclaiming "In Bach, all the seeds of music are found, as the world in contained in God."[8] And while the twentieth century might have been supposed to have consigned such Romantic notions to history, the priestly pronouncements of such performers as Albert Schweitzer and Wanda Landowska, and the competition among certain scholars to extrapolate ever more arcane theological symbolism, ever more cabalistic numerologies and ciphers from the elegant curlicues of Bach's manuscripts, have suggested that Bach the Uncanny lives on.

Come the bicentenary of Bach's death in 1950, and one admirer, that awesome hyper-dialectician Theodor W. Adorno, could take no more, duly bringing out a densely argued polemic entitled 'Bach Defended Against His Devotees'.[9] His central thrust was that, far from submitting his art to the expression of the Divine Order, Bach's music, in its idiosyncratic complexity and unpredictable spontaneity, was in fact subtly subversive of the very sacred and secular forms it was supposedly fulfilling. Indeed, when Hans Keller subsequently declared that 'The B Minor Mass does not make propaganda for God,' but, rather, its framework enables Bach to convey unique meta-musical discoveries of his own, he might have been glossing Adorno.[10] So, in another way, might Charles Rosen when he argued, 'The fashionable placing of the cantatas as Bach's principle achievement has only been harmful: it has led to an overemphasis on extra-musical symbolism' and that 'it is time to return to the old evaluation of Bach's keyboard music as the centre of his work.'[11]

Bach himself is supposed to have remarked of his unprecedented mastery simply that, "I was obliged to work hard. Whoever is equally industrious, will succeed just as well."[12] But was he being ingenuous or just a little ironical? After all, others in his time such as Handel and Telemann were quite as industrious, yet none of them synthesized such a range of past and present techniques, forms and styles into remotely so rich an idiom as he. Rosen was surely right to suggest that the primary agent of this synthesis was Bach's unique ability to invent, develop and control the most elaborate contrapuntal textures through his keyboard-playing hands (and, in the organ works, pedal-playing feet). Keller was surely right to imply that, say, the strange harmony that overtakes the 'Confiteor' in the B Minor Mass (1724-49) is not a conventional emblem of communal faith but a unique musical vision of Bach's own. And maybe Adorno himself was right even in admitting that, after one has responded in depth to Bach's 'infinitely involuted, unschematic' music, even Mozart and Beethoven could seem a little mechanical and slight.[13]

Or was this readmitting Bach the Numinous through the back door? For the notion evidently dies hard. Halfway through his millennial Bach Pilgrimage to celebrate the 250th anniversary of his birth in 2000 by performing all the surviving cantatas in different venues on their correct liturgical dates, Sir John Eliot Gardiner could be heard on Classic FM reiterating that, for many audiences, Bach seemed to fill a gap in faith. And the subsequent marketing of his recordings with devout-looking faces from all round the globe on their covers seemed calculated to back this up. But it was the Argentinian composer Mauricio Kagel in 1985 who took this to its logical conclusion. Observing that nobody believes in God any more but everyone believes in Bach, he proceeded to devise a full-length *Passion According to St. Bach*, no less. As one might expect of a composer known mainly as a droll avant-garde gadfly, the project had its surreal overtones; but it also revealed hitherto unexpected contrapuntal and expressive powers. Nobody seems to have risked actually performing it in Bach Year 2000. But we may see Sir John Eliot Gardiner getting round to it yet.

NOTES

Source: 'Beyond History', *The Independent*, 27 July 2000; rev. 2008.

1   Testimony of Friedrich Rochlitz in: *The New Bach Reader*, ed. Hans T. David and Arthur Mendel, rev. Christoph Wolff, New York, Norton, 1998, p. 488.
2   Arnold Schoenberg, 'National Music' (2), *Style and Idea*, ed. Leonard Stein, tr. Leo Black, London, Faber, 1975, p. 173. [Ed.: Interestingly, Schoenberg also praised in this context Bach's 'disregard for the "strong" beat' of the bar.]
3   Pierre Boulez, *Conversations with Célestine Deliège*, London, Eulenburg, 1976, pp. 15-16.
4   Igor Stravinsky, 'Thoughts of an Octogenarian' in: Igor Stravinsky and Robert Craft, *Dialogues and a Diary*, London, Faber, 1968, pp. 123-24.
5   *The New Bach Reader*, p. 499.
6   Cosima Wagner, *Diaries*, Vol. 1, 1869-77, ed. Martin Gregor-Dellin and Dietrich Mack, tr. Geoffrey Skelton, London, Collins, 1978, p. 336.
7   Ibid., Vol. 2, 1878-83, p. 183.
8   Natalie Bauer-Lechner, *Recollections of Gustav Mahler*, tr. Dika Newlin, ed. Peter Franklin, London, Faber, 1980, p. 166.
9   Theodor W. Adorno, *Prisms*, tr. Samuel and Sherry Weber, Cambridge, Massachusetts, MIT Press, 1981, pp. 135-46.
10   Hans Keller, 'Music 1975', *1975 (1984 minus 9)*, London, Dobson, 1977, pp. 254-55.
11   Charles Rosen, 'Keyboard Music of Bach and Handel', *Critical Entertainments*, Cambridge Massachusetts, Harvard University Press, 2000, p. 26.
12   Quoted in Forkel's Biography of Bach (1802): *The New Bach Reader*, p. 459.
13   *Prisms*, p. 141.

2 *Haydn Alone*

Quite exceptionally, he has an hour to himself. Tonight's opera is cancelled; half the cast has caught its usual fevers from the seasonal fogs – including, alas, La Polzelli, whose dark Neapolitan eyes might have beguiled the time. At least his principal violinist, Tomasini, can be left to throw together a concert. He peers round the door of his flat in the Musicians' House. His barren, shrewish wife is out, thank goodness – no doubt lavishing expensive blandishments on one of her nice priests. How often over the last 24 years has he lamented his pliancy in marrying the older sister when he longed for the younger! And how the Good Lord might have mitigated his servitude with the gift of children! But as it is … across the Hungarian marshes, across the deserted vistas of the great park, that dreaded north wind of late autumn begins to rattle at the windows; he will have to look out his thickest nightcap. For once, too discouraged even to pray, he plumps himself down at his Walter fortepiano and pulls a bundle of manuscript almost at random off the shelf above.

It falls open at a little divertimento – he'd call it 'sonata' now – in G minor.[1] When did he write it? Ah, yes, that strange period leading up to his fortieth birthday when *something* got into his music: when he found himself positively obsessed with minor keys, harsh progressions, abrupt stops and starts. He wouldn't risk such shocks today without balancing passages of brightness, of humour. A popular manner obliges one to say original things in an easy way – and besides, joy ought to be one's deepest response to God's creation.

Yet those sinfonias and *quartetti* of 15 years ago have strangely failed to go out of fashion as most music so quickly does. Connoisseurs from all over Europe seeking him out in this wilderness, this prison, this Eszterháza, are forever telling him how striking they remain – to which he will modestly reply that, shut away out here for most of the year, with an orchestra to practise on but few fellow composers to compare notes with, he was forced to become original. Indeed, how the plaintive falling progressions of the little sonata's opening melody that he has begun absently to strum match his present mood. Perhaps even now he should send it to Artaria in Vienna – who will doubtless publish it with the usual crop of misprints! Ha – a faint lift in spirits? The music moves into the relative major by way of a flurry of arpeggios and a passage of rising sequences. For the good of his soul he must look on the positive side.

And he *has* come far. Who would have imagined the wheelwright's son from rural Rohrau could rise to lead soprano in the choir of St. Stephen's Cathedral in Vienna? And how could he have foreseen on that terrible day when they threw him out into the streets, penniless at 17, that 12 years later he would be briskly sporting the livery of Vice Kapellmeister to the richest princely family in Maria Theresa's empire? If only Prince Nicolaus hadn't taken it into his head to build his Versailles in this insect-ridden swamp; if only he hadn't got bitten by the opera bug – so that his Princely Kapellmeister has virtually had to double as impresario these last, desperate 10 years. And if only the sojourn out here didn't seem to get longer and longer each year. Late November now – his younger orchestral players are almost crazy to rejoin their wives – and still no order to pack for Vienna. That old F sharp minor Sinfonia, when he got the musicians to tiptoe out gradually during the last movement, worked back in 1772. But it's not a hint he could risk again, even to so musical an employer as Prince Nicolaus.

So the precious Christmas break, being cosseted by the ladies, presenting his music to the Imperial Court – not that the strait-laced Emperor Joseph seems to approve his livelier stuff much – above all, playing quartets with Mozart, looks like being shorter than ever. Ah yes, Mozart. In his heart of hearts he has to admit that that meeting has been the shock of his life, that when he heard *Die Entführung* he knew time was up for Haydn the opera composer. And the detail, the balance, the bloom of sound in Mozart's every bar: the perfect *taste* – yes, that's the word. Thank the Lord he could yet feel admiration rather than jealousy. But then, when did he ever meet a deeper appreciation of the art beneath the genial surfaces of his own instrumental music? When Mozart is old and famous and the name of Haydn forgotten, at least he can feel some of his discoveries will go on in the music of the younger genius.

He has reached the repeat bar of the sonata movement but he plays on into its troubled second half, minor keys now all the way, like life is going to be back here after the New Year. Only yesterday, he received a letter on behalf of Count D'Ogny in Paris commissioning six new symphonies for the concerts of the Loge Olympique. Well, the Parisians have been pirating his music for decades so he might as well extract some return. And Mozart says they have grand orchestras. But when will he find a moment to write six symphonies? And if only he could escape to Paris to hear them; if only he could have accepted that invitation a couple of years back to honour and glory in London! Fingering sadly the little cadenza on a diminished seventh chord almost at the end of the movement, he reflects on the irony of the situation. Here he sits at the end of Anno 1784 at 52, Franz Joseph Haydn, the most celebrated composer in Europe, bound by ties of gratitude to a prince who depends ever more heavily upon him to stave off depression and who may live for another 10 or 15 years. What use will his release be by then, he wonders as he taps out the laconic cadential bars – what has he to look forward to?

He cannot imagine his vogue lasting more than a couple of decades at best – though perhaps his sacred music might linger in the liturgy. He has no inkling that he is father of the 'Classical Style' – the term will not be used in his lifetime. Nor in his wildest dreams can he foresee that late-twentieth-century scholars will prize even such documents as the memorandum he addressed the other week to the Prince about his little vegetable garden; or that orchestras called things like The Age of Enlightenment will be attempting to revert to the very sound of his own players as they perform the duly completed Paris Symphonies. Great Heavens! What he would give for the invention of horns that could play all the notes without perpetually changing those confounded extra lengths of tubing!

Ultimately, he must rest content with the practice of his art itself: with those moments when the patterns of notes, the ingenuities of his utmost skill, have suddenly fused together into something greater and beyond – moments when he has *understood*. He turns to the second and concluding movement of the sonata: G minor again, though over the page it will end in the major as his minor finales tend to on principle. He marked it 'allegretto' all those years ago. Now his fingers want to take its forlorn minuet subject, its accompaniment figures like distant horns, a bit slower. Against the rising wind, it sounds the loneliest music in the world.

NOTES

Source: 'A Talent for Self Doubt', *The Independent*, 27 May 1989.

1   Sonata in G minor, Hob. XVI: 44.

3   But is it Mozart? (II)

In 1793, two years after Mozart's death, a curious publication appeared under his name. Entitled *Musikalisches Würfelspiel*, or 'Musical Dice Game', this presented itself as 'Instruction for composing waltzes or German dances using two dice, without the least musical knowledge or any understanding of composition.' It comprises an apparently arbitrary sequence of 176 single bars of musical clichés – little vamping patterns, decorative turns, cadence figures – all on basic chords of C major. This is prefaced by a pair of tables numbered one to eight across (to correspond with the eight-bar halves of the standard German dance form) and two to 12 down (to cover all the possible sums of the two dice). Within these tables, the numbers one to 176 are scattered with seeming randomness. To 'play', you simply write out whichever of the 11 alternates for each bar the dice indicate, and at the end you have a jolly, if rudimentary, 16-bar dance. Actually, the 'randomness' is quite carefully rigged so that, for instance, all the fragments fit into the same overall harmonic pattern, and all the alternatives for the eighth and sixteenth bars turn out to be cadences. Yet, within the underlying set of constraints, the permutations – and resulting dances – remain pretty unlimited.

Not every scholar is convinced Mozart really devised the *Würfelspiel*, but a schematic sketch for minuets on the same principle does survive in his hand. And, trivial though it may be, it connects with much else we know of Mozart: his aptitude with numbers, his habit of thinking out music while trying complex shots at the billiards table, his love of set-dancing even. Evidently his ability to conceive, organize and hold in his head large-scale compositions depended, in turn, upon a mental knack of shuffling heterogeneous patches of material into convincing sequences within balanced forms quite as much as upon 'inspiration'.

Indeed, one can often hear this in operation. The Andante in the Piano Concerto in C, K. 467 (the so-miscalled 'Elvira Madigan'), opens with what is now popularly regarded as one of Mozart's loveliest long melodies. Yet listen again: the actual line is put together from variants of three quite disparate ideas, plus a descending sequence in the middle; the sense of unity comes almost entirely from the strongly directional underlying harmony and the regular chugging of the accompaniment.

In fact, Mozart not only put many of his individual melodies together from contrasting units, but many of his whole movements, too, on a kind of modular principle: two bars of this balanced against two bars of that, the contrast then varied or extended, leading to a cadential formula; tuttis alternating with orchestral sub-groupings – and so on. This highly sectionalized approach to composition, which originated in the reaction of mid-eighteenth-century composers against the relentlessly uniform processes of the Baroque, was widely practiced in Mozart's time, which is one of the reasons why contemporaries such as Salieri can often sound, superficially, so like him.

But come on! Mozart as mere musical fabricator? Mozart 'composing by numbers'? Of course, there is so much else. There is Mozart the contrapuntist (especially after he discovered J. S. Bach), whose command of every kind of thematic combination enabled him to knit together even the most modular structures into seemingly organic forms. There is Mozart the subtle harmonist, with incomparably the profoundest grasp of tonal structure of any composer of his age. There is Mozart the unprecedented ear who scarcely wrote a texture in his entire vast output, however richly scored, that fails to balance and 'sound'. And there is Mozart man of the theatre, whose instinct for dynamic pacing and musical characterization raised the art of opera to unsurpassable heights.

What needs to be emphasized, however, is just how much of this was owing to conscious calculation, acquired skill, cumulative mastery – and never more than today when the sound, the image, the commodity labelled 'Mozart' is globally sold on the basis of such misinformation, tackiness and transcendental hype. Generations of sober scholars have laboured to show that Mozart was neither the miraculous Dresden China child genius, nor the fated figure of Romantic myth doomed by fickle fashion to a paupers' grave – let along the divinely inspired brat of *Amadeus*. But what can they do against Hollywood and the manufacturers of 'Mozart Balls'?

Still, it is worth repeating that, for a start, Mozart was by no means the all-time prodigy of popular imagination. As a keyboard player he was easily beaten by the English infant phenomenon, William Crotch, who gave his first public performance in 1778 at the age of two. And Saint-Saëns was said to be composing and notating waltzes at the age of three, long before the five-year-old Mozart played his earliest efforts for his father to write down. What Mozart did become over the next decade was the most rigorously trained, lavishly promoted young talent in Europe, acquiring in the process an easy command over all the standard genres, compositional procedures, musical clichés even, of the day. Yet, perhaps for that very reason, he was comparatively late to find his true voice. For all the intermittent pleasures of the first 200-odd items in Köchel's catalogue, it is not until the Piano Concerto in E flat major, K. 271, composed at 22, that we reach a mature Mozart masterpiece. Schubert and Mendelssohn had already declared themselves unmistakably at 16.

Mozart's personality, as he emerged from his tight-knit professional family background and the years of youthful touring, was sociable, urban, competitive and, perhaps, just a little snobbish – after all, he had been dandled as a child on half the royal knees in Europe. His financial troubles were at least partly due to keeping up stylish appearances in order to attract aristocratic pupils, and might have been solved by a visit to London in the wake of Haydn, which was on the cards when he died. As for the 'paupers' grave', it seems communal burial was actually municipal policy at the time.

And the composer? Dare one suggest that he actually remained variable to the end? How could he not, when the exigencies of his life meant that, at the very moment he was setting down three inspired symphonies for a prospective subscription series, he might be required to break off and scribble within an hour a set of 12 German dances for a ball in the Redoutensaal the following night? That his output nonetheless contains perhaps 200 works in which supreme mastery passes over into something unique and inexplicable we call genius is wonderful enough.

But is it more wonderful than, in their very different ways, the most characteristic music of any of the other greatest masters of Western music? Let us not forget that the universal assumption of Mozart's supremacy is comparatively recent. The nineteenth century unfailingly hailed Beethoven as top composer, the earlier twentieth century, perhaps, J. S. Bach. No doubt there is something in the ambiguity of feeling beneath the graceful surfaces of Mozart's masterpieces that especially appeals in these relativistic postmodern times. Yet does one already hear the sounds of Haydn or Schubert coming up strongly from behind?

Meanwhile, let us cherish him at his ineffable best – which may mean turning a deaf ear to the kind of radio presenter who announces 'Mozart' in a voice trembling with awe and then offers, not, say, the sublime Adagio of the G minor String Quintet, K. 516, but a routine little minuet out of some early Salzburg divertimento, as if they were remotely the same sort of thing …

NOTES

Source: 'The Mozart Myth', *BBC Music Magazine*, April 2004, pp. 42-4.

4   *Wagner Takes the Stage*

Richard Wagner once told Franz Liszt that, whatever his passions demanded of him, he became for the time being – musician, poet, director, author, lecturer or anything else. In fact, that 'anything else' ranged from journalist, theatrical reformer and cultural ideologue to proselytizing vegetarian, revolutionary activist and virulent anti-Semite – a range of concerns that, under the guise of Wagnerism, exerted a vast influence over the cultural life of Europe for decades after his death. No wonder that a survey by Barry Millington concluded: 'We cannot understand Wagner's music fully without understanding him and his era.'[1] And yet, after a century in which generations of biographers, musicologists and cultural historians have toiled to do just that, we might wonder whether we are really much closer to grasping Wagner himself in all his contradictions.

Meanwhile, his greatest works have continued to move, challenge, disturb or delight audiences far removed in time, place and culture from Wagner's own – suggesting that they substantially transcended the assumptions and limits of their time. We call works that do this 'classics' and, among his many other aims, Wagner certainly aspired to create a classic art. Maybe we have a better chance of defining his achievement by asking, not what he meant then, but what he still means now.

Admittedly, the works of Romantic artists are supposed to be inseparable from their lives – think of Berlioz's *Symphonie fantastique* (1830). Yet Wagner possessed a remarkable ability to block out his personal circumstances, to give his all to his chosen dramatic, symbolic or mythological material. To understand *Die Meistersinger von Nürnberg* (1862-67) fully, we hardly need to know he faced the worst financial crisis of his life while writing it. And his affair with Mathilde Wesendonck seems to have been less the inspiration of *Tristan und Isolde* (1857-59) than the result of its composition.

We might also wonder whether all his other activities matter that much any more. For instance, Wagner was an early opponent of vivisection, but he hardly figures in the pantheon of today's animal rights campaigners; and while anti-Semitism has not gone away, one doubts whether its proponents are any longer directly influenced by Wagner's racist musings. In any case, how many, except specialists, would still willingly wade through the turgid German or English multi-volume editions of the Collected Writings?

Which leaves the musical output – or, some of it, since neither the student Symphony in C (1832) nor the early overtures, except for that to *Rienzi*, have ever established themselves in the repertoire (though the striking *Faust Overture* deserves more frequent performance). For that matter, the first three operas – *Die Feen* (1833), *Der Liebesverbot* (1836) or even Hitler's favourite *Rienzi* (1840) – hardly rate today as more than precursors. The piano pieces scattered through the output are mostly inconsequential and the later orchestral marches pompously unmemorable. We are driven back to the realization that Wagner's standing among composers depends upon no more than 12 scores. Granted, ten of them, including the four comprising *Der Ring des Nibelungen* (1853-74) are evening-length music dramas, while the *Wesendonck Lieder* (1857-58) are studies for *Tristan*, and the *Siegfried Idyll* (1870) is a spin-off from Act III of *Siegfried* (1858-71). Yet this simply underlines the fact that all that really matters to us in Wagner comes out of his involvement in the theatre – and a specific form of theatre at that.

Wagner may have aspired to unite Gluck's reformist drive for opera as drama with the symphonic impetus of Beethoven; aspired even to establish at Bayreuth a musical theatre that would become the conscience of the German nation in a way that the theatre of Aeschylus had served ancient Athens. Yet the dramatic themes and musical imagery of his stage works derive mainly from the world of early-nineteenth-century Romantic opera, with its gothic chivalry and wild evocations of Nature, its omens, apparitions, talismans and potions, its dramas of black magic and love unto death.

And here the historians might be thought to have a point. For while Wagner grew up in the Romantic world of Weber, the whole cultural climate had changed by the time he came to realize his later music dramas. Europe after 1850 was an increasingly industrialized, imperialistic culture with a bias in the performing arts away from the extravagancies of Romanticism towards detailed Realism. It is often argued that the perennial problems of staging Wagner stem from the fact that, while his conceptual and musical thought kept pace with the changing times, his ideas of performance remained stuck in the old Romantic theatre. After minutely supervizing the accident-prone first complete staging of *The Ring* in 1876, with its craggy landscapes, horned helmets and Rhine Maidens trundled around on trolleys, Wagner despairingly told his associates it would all have to be done differently next time.[2] Sadly, he died before showing us how.

More seriously, it could be argued that Wagner's range of subject and tone was circumscribed by the irrational emotionality of his Romantic heritage: Nietzsche complained that someone in Wagner's operas always wanted to be saved. And certainly, if one approaches *Tristan* from the human comedy of Mozart's *Così fan tutte* (1790) or the historic sweep of Mussorgsky's *Boris Godunov* (1868-72) or the harsh realism of Berg's *Wozzeck* (1914-22) it can seem a hothouse theatrical bloom. But this would be to underrate how Wagner transformed his Romantic themes and materials. Take the device of the fatal ring. In Weber's *Euryanthe* (1823), this is a mere cog in the plot. By the end of Wagner's *Götterdämmerung* (1869-74), it has become a psycho-economic power-symbol of the most complex significance for the later-nineteenth-century world of Marx and Freud. And when W. H. Auden joked that the beginning of the second act of *Die Walküre* resembles 'a Victorian breakfast scene, Wotan meekly cracking his morning egg behind *The Times* while Fricka furiously rattles the teacups', he was really hinting at how closely, beneath the mythological surface, Wagner approaches the bourgeois realism of Flaubert and Ibsen.[3]

He was, after all, an artist who developed tremendously over his creative life. Only the first three mature music dramas stand directly in the early-Romantic tradition. Of these, *Der fliegende Holländer* (1840-41) concerns the redemption of an unquiet spirit by love; *Tannhäuser* (1843-45) tackles the conflict between love sacred and profane; while *Lohengrin* (1846-48), with its pageantry and swan-knight, is about … well, exactly what? Already, one has a sense of plot and symbolism coming slightly apart, acquiring a looseness and latency that opens them to a variety of interpretations. Indeed, with his last music drama, *Parsifal* (1877-82), we reach a work so complex and ambiguous that nobody seems to agree what it all means. But then, as Wagner clearly realized, the lasting vitality of great works often lies in their very inconsistencies and imperfections, which challenge interpreters to make newly coherent sense of them.

Meanwhile, armed with the epic theatre doctrines of his manifesto *Oper und Drama* (1851), he had embarked upon *The Ring* in 1852, only to break off after Act II of *Siegfried* in 1857 in order to compose that utterly opposite pair of music dramas, *Tristan* and *Die Meistersinger*. If the treatment of the theme of the fulfilment of love in death in *Tristan* attains an obsessive intensity far beyond anything in early Romantic opera, the leisurely romantic comedy of *Die Meistersinger* might seem exceptional in Wagner's work – until one notices that, like *Parsifal*, it concerns the renewal of a community by an unlikely outsider. When he resumed work on *The Ring* in 1869, the enriched tonality of *Die Meistersinger* duly flowed into the jubilant final scene of *Siegfried*, just as a post-*Tristan* chromaticism compounded the terminal glooms of *Götterdämmerung*.

And the key to all this? As a youth, Wagner aspired to be a playwright even before a composer, and he evidently had a feeling for large-scale dramatic timing long before he developed musical skills to match. He certainly always started from the dramatic idea, first making a prose sketch, then writing his libretto, or 'dramatic poem'. The music was supposed, as far as possible, to flow directly from the words, symbolism and structure of the libretto – not just in terms of immediate melody, gesture, colour and atmosphere, but also in its longer-term shape and direction.

In this he evolved a new and opposite principle of music drama to his greatest contemporary, Verdi, who inherited a range of traditional operatic forms and formulae that he gradually adapted and combined to his own purposes over a long career. But this meant that whereas Verdi always had a background form to guide his musical invention, Wagner – at least after *Lohengrin* – had to depend from moment to moment on spinning out whatever musical idea that text happened to suggest. His system of so-called leitmotifs – brief musical ideas associated with particular characters, events or symbols in the drama – is often described as a subtle means of commenting on the dramatic predicaments or psychological motivation of his characters. However, it may have originated as a simple means of filling in his vast time spans. If a character mentioned the curse on the ring, and Wagner had already invented the curse-motif some way back, then at least he had a bunch of notes or harmonies to help him fill the next few bars. This method he enhanced by a symbolic use of harmony – notably the contrast between diatonicism (light, health, goodness) and chromaticism (darkness, sickness, evil) – so that, in the *Ring*, leitmotifs grow more chromatic in shape and harmony as corruption spreads. The most radical outcome of his approach, first fully attained in *Tristan*, was what Wagner called 'musical composition as the art of transition' – the idea of a ceaselessly changeable flow reaching stability, if at all, only at the end.[4]

Of course, other composers have sought a union of words and music by writing their own librettos. Yet Wagner's achievement surely remains unique in its daring, mastery and completeness. He was, on top of all his other multifarious activities, one of the best-read composers ever. The works of the Ancient Greeks, the Medieval Romances, Dante, Shakespeare, Goethe, Schopenhauer, Nietzsche and many others all fed into the subsoil of his dramatic imagination. The dramatic poem of each mature music drama duly conjures into being its own musical world. So the luminously sweet *Lohengrin* style substantially differs from the rough-hewn heroic *Ring* style, just as the sliding harmonies of the *Tristan* style contrast radically with the hearty counterpoint of the *Meistersinger* style – and all of them differ from the eerie phosphorescence of the *Parsifal* style. These differences were heightened by Wagner's evolving concept of orchestration as he moved from the strong colour contrasts of Weber by way of the more sonorously blended texture of his middle years to the diffused ideal of his late music. Claude Debussy described *Parsifal* sounding 'as though lit from behind'.[5]

For true Wagnerians, those complementary worlds of concept and drama, expression and sound, add up to something so vast it dwarfs the achievements of any other composer. Anti-Wagnerians tend to resist this very power and bigness as coercive, as seeking to influence its audience not only as individuals but also in the mass – hence his appeal to certain totalitarian tendencies. Those in between (such as this writer) might argue that, while Wagner stands among the greatest composers, he had very real limitations; that there are areas of musical thought and feeling and, indeed, concepts of musical theatre that lay quite outside his scope. To think of the wholly 'other' musical worlds of, say, Monteverdi or Haydn, Mozart or Stravinsky, may help to put Wagner's in perspective – which is not to deny that what he did, he did supremely well.

NOTES

Source: 'Composer of the Month [Wagner]', *BBC Music Magazine*, December 2004, pp. 44-8.

1   Barry Millington, 'Richard Wagner', *BBC Music Magazine*, March 1995.
2   See: *Cosima Wagner's Diaries*, Vol. 1: 1869-77, ed. Martin Gregor-Dellin and Dietrich Mack, tr. Geoffrey Skelton, London, Collins, 1978, pp. 921-22.
3   W. H. Auden, quoted in: *Robert Craft, Stravinsky: Chronicle of a Friendship*, rev. ed., Nashville, Vanderbilt UP, 1994, p. 344.
4   Letter to Mathilde Wesendonck, 29 October 1859, reprinted in: *Wagner: A Documentary Study*, ed. Herbert Barth, Dietrich Mack and Egon Voss, London, Thames and Hudson, 1975, p. 189.
5   *Debussy Letters*, sel. and ed. François Lesure and Roger Nichols, tr. Roger Nichols, London, Faber, 1987, p. 262.

5   *Brahms and Antipathy*

It was Thomas Adès, interviewed in July 2001, who set the whole argument going again.[1] "I think that Brahms is unable to allow his ideas and material to breathe within his structures; as if he deliberately disables his instinct," he remarked – apparently unaware that the co-founder of the Aldeburgh Festival he was then directing was saying much the same thing 50 years before. For, according to Hans Keller, 'Britten resented the lack of spontaneity in the writing, in particular in those passages where Brahms seems to interrupt a melody abruptly in order to avoid what he may have thought of as sentimental writing.'[2] Nor was this so different from Tchaikovsky's complaint during Brahms's lifetime that 'he never makes a statement or … if he does begin to say something, he never finishes it; his music consists of little bits of something, artificially stuck together.'[3]

Composers, doubtless, tend to be occupationally biased, endorsing fellow composers who share their creative aims and sound worlds while fending off those whose 'otherness' seems to raise questions or to pose a threat. And what could seem more opposite to the clear, bright colours of Tchaikovsky, the thin, sensitized textures of Britten, or the vast, resonating spaces of Adès, than the richly blended, mahogany-dark density and glow of the characteristic Brahms sound? Of course, that sound was subsequently to touch a wide range of other composers from Reger to Rubbra, even from Schoenberg to Elliott Carter. And it was, of all people, Ravel who remarked, 'Brahms's superiority is clearly seen in one respect, namely, his orchestral technique, which is extremely brilliant.'[4]

Yet even Elgar, who loved Brahms's Third Symphony (1883) to the point of virtually quoting it in the finale of his own First (1908), felt obliged to criticize some of its scoring as uneven, awkward and heavy.[5] And the strictures of Tchaikovsky, Britten and Adès run deeper than just the sonorous texture of it all, carrying an implication that Brahms was unable to let go, either technically or expressively, because he was deeply inhibited. Post-Freudian biographers have usually located these inhibitions in his allegedly troubled childhood, his proclamation by Schumann as the coming genius at too tender an age, or his frustrated passion for Clara. Indeed, Keller went so far as to suggest that Brahms's very popularity rests upon his genius to appeal to comparable neuroses in us all. Yet in his own time, Brahms's guardedness was put down rather to an innate conservatism, his supposed attempt to shore up Classical tradition against the Wagnerian flood tide. 'Everything he has ever done is just one gigantic variation on the works of Beethoven, Mendelssohn and Schumann,' proclaimed his most virulent composer-critic, Hugo Wolf, who proceeded to attack the Fourth Symphony (1885) as running the gauntlet 'between "can't do" and "wish I could" through four movements.'[6]

Actually, Brahms knew and admired much of Wagner's music, while the latter conceded that Brahms's *Handel Variations* (1861) showed what could still be done with the old forms by someone who really understood them. What evidently disturbed Wagner, after confidently proclaiming the death of the symphony, was the belated appearance, innovatory complexity and, not least, colossal success of Brahms's First (1876); soon he, too, was talking of returning to symphonies after completing *Parsifal*. And this hints at something radical behind Brahms's apparently cautious stance.

A symptom of that caution, to be sure, was Brahms's refusal to give interviews or write programme notes, which means we have to search for his views in his correspondence and the memoirs of his associates. But he did remark: "Neither Schumann, nor Wagner, nor I was properly schooled. Talent was the decisive factor. Each of us had to find his own way. Schumann took one path, Wagner another and I took a third."[7] What he seemed to be suggesting was that the traditional criteria of musicality and the old disciplines for nurturing talent had somehow got lost in an ever more complicated nineteenth-century world and that, from then on, composers would have to consciously recreate their own traditions from whatever elements of the past or present still seemed to have some potential in them. Hence Brahms's obsessive interest in the manuscripts, sketches, even exercises of his fellow composers, past and present. Hence his combing the Renaissance, Baroque, Classical and early Romantic periods, to say nothing of the folk and popular musics of his own day, for materials and procedures to put together in new contexts that he hoped might yield fresh expression. Hence the unprecedented allusiveness of his style, which, Wagner jeered, sounded like cabaret songs one day, mock-Handel the next, Jewish-Hungarian gypsy music on yet another or pseudo Beethoven's Tenth.

Whether this artistic self-consciousness was rooted more in Brahms's personal psychology or in a realistic grasp of historical process, it represented a new, even potentially Modernist spirit in music – as Schoenberg was happy to acknowledge in his famous lecture 'Brahms the Progressive', in which he sought to suggest that Brahms's intensive development of Beethoven's motivic techniques already brought music to the verge of 12-tonery.[8] Stravinsky duly dismissed Schoenbergian serialism as 'rooted in the most turgid and graceless Brahms'.[9] Yet, more surprisingly, he also confessed in a 1939 interview to a 'great feeling for Brahms … You always sense the overpowering wisdom of this great artist even in his least inspired works.'[10]

And that is surely the heart of the matter. By ceaselessly probing and cumulatively mastering the profoundest secrets of his art, Brahms emerged as perhaps the greatest conscience-figure in Western composition since Bach. And conscience-figures are rarely easy to live with – or to shake off. When Tchaikovsky lamented his inability to disguise the seams in his own music, he was implicitly acknowledging the ideal of integration that Brahms stood for. And on finally confessing his distaste for Brahms's music to the man himself at a meeting in Hamburg in 1888, he was overwhelmed by the self-deprecating generosity of the response.

Britten was evidently a fan until his late teens when he suddenly felt Brahms stood in the way of his own natural development. Yet he admitted continuing, periodically, to play through the whole of Brahms, "to see if I'm right about him; I usually find that I underestimated last time how bad it was!"[11] How piquant, therefore, to catch Britten half-remembering the plaintive second subject of the scherzo of Brahms's Second Piano Concerto (1881) – same key, register, scoring, general shape – in his 'Dawn' Interlude from *Peter Grimes* (1945), or launching his 'Cello and Piano Sonata in C (1961) with an 'inhibited' hesitation comparable to Brahms's E minor Intermezzo, Op. 116, No. 5 (1892). And Adès? Having declared, "the thing I can't forgive Brahms for is his self-pity," and having set Alfred Brendel's little satire about Brahms's ghost to a phantasmagoria of Brahmsian techniques and allusions (*Brahms*, 2001), he might be supposed to have got shot of him. How, then, to account for so many harmonic and textural echoes in his contemporaneous Piano Quintet (2000), and, in particular, for a lilting figure that, more than once, seems about to turn into the first-movement second subject of the Double Concerto (1887) … by Brahms?

NOTES

Source: 'Bashing Brahms', *BBC Music Magazine*, July 2002, pp. 32-3.

1   Thomas Adès in interview, *BBC Music Magazine*, July 2001.
2   Hans Keller, cited in: *Alan Blyth, Remembering Britten*, London, Hutchinson, 1981, p. 88.
3   Alexandra Orlova, *Tchaikovsky: A Self-Portrait*, tr. R. M. Davison, Oxford, OUP, 1990, p. 191.
4   Maurice Ravel, 'The Lamoureux Orchestra Concerts' (*Revue musicale de la S. I. M.*, March 1912) in: *A Ravel Reader*, ed. Arbie Orenstein, New York, Columbia UP, 1990, pp. 344-48.
5   Edward Elgar, *A Future for English Music*, ed. Percy M. Young, London, Dobson, 1968, p. 103.
6   Hugo Wolf, 'Brahms's Symphony No. 4' (*Wiener Salonblatt*, 24 January 1886) in: *The Music Criticism of Hugo Wolf*, tr. and ed. Henry Pleasants, New York, Holmes & Meier, 1978, pp. 184-87.
7   Brahms in conversation with Richard Heuberger, in: Imogen Fellinger, 'Brahms's "Way": A Composer's Self-view', *Brahms 2: Biographical, Documentary and Analytical Studies*, ed. Michael Musgrave, Cambridge, CUP, 1987, p. 49.

8   Arnold Schoenberg, 'Brahms the Progressive' (1947), *Style and Idea*, ed. Leonard Stein, tr. Leo Black, London, Faber, 1975, pp. 398-441.

9   Igor Stravinsky and Robert Craft, *Memories and Commentaries*, London, Faber, 1960, pp. 122-23.

10   Vera Stravinsky and Robert Craft, *Stravinsky in Pictures and Documents*, London, Hutchinson, 1979, p. 204.

11   The Earl of Harewood, 'The Man' in: *Benjamin Britten: a Commentary on His Works from a Group of Specialists*, ed. Donald Mitchell and Hans Keller, London, Rockliff, 1952, p. 6.

12   Adès, 2001.

6   *Poulenc* en collage

In January 1945, as London lived out the final months of the Second World War, Francis Poulenc arrived from recently liberated Paris to play in a performance of his Concerto in D minor for Two Pianos and Orchestra (1932) at the Albert Hall. His fellow pianist was none other than the brilliant young Benjamin Britten and the two composers struck up an instant friendship. Both were committed to ideals of lucidity and directness in musical expression, rather than to technical originality for its own sake. And both were involved in long-standing song-recital partnerships: for Poulenc's 25-year collaboration with the great French baritone Pierre Bernac was to prove as close (except that they were never lovers) and productive as Britten's relationship with the tenor Peter Pears.

In fact, the Englishmen had already performed Poulenc's finest song cycle *Tel jour telle nuit* (1937) two years before. In 1956, they inveigled him to the Aldeburgh Festival and two years later mounted a riotous Festival production of his wickedly transvestite *opéra-bouffe*, *Les mamelles de Tirésias* (1944). Poulenc was too preoccupied with personal problems to participate in the latter, but it suggests the warmth of the friendship that, in requesting production snaps, he told Britten, 'I want to see Peter in a dress'.[1] And 18 months after Poulenc's unexpected death from a sudden heart attack at only 64, Britten and Pears put on a memorial concert at the 1964 Aldeburgh Festival. In their joint tribute, they hinted that their late friend had been a rather more complex character than many assumed: 'To the average Englishman, Francis Poulenc's music may have appeared that of a typical French composer: witty, daring, sentimental, naughty. In fact, Poulenc was very easily depressed, shockable, unsure and liable to panic.' But they could not help adding, 'One of his most adorable qualities was that he was incapable of being anything but himself.'[2]

Complex he certainly was. Although homosexual in orientation, with a penchant for guardsmen, chauffeurs and other members of what were once known as the 'lower orders', he also fathered a daughter in his forties, keeping in affectionate contact with both mother and child for the rest of his life. Nor were the complexities entirely admirable. Born into more than comfortable circumstances – his father was a director of what was to evolve into the Rhône-Poulenc pharmaceutical conglomerate – he could become querulous if deprived of life's little luxuries. Though certainly no collaborator during the German Occupation, neither did he risk any real involvement with the Resistance as the magnificent choral cycle *Figure humaine* (1943), written in anticipation of the ultimate Allied victory, might vicariously suggest he had. And in the mid-1950s, his obsession with his largest project, the three-act opera *Dialogues des Carmelites* (1956), plus a debilitating crisis over his latest boyfriend, reduced him to such supine self-pity that even the long-suffering Bernac threatened to quit unless he pulled himself together. Yet somehow Poulenc's sense of creative purpose kept him intact. As he himself ruefully observed, 'Perhaps the heart of the matter is that the worst of myself is the best of myself.'[3]

Confronted by such helpless candour, not even the sometimes puritanical Britten and Pears seem to have been bothered by the personal contradictions. Yet the contradictions in his music have bothered many over the decades. Even in the centenary year of his birth, with the best of his songs, piano pieces, instrumental works, ballet scores, concertos, operas and sacred settings more widely performed, broadcast, recorded, studied and, indeed, loved than ever before, it was still possible to encounter musicians or listeners for whom an enthusiasm for Poulenc was not quite respectable.

Not being quite respectable was, of course, part of the populist image Jean Cocteau sought to drum up for that journalistic figment, the group *Les Six*, just after the First World War. And even among this actually rather disparate association of composers, with their anti-bourgeois stage projects and jolly jaunts to the circus, Poulenc, as the youngest member, seemed very much the gadfly with his handful of saucy little wrong-note salon successes such as the cod-ethnic *Rhapsodie nègre* (1917) or the raucous Sonata for Two Clarinets (1918). It was the vastly fertile Darius Milhaud with his experimental *Études* in every key at once and the Swiss-born Arthur Honegger with his modernist enthusiasm for rugby matches and express trains who were expected to develop into the heavies of the new aesthetic. Few could have foreseen the reawakening of Poulenc's religious feelings in the 1930s, or his graduation to large-scale sacred and operatic composition after the Second World War. But by then, the French scene was increasingly dominated by Olivier Messiaen and his star pupil, Pierre Boulez. And while the open-minded Poulenc proved sympathetic even to this more doctrinaire phase of avant-garderie, declaring Boulez 'a true musician', the compliment was not returned.

Meanwhile, the critical charges against him accumulated: that Poulenc was essentially a pampered amateur who never fully achieved artistic maturity or wholly mastered the techniques of composition; that his music is such a grab-bag of other composers' ideas that it lacks all integration of its own; that in attempting wit or seriousness he too often delivered merely mawkishness or triviality. Moreover, it is now evident from the clear-headed self-assessments to be found scattered through his marvellously vivacious *Selected Correspondence* (superbly translated and annotated by Sidney Buckland) that Poulenc conceded many of these criticisms himself. Could it be that, in his heart of hearts, he realized they were ultimately beside the point?

It is, after all, a mark of major talent somehow to turn even the most drastic limitations to positive advantage. Poulenc emerged as an accomplished pianist with an omnivorous ear. But he missed a conservatoire training and the compositional facility that might have brought. Even his most apparently spontaneous songs and piano pieces seem to have emerged from a hesitant process of sketching little patches and gradually assembling them into longer structures. Yet instead of trying to smooth over the joins, Poulenc evidently decided quite early on to flaunt them, defiantly filling the gaps in his sonata forms where thematic development was traditionally expected with self-contained middle sections of new material, and emphasizing the sudden jolts and jump-cuts in his continuities.

The major limitation of this method was that it remained difficult to achieve really large-scale forms without the aid of a potentially dramatic concept, such as the solo-orchestral opposition of concerto form, or by means of ballet scenarios, operatic libretti or sacred texts. Only once did Poulenc attempt anything remotely approaching symphonic form, in the so-called Sinfonietta (1948) – an early commission for the BBC Third Programme delivered, symptomatically, one year late and subsequently dismissed by one English critic as resembling 'the random jottings of a gifted theatre composer'.[4] On the other hand, the method of juxtaposing and cross-cutting, with its minimizing of transition passages, enabled Poulenc to pack striking contrasts and contradictions of tempo, tonality and, not least, mood, into the tightest time spans – with the endings of works often proving especially unpredictable. Indeed, there are pieces, such as the incredibly patchwork *Concert champêtre* (1928) for harpsichord and orchestra, commissioned by the great Wanda Landowska, that sound consciously contrived to test just how many disparities could be jammed into a single structure without its actually falling to bits.

And the variety of musical content with which Poulenc filled his structural collages was even more extreme. 'I am very well aware that I am not the kind of musician who makes harmonic innovations like Igor [Stravinsky], Ravel or Debussy,' he wrote to a friend in 1942, 'but I do think there is a place for new music that is content with using other people's chords'.[5] Yet other people's chords were the least of it. In addition to the neo-Baroque and neo-populist clichés that were stock-in-trade to many French composers between the wars, plus his more personal feeling for Renaissance choral music and the eighteenth-century French keyboard composers, one can find scattered through his magpie output quite specific allusions to, and cribs from (wait for it): Monteverdi, Gluck, Mozart, Beethoven, Schubert, Schumann, Brahms, Gounod, Offenbach, Massenet, Chabrier, Debussy, Satie, Ravel, Chopin, Falla, Mussorgsky, Tchaikovsky, Prokofiev …

And, overwhelmingly, most of all from Stravinsky, who Poulenc claimed as his spiritual father, without whose example he might never have become a composer. It is common enough for rising talents in search of their own styles to imitate admired seniors, but Poulenc's identification was much closer – and lifelong. If an early success such as his ballet *Les biches* (1924) pinches snippets from such Stravinsky scores as *Pulcinella* (1920) and *Ragtime* (1918), to say nothing of a whole passage from *Fireworks* (1908), a mature work such as the ever-popular *Gloria* (1959) opens with a still more blatant theft of the beginning of Stravinsky's Serenade in A (1925). One gets the impression that, within days of the appearance of each new Stravinsky score, Poulenc had assimilated its every gesture, texture, harmonic sequence and chord-spacing through his piano-playing fingertips, duly transmuting his findings into a kind of admiring or naughty commentary on the Master in his own next piece. His last and finest sacred work *Sept répons des ténèbres* (1962) even runs, startlingly, to a passage of austere 12-tonery prompted by Stravinsky's late *Canticum sacrum* (1955). Evidently Poulenc kept on cribbing to the end. Indeed, the notoriously litigious Stravinsky could justifiably have sued him over and over for plagiarism. Instead, quite exceptionally, he proved indulgent, even, astonishingly for a man so stingy of praise, once telling Poulenc, 'You are truly good, and that is what I always find again and again in your music'.[6] Stravinsky's development between the wars was widely misconstrued as a decline; no doubt he realized the genuine insight behind Poulenc's plunderings and appreciated the support.

But interspersed throughout Poulenc's collages, one also finds usages of a kind unparalleled in Stravinsky: in fact, an obsessive vein of self-quotation. At the back of his mind Poulenc evidently kept a stock of a dozen or so cut-and-dried turns and textures he seemed prepared to shove regardless into the most touching *mélodie*, frivolous ballet sequence or agonized sacred chorus. The stock included a kind of desperate silent-film chase music, which one hears, for instance, in the first allegro of the curiously hybrid choreographic concerto for piano and 18 instruments, *Aubade* (1929), and a variety of clangorous chord changes redolent of church bells, which appear at their most acidulous in the darkly imposing Sonata for Two Pianos (1953). Then there is a languorous, sinking chord progression, deriving perhaps from Ravel, which insinuates itself into many of his longer tunes, such as the bucolic opening of his Aesop ballet *Les animaux modèles* (1942), plus various *déraciné* Classical cadences and Romantic vampings – anyone who knows their Poulenc could continue the list.

The constant recurrence of these formulae might simply be construed as a failure of invention. But the care with which Poulenc varies them to fit their different contexts suggests, rather, that he consciously wants us to make connections between works – that his ultimate concern is less with music as a series of self-contained pieces than as a medium, a continuous focus, whether sublime or banal, to life as it is lived. From his many affectionate reminiscences, it is evident that his ideal of this life related back to his childhood in Nogent sur Marne, where he could wander back and forth between strumming

Chopin in the *haute bourgeois* salon and observing the plebeian picnickers along the riverbank with their accordions and *bal musette* melodies. Such a technique, such a background certainly suggests why Poulenc's output seems to become increasingly interesting and indeed necessary, its limitations and faults to matter less, the more of it one gets to know.

It might, then, seem perverse to insist all the same that his stance was essentially Modernist. But this was a French composer who not only kept up with Stravinsky, respected Schoenberg, came to love Webern and Berg and took in the 1950s avant-garde with an acute ear, but who also avidly followed the latest in art, design, theatre and literature. Unlike Britten, for instance, the majority of his nearly 150 songs were settings of contemporary poets such as Apollinaire, Max Jacob and Paul Eluard. And it is clear by now that the ironic sensibility with which he juxtaposed his incongruous musical materials captured the complex spirit of his time as well as any composer. And perhaps subversively as well. For it could be argued that, by emphasizing the discontinuity within his works while simultaneously emphasizing connections between them, he was offering a rather radical critique of the traditional notion of what a work actually is. In which case, we may have yet to grasp the full significance of Poulenc's idiosyncratic achievement.

NOTES

Source: 'Composer of the Month', *BBC Music Magazine*, January 1999, pp. 41-5.

1   Francis Poulenc, *'Echo and Source': Selected Correspondence 1915-63*, tr. and ed. Sidney Buckland, London, Gollancz, 1991, p. 253.
2   Benjamin Britten and Peter Pears, 'Francis Poulenc 1899-1963' (*Aldeburgh Festival Programme Book*, 1964), in: *Britten on Music*, ed. Paul Kildea, Oxford, OUP, 2003, p. 254.
3   Poulenc, ed. Buckland, p. 213.
4   David Drew, 'Modern French Music', *European Music in the Twentieth Century* (1957), rev. ed. Howard Hartog, London, Penguin Books, 1961, p. 279.
5   Poulenc, ed. Buckland, p. 130.
6   Ibid., p. 94.

7 *The Case of Ruth Crawford Seeger*

Do we really progress? Reviewing a London concert in *The World* in 1892, Bernard Shaw recorded: 'When E. M. Smyth's heroically brassy overture to *Antony and Cleopatra* was finished, and the composer called to the platform, it was observed with stupefaction that all that tremendous noise had been made by a lady.'[1] With her suffragette militancy and masculine tweeds, Ethel Smyth was no ordinary lady, of course. But had she actually been a man, we might better remember her as the composer of the grandly symphonic Mass in D that she completed in 1893, and rather less as the mere butt of those wicked wits, Virginia Woolf and Sir Thomas Beecham.

At least her appearance stirred the prophetic strain in Shaw. 'The day is not far distant,' he declared, 'when everything that is most passionate and violent in orchestral music will be monopolized by women as it is now in novel-writing.' Or was he just teasing? 'I shall not say there is any likelihood of our ever seeing a female Mozart or Wagner, lest I should hurt the feelings of many male composers who are nothing like so clever as Miss Smyth ...'[2] To which one might respond that the twentieth century has hardly thrown up an abundance of male equivalents to Mozart or Wagner either, though a number of striking women composers have more or less managed to pursue professional careers in the wake of Dame Ethel. Yet the suspicion lingers that the odds, in getting commissioned, performed, taken seriously, have remained, if more subtly, against them.

Or not so subtly. Even in 1975, *Time* magazine was evidently capable of proclaiming 'Men compose symphonies, women compose babies'. Actually, there never seems to have been a lack of primary talent among women – from the ecstatic twelfth-century monodies of Hildegard of Bingen to the post-war serial strivings of Elisabeth Lutyens; from the *clavecin* music of Elisabeth Jacquet de la Guerre which so ravished Louis XIV to the enchanting curiosities of Judith Weir. Yet the fate of Fanny Mendelssohn only suggests how many other aspirants over the centuries must have been frustrated. Brought up in the most enlightened circumstances and almost as gifted as her younger brother Felix, she was none the less virtually sacrificed to his glorious career – some of her songs were actually published under his name. At her death, most of her music remained in manuscript and has only recently been explored.

Behind the social and professional prejudices that made for such suppression, feminists would doubtless detect a more atavistic male fear: that if women should actually succeed in composing both babies and symphonies, what then? How else to explain Mahler's notorious insistence that his young bride, Alma, should renounce her own compositional aspirations and devote herself to his? Granted, he ultimately relented – chided for his view of women by Sigmund Freud, no less. And one might have thought such attitudes had become rarer in our ostensibly more liberated era. Or has that liberation brought problems of its own? Consider the case of Ruth Crawford Seeger.

Born in 1901, daughter of a Midwest Methodist minister and variously raised in small-town Ohio and Florida, she proved gifted enough to enter the American Conservatory in Chicago in 1920. There she received a traditional training while absorbing more modernist and mystical enthusiasms of her piano teacher Djane Herz, a direct link with Scriabin. But if such early Crawford scores as her *Music for Small Orchestra* (1926) contain their darkly numinous textures, they also show a leaning towards constructivist schemes and atonal harmony. In due course, this was to attract the attention of that ubiquitous impresario of radical American music, Henry Cowell, who found a patroness to bring her to New York. Soon such pieces as her fiercely rhetorical Suite No. 1 for Five Wind Instruments and Piano (1927) began to be heard among works of Charles Ives, Edgar Varèse, Carl Ruggles and Cowell himself in what was then known as the Ultra-Modern manner. In 1930-31 she became the first woman to receive a Guggenheim fellowship, travelling to Europe to consult Bartók and Berg and drafting what were to remain her three terse masterpieces: the *Three Chants* (1930) for women's chorus, the *Three Songs to Poems by Carl Sandburg* (1930-32) for contralto and three ensembles, and the extraordinary String Quartet (1931).

For, already, events were in train that would stop her in her tracks. In 1929, Cowell had arranged for her to take some lessons with his own teacher, Charles Seeger. A mind of commanding scope, Seeger had been a conductor and composer until most of his music was lost in a fire, and he was to end up as one of the founding fathers of ethnomusicology. But in the 1920s he was very much the theorist of the Ultra-Moderns, seeking through his concept of 'dissonant counterpoint', to establish the basis of an authentically American new music independent of European influence. Initially, Crawford was put through a strict course of permutational schemes and anti-tonal part-writing, which she developed in her four *Diaphonic Suites* (1930-31) for one or two instruments. Gradually lessons turned into a collaboration on Seeger's projected treatise, and then into a romance. After Seeger had divorced his first wife, he and Crawford were married in 1932.

Meanwhile, however, the Great Depression was spreading its blight. Like many left-leaning artists and intellectuals, the Seegers came to feel that high Modernism had failed to answer the urgent needs of ordinary people. For a time, they involved themselves in composers' collectives and agitprop music under the influence of their friend, Hanns Eisler. Then, in 1936, Seeger was summoned to Washington to serve in the Federal Music Project as part of the New Deal enterprise to create an inclusive and optimistic all-American culture. To this Crawford was to contribute over the next 15 years by collecting, transcribing, editing, arranging and publishing hundreds of American folksongs, while simultaneously pioneering their use in basic musical education – not least, in that of her own children. In marrying Seeger, she had become stepmother of his son Pete, who in due course was to emerge as the leading light of the post-war folk- and protest-song revival. And two of her own four children by Seeger would also make their impact: Mike Seeger as an advocate of Deep South folk music, and Peggy Seeger with her husband, Ewan MacColl, as stars of the British folk revival. Indirectly, Crawford's selfless work in traditional music was to exert a huge posthumous influence.

What of her own music? In 1938, she revised the String Quartet for publication, also arranging its slow movement for string orchestra. The following year she fulfilled a radio commission with a brief but joyous orchestral folksong fantasia entitled *Rissolty, Rossolty* – her sole tonal piece. But for the most part, she seems to have reasoned, as many creative women have to, that, with luck there would still be time enough for her more radical music in later life. In 1952 she at last got round to completing a new Suite for Wind Quintet full of implacable ostinatos and hard-edged invention. Might she have gone on to assimilate the still newer innovations of the post-war avant-garde? Alas, within months she was dead from cancer at 52 – only nine years after Dame Ethel herself.

It is tempting to imagine that, had time allowed, she could have come as close as any woman to balancing and fulfilling the demands of creativity and childbearing, of professional achievement and social commitment, of sustaining tradition and advancing the new. But it is not so simple. What of the role of Charles Seeger? In submitting Crawford's already striking talent to a disciplined fine-tuning, he may have enabled her briefly to realize her most striking pieces; but, in marrying her, did he also subordinate that talent to his own desire for a renewed family life? In any case, how had Crawford managed to establish herself in a notoriously masculine and, in the era of Ives, Varèse and Ruggles, aggressively macho profession? Was it by denying her femininity in pursuing as hard and uncompromising a style as any of them? Back in 1953 when she died, such matters were difficult to determine, since, apart from the String Quartet (already an acknowledged influence on the teeming heterophonies of Elliott Carter's mighty String Quartet No. 1, 1951), most of her exiguous catalogue remained unpublished and little known.

Only over the last couple of decades has the true quality and stature of her achievement become apparent with the publication of Judith Tick's detailed and sympathetic biography;[3] the appearance of studies by David Nicholls and Joseph N. Straus revealing the conceptual and technical ingenuities Crawford packed into a surviving catalogue of a mere 15 works;[4] the belated edition of her pioneering monograph *The Music of American Folk Song* (originally intended as an appendix to *Our Singing Country* by John and Alan Lomax);[5]

and not least the recording of all her music under the devoted supervision of Oliver Knussen and others. By now, it is clear that the half-dozen best of her pieces stand with a handful of scores of Varèse and Ruggles as the essential classics of the Ultra-Modern era. Maybe she lacked a little of their visionary grandeur; but then she never had their chance to get her hands on a large orchestra – let alone to wax passionate and violent with it, as Shaw prophesized. Yet her achievement was arguably more various in its radicalism and more steely in its definition.

The four *Diaphonic Suites* already exemplify her special talent for teasing agile and characteristic discourses from the most cerebral schemes while the polymetric superimposition of abstract phonemes in the *Three Chants* prove uncanny studies in sophisticated primitivism. The *Three Songs to Poems by Carl Sandburg* achieve a remarkable textural complexity and depth through their sharp foreground imagery for voice, oboe, piano and percussion shadowed by two spatially separated background ensembles. And the String Quartet is *sui generis*. The four independent lines of its opening movement not only anticipate the Carter of twenty years later but actually sound like him too. The ductile rhythmic palindrome of its finale equally pre-dates the constructivist schemes Conlon Nancarrow would carry through in his pianola studies of the 1950s. As for the slow movement, with its cross-pulsating clusters, gradually shifting according to internal movements of parts and eventually rising to a climax of searing intensity: this achieves a sound and structure all but unheard before in Western music – epitomizing a pioneer who lived the cultural contradictions of her American era, impressively challenged gender stereotypes, and whose lapidary art still has things to teach composers now.

NOTES

Source: *The Independent*, 15 February 1992 and 3 July 2001; rev. 2008.

1   Bernard Shaw, 'Mr. Henschal in a Bad Light', *Shaw's Music*, Vol. 2 (1890-93), ed. Dan H. Laurence, London, The Bodley Head, 1981, p. 557.
2   Ibid., p. 557.
3   Judith Tick, *Ruth Crawford Seeger: A Composer's Search for American Music*, New York, OUP, 1997.
4   David Nicholls, *American Experimental Music 1890-1940*, CUP, 1990, in particular, 'On Dissonant Counterpoint', pp. 89-133; Joseph N. Straus, *The Music of Ruth Crawford Seeger*, Cambridge, CUP, 1995.
5   Ruth Crawford Seeger, *The Music of American Folk Song*, ed. Larry Polansky with Judith Tick, Rochester N. Y., University of Rochester Press, 2001.

8   In Search of Walton

But what could there still be to search *for*? No idiom, surely, remained so
changelessly identifiable across the twentieth-century decades. For thousands,
this very recognition sustained his output, together with not so many works
of Shostakovich and Britten among younger composers, as the furthest
excursion into modernism from which they could derive any certain joy. The
critical reaction is almost as longstanding – initiated by Colin Mason's doubts
about the 'merely exotic' Violin Concerto (1939),[1] or perhaps even earlier by,
of all people, Constant Lambert when he argued that the finale of the First
Symphony (1932-35) provided 'a physical rather than an intellectual answer to
the questioning and agitated mood of the opening'.[2] By 1960, when the Second
Symphony collected some of the worst notices in William Walton's career, his
imperviousness to the implications of the Second Viennese School, let alone
Darmstadt, was axiomatic among younger commentators, though in 1976, in
the course of a review wondering 'why Covent Garden was bothering itself
with such a hopeless old dodo as *Troilus and Cressida* [1949-54]' the critic of
the *Sunday Telegraph* could be read diagnosing 'the disappointing failure to
evolve that has marked almost Walton's entire post-war output' as:

> Less the inability to absorb avant-garde elements that has sometimes
> been alleged – after all, composers such as Britten have drawn vibrantly
> new sounds from even more traditional techniques – than a refusal to
> take risks with the idiom of which he was already master.

Nevertheless the writer of these words (in fact, this author) ought to have
known better. For the continual questioning of received opinion is among
the first duties of any critic; and on further thought, neither the established
view of Walton's musical personality, nor the implicit view of musical history
against which he has been judged, quite adds up. Maybe, when the young
Britten himself remarked, "I do not see why I should lock myself inside
a purely personal idiom,"[3] he was already implicitly criticizing his, at start,
almost equally precocious older contemporary. If so, he was assuming that
Walton's relation to the composers he admired must be equivalent to his
own. To be sure, figures as disparate as Stravinsky, Sibelius and Elgar have
been commonly cited as agents in Walton's maturing. Yet, though Michael
Kennedy for one has sought to establish a more general parallel in his career
with Elgar,[4] he and Frank Howes agree that such influences were incidental
to the emergence of a singularly independent, even solitary artist.[5] And
considering how struck the very young Walton of *Façade* (1922) evidently
was by the Stravinsky-Diaghilev ethos in its post-1918 phase of cosmopolitan

chic – all those 'portraits' of popular genres and 'postcards' of national styles – and his absorption of such technical devices as the irregular accenting of a continuous fast pulse, as in *Portsmouth Point* (1925), it is indeed surprising how little his pre-war music actually sounds like Stravinsky. One passage that briefly does – the stuttering winds and frilly strings between letters I and J of the delectable *Siesta* (1926) for small orchestra – anticipates the Stravinsky of the early 1940s, which ought to stand as a caveat to influence-pickers.

The oft-claimed Sibelius influence on the First Symphony, especially its opening movement, is even more in need of qualification. Granted the invocation of such procedures as ostinato and pedal point at the start and the *Tapiola*-like reiterations at apostrophes throughout the work, the only extended stretch of Sibelius at all resembling the gallopings of Walton's first movement is the opening half of *Nightride and Sunrise* (1907) – of which, certainly, he could have heard the earliest British broadcast in October 1931, a few months before embarking on the Symphony. But the extreme motivic economy of *Nightride*, as of most Sibelius after the early 1900s, is contrary to Walton's thematic copiousness here, while his deployment of pedal points as a series of discrete steps in a tonal process of marked instability is quite distinct from Sibelius's habitual usage as a link between contrasting keys (as in the mediant pedals through the E flat, G and B key-cycle of the Fifth Symphony's opening movement).

As regards Walton's known affection for the then out-of-fashion Elgar, one can certainly find traces before the downward strutting tutti figure and accompanied cadenza of the Violin Concerto's finale - the pattering chord antiphonies between woodwind and strings at figures 11 and 16 of the first movement of the 1927 Sinfonia Concertante surely derive from Elgar's Introduction and Allegro for Strings (1905). Yet the contrast in spirit between *Crown Imperial* (1937) and Elgar's ceremonial marches is palpable: not only is Walton self-consciously assuming the style and afflatus of slow melody that came spontaneously to Elgar, but the jubilation of the bouncier passages is as suggestive of a source of his own – the Babylonian praises in *Belshazzar's Feast* (1931) – an irony that seems to have been lost on the English establishment.

If such imputed influences are by no means the simple matter they might seem, neither are they, of course, the only ones. When Hugh Ottaway suggested that the Viola Concerto (1929) may have been modelled on the form of Prokofiev's First Violin Concerto (1917) – and the parallels between their respective outer movements are sometimes striking – he failed to mention that the earliest British performance of the Prokofiev was not till 1932 (though possibly Walton could have seen a score – his earlier musical self-education seems largely to have been a matter of silent score-reading in the Radcliffe Camera).[6] Yet the transparency and astringent sweetness of the Prokofiev are surely evident in the first movement of the Violin Concerto, as they are in Britten's contemporaneous Concerto and the later concertos of Shostakovich (but then the importance of this most lyrically perfected of all Prokofiev's works in furthering the tradition of the 'thin' string concerto, the Mendelssohn-Sibelius tradition in which the soloist leads as distinct from the bigger, symphonic tradition of Beethoven, Brahms and Elgar, is a topic in itself). As for the Viola Concerto, Walton himself acknowledged a source in the *Kammermusik* No. 5 (1927) of his first soloist, Paul Hindemith: "I was surprised he played it. One or two bars are almost identical"[7] – fair comment, since Hindemith's second movement ends with the double-stopped, false-related parallel sixths that are among the basic données of the Walton. Indeed, the affinity with his German peer, expressed not only in the rising fourths of the Viola Concerto scherzo or the First Symphony fugue, but more generally in a certain bluff, contrapuntal dryness of texture, is so special a feature of early Walton up to the mid-1930s that one can only feel his 1962 'Mediterraneanizing' of the Viola Concerto by manifold textural lightenings and the addition of a harp, though in no way altering its substance, amounts to a compromising of its character.

But it is the continuing evidence of traffic with other composers – more so, possibly, than in later Britten – *after* the Violin Concerto, when Walton is widely considered to have settled for self-repetition, that is intriguing. Some of the hints are quite specific. The opening of the slow movement of his String Quartet in A minor (1947) with an arching cello melody against a violin pedal third, and the movement's climax of aspiring thirds at figure 63, are too close to the Andante of Britten's own First String Quartet (1941) to be entirely coincidental (there is more than a suggestion of '*Départ*' from *Les Illuminations* (1940) in the opening phrases, too). Again, the vague procedural parallel one senses between the revolving of the chromatic motif of the Second Symphony's first movement against its shimmering background and the diatonic motto with chugging accompaniment of Stravinsky's Symphony in C (1940) is confirmed by Walton's virtual appropriation of Stravinsky's irregular, peremptory final chord alternations near the end.

Other resemblances, perhaps, are to be treated more cautiously. Suspicions, raised by some distinctly *Suite en Fa* (1926) inflections in the other movements of the Partita (1958), that Walton may have been indulging a penchant for Albert Roussel around the mid-1950s, are strengthened by the similarity of the viola melody of its middle movement to a line in the introduction to Roussel's *Bacchus et Ariadne* Suite No. 2 (1930), and of the slow movement climax of the Second Symphony to moments of Roussel's Third (1930). The tolling low Cs with tam-tam and lamenting English horn that open Act 3 of *Troilus* could have been prompted by Mahler's 'Abschied' from *Das Lied von der Erde* (1909), just as the falling tetrachord of a pair of semitone-linked fourths that introduces the 12-note row tailpieces to the variations of the Violin Sonata

(1949) could have been derived from Berg. Some of these may indeed be accidental conjunctions, but many other instances could be substituted, and they clearly differ in kind from such explicit references as the parodies in *The Bear* (1967) or the Britten-Pears skit offered by the Pandarus music in *Troilus*.

Now there is something deeply paradoxical about a style that, though never other than its apparently unevolving self, presents continual clues as to what its composer had been recently hearing. Evidently, Walton's musical explorations did not cease with the embarkation for Ischia. It was, appropriately enough, on *Desert Island Discs* that an explanation of those mysterious manifestations of the notes B-A-C-H over *sul ponticello* frissons in the fifth of the *Variations on a Theme by Hindemith* (1963) offered itself – when Walton chose, as his single out of the eight, Schoenberg's Variations for Orchestra, Op. 31 (1928) because "I might eventually learn to understand them," or words to that effect. A critic-induced anxiety not to fall behind, then? "I keep a very large gramophone collection and I torture myself listening to the latest records of contemporary music," he once remarked.[8] But the assurance of an ear that scarcely allowed him to compose a note for decades that does not 'sound' compelled him to add, "On the whole I find a great deal of it monotonous, overlong, boring ..." and in any case, most of his allusions are to composers of his own generation or earlier. A closer comparison might be drawn with Stravinsky's habitual borrowing of stylistic elements to variegate an inborn fixity of shape and gesture, or with the indirect doctrine of self-realization through the copying of models of Ravel – yet another composer to be variously sensed behind much of Walton's music if, for the most part, fugitively (the outrageous Mussorgsky-Ravel bell-crib of bars 63-71 of the *Gloria* (1961) is an exception). Yet Walton's references are surely less functional than those of Ravel or Stravinsky, more in the nature of companionate signals from a self-isolated, literally insular composer to others, on the mainland as it were, in the Great Community of composers.

That he needed to maintain such a balance – in his life as in his work – for so long, suggests its centrality to his creative motivation. When, in a discussion of the 'inhibited attitude towards a largely diatonic idiom' of many of Britten's contemporaries, Donald Mitchell remarks, 'Walton is a good example of a composer who almost aggressively attempts to suppress, or at least disguise, his diatonic tendencies – hence his often self-destructive rhythms and his frequently cloying chromaticism,'[9] he can be countered by diatonic Walton from *Portsmouth Point* to the recomposition for brass band of his ballet suite, *The First Shoot* (1935, rev. 1980). But in more general terms, the argument is suggestive. Whatever extra-musical explanations future biographers may extrapolate, the salient musical fact of Walton's career is that his natural gifts and technical flair were matched, almost from the start, by a corresponding difficulty, even suffering, in the act of composing. If this reflected a deep, perhaps irresolvable conflict between the urge to expression and the fear of self-exposure, then one can better understand the stylistic tensions of his unfolding: the early self-realization through the indirection of parody in *Façade* and the inclination towards such 'objective' composers as Stravinsky and Hindemith rather than the uninhibitedly aggressive Bartók or the expressionistic Viennese whose influence, briefly admitted in the String Quartet (1922), rapidly resulted in that work's embarrassed withdrawal.

One can also understand Walton's avoidance throughout his career, with one significant exception, of intimate writing for the human voice. His most striking innovation here, the rhythmicized speech of *Façade*, is also the most stylized; it is notable how the two settings he subsequently turned into songs already lose incisiveness with the addition of pitches. The later song sets are predominantly extrovert, while the choral writing, where it is not simply fulfilling the motions of cathedral music (the least changeable or interesting side of his output), tends towards florid public utterance, as in *Belshazzar's Feast* (1931). Admittedly the savagery of the latter might tempt one to compare it with the psychological release of *The Rite of Spring* (1913): the moment Walton sent his (Anglican) past to blazes – except that he first endorses it in the post-Parry choral turns of 'By the waters of Babylon'. Even in the unbridled stretches of the First Symphony, patently the result of an upwelling perturbation, the directness of expression is qualified by the assumption of a 'bardic' rhetoric and – if the criticism may be hazarded of so admired a work – by a certain sense of protesting too much.

Nonetheless, the Symphony was notoriously his most tortuous birth. If the music came marginally more easily from the 1940s to the 60s, this surely represented Walton's recognition of the principle of variation, both structurally and in detail, as the most fruitful response to his creative tensions, the optimum 'distance' from which to handle his expressive promptings. Of course, it was evident from fairly early on that he was the kind of composer in whom certain types of texture and gesture were liable to recur from work to work – so the Violin Concerto opens with a becalmed clarinet quasi-echo of the Symphony's initial ostinato and closes with a miniaturized recapitulation of the earlier work's grandiosity. Perhaps a few of these recurrences – the *con malizia* trumpet snarlings and febrile octave-doubled trills, or the jaunty plunging major seventh chords down progressions of thirds – ultimately came close to justifying charges of self-imitation. Yet one has only to compare the relatively flavourless Siciliana in the quickly written ballet *The Quest* (1943) with the manifold cross-currents of the atmosphere and feeling in the exquisitely worked central movement of the Partita, to realize how this approach has as often resulted in an enhanced richness and subtlety even in the lightest of contexts.

But it is on the larger scale that Walton diverges most from the precedents of his equally 'indirect' peers. Not obviously constrained within Stravinsky's formal limits, nor on the other hand inclined to the total stylistic submissions of Ravel, he can be seen in the first part of his development, rather, in the process of synthesizing stylistically and defining formally a set of models of his own for varied future realization. If the composition of *Scapino* (1941) may be suspected of having virtually completed this first phase, then is it not surprising that variations *per se* almost immediately start appearing – first in the passacaglias of *The Quest* and *Henry V* (1944), later in the five big sets from the Violin Sonata (1949) by way of the 'Cello Concerto (1956), Second Symphony (1959-60) and *Hindemith Variations* to the *Improvisations on an Impromptu of Benjamin Britten* (1970), but also implicitly in the recomposition involved in the Sonata for Strings (1972) arrangement of the 1947 Quartet and the 1976 *Varii capricci* orchestration of the Bagatelles for Guitar (1972).

From this perspective, it is not the similarities but the structural variations between the three string concertos that are critical. Thus the achievement of the 'Cello Concerto's opening movement in sustaining an ample, seven-minute unfolding without any obvious principle of dramatic contrast is the more remarkable heard against the abrupt switches in tempo of the first movement of the Violin Concerto or the progressive evolutions of that of the Viola Concerto (even if one may think the work's slow epilogue is, after all, determined less by its own necessity than by consistency with the earlier concertos). Curiously, if one played this movement at about three times the speed, one would have something approaching the comedy overture model established by *Scapino* and varied in the robust first movement of the Partita, the featherlight *Capriccio burlesco* (1969) and, most importantly, in the opening movement of the Second Symphony, where the trapping of its gestural fun and games in a singularly constricted and dissonant harmonic field produces as unsettling an effect as anything in Walton. But then the Second has surely been misprised: the point about the 12-tone row in the finale is not that Walton fails to exploit it serially, but that it prompts him towards some variations of exceptional concision and harmonic adventurousness.

If his most complex feelings, then, tend to be infolded in his various detailing, and the development of his musical thought is mainly to be discerned in structural variation between works, one can perhaps more readily understand why, despite its incidental excitements and beauties, *Troilus and Cressida* fails to fulfil its apparently intended function as crowning opus – aside, that is, from the too, too lovely diction and deadly well-madeness of Christopher Hassall's libretto. In seeking, out of the emotional security of his married happiness, at last to compose vocal settings of a direct expressiveness, Walton was foregoing precisely the inhibitions that had for so long helped to define the very character of his music, while at the same time attempting the one genre for which he had established no previous structural models of his own. Or so one listener would rationalize what seems to him the opera's lack of idiosyncratic electricity. On the other hand, such a view of his musical character could help to explain why works so finely wrought as the *Hindemith Variations* – packed with such cogent individuality as, to choose at random, the bassoon and then horn progressions that open Variation VII – continue to be dismissed in certain quarters as without contemporary relevance.

In his brilliant study *Between Romanticism and Modernism*, Carl Dahlhaus described how the late-eighteenth-century practice of form as a balance of (not, in themselves, very individual) parts defined by function was gradually replaced, through the growing cult of originality, by 'the concept of musical form as something which presented the history of a musical theme' – the attempt, that is, to generate every aspect of a work from an original motif, whether by 'real sequence' (Wagner) or 'developing variation' (Brahms).[10] Now it is notable, not only the extent to which Walton's forms depend on a balance of parts defined by function and how their carrying and 'slanting' of an element of cliché has always helped to express the more convivial side of his personality, but also how relatively small a role motivic generation has played in shaping his large structures. As often as not, his basic material comprises quite extended melodies, tending to a mode of construction, moreover, which (*pace* Michael Kennedy) is at the furthest remove from Elgar. A typical long Elgar tune, whether of the *Pomp and Circumstance* or 'Cello Concerto variety, is paradigmatic of developing variation: a single motif put through a series of varied sequential hoops. A Walton melody rarely consists of fewer than two basic elements, being generally assembled from a number of contrasting, balancing figures to fill the allotted formal space in a way more nearly analogous with … Mozart! As if by confirmation, the one disappointment among his orchestral works is his attempt to make something of a purely sequential, monorhythmic, not to say circular tune – the Britten Impromptu upon which he based his *Improvisations*. So that while one can understand – not least in the light of that luxuriant bitonal shimmering that enveloped Walton's work in the late 1940s and then rather mysteriously evaporated from it again after the Second Symphony – Hugh Wood's dismissal of the post-war music for an 'impotent romanticism of a vaguely Gallic cast,'[11] one is inclined to take Walton's self-characterization as 'a classical composer with a strong feeling for lyricism' the more seriously.[12]

Admittedly, the cult of originality still haunts criticism; it is not so long since developing variation achieved its apogee in the serial ramifications of Pierre Boulez and Milton Babbitt and it may be some while yet before a redress of what Dahlhaus calls the 'one-sided' dependence of form itself upon the musical idea prompts the reassessment of a composer such as Walton. But if he is to be left among the conservative also-rans of the twentieth century who kept up the standard genres – somewhere in between Prokofiev and Roussel, Shostakovich and Samuel Barber – at least we should recognize that for accessibility, professionalism and the integrated mediation of a singularly complex musical personality, his variations, concertos and symphonies stand among the very best of their kind.

NOTES

Source: *The Musical Times*, Vol. 123, No. 1669, March 1982, pp. 179-84; rev. 2008.

1   Colin Mason, 'William Walton' in: *British Music of Our Time*, ed. A. L. Bacharach, Harmondsworth, Penguin Books, 1946, p. 146.
2   Quoted by Hugh Ottaway in 'Walton' from: *The New Grove Dictionary of Music and Musicians*, Vol. 20, ed. Stanley Sadie, London, Macmillan, 1980, p. 197.
3   Quoted by Hans Keller in 'The Musical Character' from: *Benjamin Britten, A Commentary on His Works from a Group of Specialists*, ed. Donald Mitchell and Hans Keller, London, Rockliff, 1952, pp. 329-30.
4   Michael Kennedy, 'William Walton: A Critical Appreciation' in: Stewart Craggs, *William Walton: A Thematic Catalogue*, Oxford, OUP, 1977, p. 2.
5   Frank Howes, *The Music of William Walton*, Oxford, OUP, 1974.
6   Ottaway, 'Walton', 1980, p. 197.
7   Quoted in: Geoffrey Skelton, *Paul Hindemith*, London, Gollancz, 1975, pp. 97-8.
8   Quoted in: Murray Schafer, *British Composers in Interview*, London, Faber, 1963, p. 82.
9   Donald Mitchell, 'The Musical Atmosphere' in: Mitchell and Keller, 1952, p. 34.
10 Carl Dahlhaus, *Between Romanticism and Modernism*, Berkeley, California UP, 1980.
11 Hugh Wood, 'English Contemporary Music' in: *European Music in the Twentieth Century* (1957), rev. ed. Howard Hartog, London, Penguin Books, 1961, pp. 146-47.
12 Schafer, 1963, p. 79.

9   *The Once and Future Tippett*

In one of his last articles, Sir Michael Tippett recalled his excitement as a student at the Royal College of Music in the mid-1920s on singing in an early performance of *The Hymn of Jesus* (1917) by Gustav Holst.[1] Not only was the choral writing 'wonderfully daring,' but Holst had also succeeded, Tippett felt, in going back to the basic sources of religion through his choice of text from the Apocryphal Acts of St. John, his incorporation of plainsong and, most importantly, through his reconnection of dance with religious ecstasy. Like Stravinsky and Picasso, he argued, Holst was destined to be an artist driven by 'the compulsion to change from and be enriched by experience and to discover new content and new styles'. True, he died comparatively young: 'What he did manage, even early on, however, was a sort of odd intermingling of disparate ingredients which, when also properly cohesive, attests to the quality of a vision.'

Suggestive though these words may be of Holst's still incompletely understood achievement, the artist they most evoke is surely Tippett himself. An 'odd intermingling of disparate ingredients,' both musical and extra-musical, was noticed in his output almost from the start. The sometimes abrupt shifts of aim and focus that marked his artistic development certainly tell of a compulsion to discover new content and styles, and many of his major projects aspired to the quality of a vision. The question that continues to hover over the re-exploration of his output prompted by his centenary year was to what extent, and how often, he managed to achieve an amalgam of those odd interminglings and disparate ingredients that we recognize as 'properly cohesive'.

Maybe it is still too soon to say. Until 1998, Tippett was still among us as his familiar, loquacious self. And it is not so long since he brought forth his last major work, *The Rose Lake* (1991-93), on his ninetieth birthday. While that piece has achieved a fair number of performances and two commercial recordings, the chequered reception history and slow acceptance of some of his most remarkable earlier scores should stand as a caveat to sweeping judgements, even now. It is not only that the press sometimes reacted crassly to apparent anomalies in Tippett's librettos or complexities in his musical technique that later proved to have their own logic, but also the way that Tippett's changes of direction disconcerted precisely those listeners who thought they loved and understood his music best.

In contrast with a composer such as Benjamin Britten, whose innate musicality was nurtured from the start, perhaps the key to Tippett as an artist is that he was essentially self-created. By his own account, he seems to have fallen in love with the *idea* of becoming a composer before he had much musical experience or any evidence of real talent. And decades later he was to insist, 'Looking back, the drive to make musical and theatrical artefacts was always strong, but absorbed into it was an intellectuality which I could never refuse.'[2] Thus, where for Britten music was the given thing, to be adapted according to textual or social function, for Tippett it was more of an endpoint, the medium in which the impressions, thoughts and intuitions of a complex mind could most nearly be resolved. And where Britten cleaved increasingly to the idea of the composer as a servant to the community, Tippett seemed to view his role as more in the nature of a seer, conveying to audiences, through his sonorous image-making faculty, intimations of the collective psyche or the ineffable beyond.

His initial struggle, however, was to acquire even a modicum of musical competence. Brought up in rural Suffolk before and during the First World War, with radio still to come, he had little to go on but the Edwardian drawing room songs his mother sang and his own inchoate improvisings at the piano. Not until the age of 14 did he hear a symphony orchestra; not until he arrived at the Royal College at 18 was he able to begin exploring the standard repertoire. And only then did he start composing intensively, taking another decade to achieve a manner he could recognize as his own. "You never have it all," he would tell aspiring young composers in later years, recalling that long melodic lines and lively rhythms came comparatively easily to him whereas it took years of effort to acquire a comparable grasp of harmony and form.

At first, it was the overwhelming impact of Beethoven that inspired him, offering not only strong models of harmony and form, but suggesting how a compositional career might be projected in terms of complementary opposites: the abstract drama of symphony versus the human drama of opera, the grand public vision of oratorio versus the private metaphysical communing of string quartet, and so on. Yet almost as vital in helping him find himself was the practice, not only of Holst, but also especially of Stravinsky, of animating their forms through the citation and juxtaposing of many different procedures and styles from the historical past. Behind this, though he alluded to it less often, Tippett seems to have believed that to come to maturity, a composer, in a certain sense, needed to relive the development of Western music, rather in the way the child in the womb recapitulates the stages of evolution. It is striking that while this earlier output teemed with influences from Classical, Baroque, Renaissance and even Medieval music (to say nothing of folksong and traditional spirituals), up to his early fifties it showed little sign of anything more 'advanced' than middle-period Stravinsky, Bartók and Hindemith. Only then did Tippett seem to feel he had earned the right to come up to date, with the abrasive (and unexpected) onslaught of his second opera, *King Priam* (1958-61).

If his first decade after leaving the Royal College was a matter of mastering such classical procedures as the Beethoven sonata allegro and Baroque fugal technique together with a variety of historical influences, it already established his creative process as a kind of assembly job of different elements that he would gradually attempt to combine into a unified whole. One thinks of the gaudier collage structures among his later works as exemplifying this approach, but it is already evident in his first outright masterpiece, the Concerto for Double String Orchestra (1938-39). Here, the opening sonata allegro has a Classical head-motif but articulated in contrapuntal cross-rhythms suggestive at once of Elizabethan madrigals and early jazz, while the slow movement, clearly modelled on that of Beethoven's String Quartet in F minor, Op. 95 (1810), complete with chromatic fugato, takes as its opening the paraphrase of a Scottish folksong, which Tippett inflects with a Bessie Smith-style 'blue' note.

If the projected work was to be large-scale and text-based, such as an oratorio or opera, the process of assembly could take years: a slow gathering of likely dramatic, literary, philosophical, psycho-social, political and mythological materials out of his reading, theatre-going, even cinema- and television-viewing, from which specifics of genre, action and text would be teased long before he began composing: "The notes come last, and are easy," he once remarked.[3] As a result, his creative process tended to move forward as on a multiple conveyor belt; while one major piece was being written, the next would be in active preparation, while still a third would be in its early stages of conception. Occasionally there were hold-ups: the composition of his first opera, *The Midsummer Marriage* (1946-52), was protracted by the demands of his musical work at Morley College and by illness; that of his fifth and last, *New Year* (1985-88), by a serious cancer operation. But usually he could predict – with surprising accuracy for an artist so dependent on the vagaries of visionary inspiration – just what he would be working on years ahead and when he expected to deliver it.

This, in turn, reflected the artistic psychology he had forged for himself in the process of mastering his métier. After the disintegration of a love affair in the mid 1930s left him devastated, he appears to have concluded, through a process of self-analysis along Jungian lines, that for the type of artist he aspired to be, the price of continuing creativity would have to be the avoidance of intense personal entanglements in the future – as he put it, somewhat chillingly, 'the composer, slowly being dehumanized in favour of the Muse or the God'.[4] In the event, he continued to attract a succession of companions and young supporters while retaining a bemusing ability to comment on his self-absorption as though he were someone else. But he must also have felt his acceptance of his essential apartness as an individual was quickly justified by the deep collective feeling it enabled him to tap into and convey to wartime and post-war audiences with his first oratorio, *A Child of Our Time* (1939-41).

Indeed, the virile and still-underrated First Symphony (1945) Tippett brought forth on turning 40 sounds like the celebration of a hard-earned artistic and personal maturity. As a man of social conscience, he had proved himself by going to prison for his uncompromising pacifism in 1943; as a composer, he now had a catalogue including not only the symphony and the oratorio but also a piano sonata, two fine string quartets and the floridly Purcellian solo cantata, *Boyhood's End* (1943), composed for his new-found friends, Benjamin Britten and Peter Pears. Now he felt on the verge of what he later called 'one's little period in which everything is flowing',5 that huge surge of vitality and lyricism that was to carry him through *The Midsummer's Marriage*, the song cycle *The Heart's Assurance* (1951), the *Fantasia Concertante on a Theme of Corelli* (1953), the Piano Concerto (1953-55), the Sonata for Four Horns (1955) and the Second Symphony (1956-57).

For not a few listeners, the output from the mid 1930s to the late 1950s, when his richest, most generous imaginings were still held in focus by relatively traditional techniques, remains the authentic Tippett. With the shock of *King Priam*, in which he suddenly abandoned all the symphonic continuities he had mastered for anti-developmental structures of harsh juxtaposition, he seemed to embark upon a strategy of ever higher stakes: attempting in the glittering superimpositions of *The Vision of Saint Augustine* (1963-65) to articulate the experience of eternity; seeking in the cinematic cross-cuttings of *The Knot Garden* (1966-69) and the Expressionist confrontations of *The Ice Break* (1973-76) to diagnose respectively all the ills of modern society and the anxieties of the Cold War; challenging the optimism of Beethoven's Ninth in his own Third Symphony (1970-72) and working up to nothing less than an emblematic history of the world in *The Mask of Time* (1980-82).

Tippett's music never lacked for detractors, of course. Some of his finest scores from the 1950s were initially criticized for 'amateurishly crowded textures', 'over-intellectualism', and so on. On the other hand, it would take a fervent enthusiast indeed to assert that, in his ambition to encompass so many conceptual ideas, so many stylistic allusions, the later Tippett never lapsed into patches of summary structure, unfocussed harmony or scrappy invention. What no one could ever deny was his ability, to the end, to illuminate even his most rebarbative scores with sudden, vibrant sonorous images, whole passages of genuinely visionary resonance. One thinks of the single, quiet chord that concludes *The Ice Break*, the radiant final pages of *The Mask of Time*, that brazenly heroic farewell salute to light and life at the apex of *The Rose Lake*. Maybe it was for moments such as these that Tippett was prepared to risk everything.

As he retreated from conducting and actively promoting his music, then ceased composing and finally died in 1998, it nevertheless began to look as though only a handful of earlier works – the Double Concerto, *A Child of Our Time*, the *Corelli Fantasia* and a few instrumental pieces – were destined to hold firm in the international repertoire. Yet the proliferation of performances marking his centenary in 2005, beyond the expectations even of his publishers, seems to have put far more of his output back into currency. What of its future influence? At a time when a later work such as *The Knot Garden* begins to look and sound more cohesive, less merely trendy, then it seemed to many in the past, it could be that his operatic innovations will prompt further experiments in the musical theatre, which he himself believed the likeliest site of new musical developments.[6] But for composers to come, perhaps his most inspiring legacy will always be the *way* he developed: showing how, by patiently working, step by step, on a modest initial talent, an artist of genuine idealism could eventually aspire to the creation of works of the richest content and on the grandest scale.

NOTES

Source: 'The Past and Future Tippett: A Centenary View', programme book for the revival of *The Midsummer Marriage* at the Royal Opera House, Covent Garden in November 2005.

1   Michael Tippett, 'Holst' in: *Tippett on Music*, ed. Meirion Bowen, Oxford, OUP, 1995, pp. 73-5.
2   Michael Tippett, *Those Twentieth Century Blues: An Autobiography*, London, Hutchinson, 1991, p. 16.
3   Remark to the author, summer 1970. See also: Murray Schafer, *British Composers in Interview*, London, Faber, 1963, pp. 97-8.
4   *The Selected Letters of Michael Tippett*, ed. Thomas Schuttenhelm, London, Faber, 2005, p. 366.
5   Remark to students at the Wardour Castle Summer School, August 1964.
6   Michael Tippett, 'Dreaming on Things to Come' in: *Tippett on Music*, 1995, pp. 307-09.

10   *The Britten Aesthetic*

'Mr. Britten's cleverness, of which he has frequently been told, has got the better of him and led him into all sorts of errors, the worst of which are errors of taste,' complained William McNaught in *The Musical Times* for September 1938.[1] Whether the charge could have been so easily levelled ten, or even five years later is another matter. As one scans the first production designs of Kenneth Green, John Piper or Annena Stubbs, the verse librettos of Ronald Duncan or William Plomer in David Herbert's T*he Operas of Benjamin Britten*,[2] it is difficult not to think of Britten's activities as epitomizing English taste over the next three decades – difficult not to link the *Serenade* for tenor, horn and strings of 1943 with, say, the nocturnal neo-Romantic convolutions of Dylan Thomas or Graham Sutherland, or the handling of low-life caricature and heightened 'spirit of place' in *Peter Grimes* (1945) with the Dickens films of David Lean. Nor was this centrality limited in milieu; if *The Turn of the Screw* (1954) evokes such delights of the 1950s intelligentsia as *The Architectural Review* on 'pleasing decay', the colossal success of the *War Requiem* (1961) undoubtedly floated – to Britten's own dismay – upon the queasy tide of First World War nostalgia that swept the mass media in the early 1960s. By the later 1960s, admittedly, newer notions of 'authentic performance' and 'community arts' were threatening to shunt the whole Aldeburgh aesthetic – Purcell to brass rubbing – into a cultural siding, though from this time on Britten seemed increasingly preoccupied with laying bare his own artistic soul.

What McNaught stigmatized as 'cleverness' represented, nevertheless, a quality of sensibility quite new in English music – and one that evidently continued to disturb some listeners to the end. After the musical triumph of *Grimes*, criticism admittedly tended to take more surreptitious forms; when *Scrutiny* savaged Britten in 1953, for instance, it was less upon the predictable grounds of 'immaturity' than as a symptom of an alleged ex-public school cultural conspiracy.[3] Even so, the phobia he understandably developed over such attacks was to kill at least two major projects prematurely leaked to the press during the 1960s, according to Peter Pears's preface and Colin Graham's article on the later productions: a *King Lear* and an *Anna Karenina* that had reached draft libretto stage. And behind all this lurked the imputation of Britten's homosexuality, a factor only openly discussed after his death by that self-confessed 'heterosexual without homosexual interests', Hans Keller, on Radio 3 and later in his remarkable long introduction to Herbert's book.

Pointing to Britten's use of boys' voices and the success of the texture of *Billy Budd* (1951) 'in unfolding contrasts within the self-imposed limitation of male voices the like of which the heterosexual Richard Wagner did not find easy to realize in all those hours of all-male *Siegfried*' (Woodbird and

Brünnhilde apart, that is), Keller contends that 'however little Britten may have been alive to the fact, his psychosexual organization placed him in the position of discovering and musically defining new truths which, otherwise, might not have been accessible to him at all.' This recognition of Britten's 'straightforwardly homosexual genius', however, is only part of a broader argument based upon Schiller's distinction of the naïve and (as Keller puts it) 'sentimentalic' artist: naïve composers (for instance, Mozart, Bruckner, Britten) being revealers of the given thing, excelling in musical statement; sentimentalic composers (Beethoven, Brahms, Schoenberg) being seekers, excelling in musical development. The operatic pre-eminence of Britten, like that of Mozart, accordingly sprang from overcompensation – a resort to stage drama to offset their unease over the purely musical drama of sonata development – though Keller adds that ultimately they had it both ways by transferring operatic procedures into their later chamber music. But, he continues, there is one important difference: where the naïve Mozart and the sentimentalic Haydn could happily coexist in the eighteenth century, the naïve temperament ran counter to all accepted twentieth-century notions of growth and change both in the art and the individual artist – a situation complicated by the apparent fragmentation of the musical language, which forced even the naïve artist into the stance of seeker, at least at the outset of his career.

In so far as John and Myfanwy Piper's accounts of working with Britten, as designer and librettist respectively, on *The Turn of the Screw*, *Owen Wingrave* (1971) and *Death in Venice* (1973) confirm his concern with every conceivable aspect of dramatic pacing and atmosphere; in so far as Britten's evolution proceeded through his operas rather than his concert works, at least until the culmination of the Third String Quartet (1975), the over-compensation theory seems to hold good. But the suggestion of a naïve bias also helps to explain the ambivalence of his reception. Even with the dogged Vaughan Williams before them as an ideal of insular integrity, the critics of the 1930s and 1940s should not have been thrown by Britten's provisional eclecticism – his expressed refusal to lock himself within a narrow personal idiom – not in itself, at least. Such an approach has a long enough English tradition: the Continental importations of Morley and Purcell, the echoes of *Parsifal* and Brahms's Third behind so much of Elgar – the presence of Ravel in the background of Vaughan Williams, for that matter.

But whereas the sentimentalic talent presumably tends to select influences out of some conscious sense of what needs to be done, some feeling of responsibility to the art, the historical moment or whatever, the influences upon the naïve artist are likely to be more in the nature of selective affinities, predilections that help to reveal – to others and to himself – what he already is. And in two respects, Britten's selective affinities proved worrying: not only were the composers he absorbed mostly rather out of fashion in Britain during his earlier years, but there seemed virtually no stylistic connection between them. If Mahlerian texture, for instance, was merely 'post-Wagnerian' and Rossinian coloratura manifestly 'trivial', how was it possible to take seriously a work such as *Our Hunting Fathers* (1936) in which the two elements were so impudently thrown together? McNaught, to do him credit, was to hail the *Sinfonia da Requiem* (1940) as the harbinger of Britten's maturity, Mahlerian affinities notwithstanding, though the critic can hardly have foreseen the extent of a synthesis that would enable Britten five years later to deploy, in the high string lines of *Peter Grimes*, the stock turns of early nineteenth-century bel canto to evoke the very feel of the grey East Anglian dawn.

If Britten continued to disturb some even after *Grimes*, it must surely have been less for the provenance of his influences than for the nakedness of their integration. How far his emergence as a 'thin' composer depended upon a conscious decision is difficult to divine, though, by his own account (in the BBC Radio 3 'Britten Sunday' in 1973) something of a Mozartean epiphany appears to have switched his youthful enthusiasm from Beethoven and Brahms to the 'slender' sound of such composers as Schubert, Verdi, Mahler and – for a time – Stravinsky. His lifelong quest for 'simplicity', with its social as well as artistic implications, could certainly be seen – if paradoxically – as the closest approach to a sentimentalic trait in his musical character, possibly even inhibiting the flow of his invention by the 1960s. Be that as it may, listeners who habitually equate musical 'substance' with density of texture are always likely to experience a difficulty over Britten: the fact that his music rarely involves more than two dynamic compositional elements simultaneously – a third already usually comprising a merely static or background ostinato pedal. That the best of his pieces nonetheless contrive to stand up to repeated listening disturbed even the awesome Adorno into attacking the 'triumphant meagreness of Benjamin Britten' for a 'taste for tastelessness, a simplicity resulting from ignorance, an immaturity which masks as enlightenment, and a dearth of technical means.'[4]

This simplicity is more apparent than real, of course. Undriven – at least directly – by an urge towards elaborate development within a piece or a search for technical innovation within the art, a 'thin-naïve' composer is likely to concentrate upon expressing himself through the slanting of the received language; and not just in the satirical sense of the 'wrong notes' inserted by composers such as Prokofiev and Shostakovich into traditional genres – though early Britten shows a measure of this, too. If the wrong notes in Britten's music have a propensity for ultimately sounding right after all, this springs, as any analyst soon discovers, from a remarkably complex and volatile relationship between such stable concepts as key and mode, and the flexible devices of false relation, intervallic permutation and dissonance prolongation – or however one is to pick apart the elements of Britten's grammar of pitch.[5] What differentiates his achievement from such another accomplished selector of the 'right wrong note' as Aaron Copland is not only his mastery of stage drama – the extra-musical compensation for his fancied limitations – but also of the vastly suggestive shadow area between *Wort und Ton* variously embodied in musical affect and atmospheric overtone, 'word painting' and intervallic symbolism.

And leitmotif – for, as Keller points out, the Wagnerian technique, variously modified, runs through all the operas despite their ostensibly Verdian or, later, quasi-oriental form schemes. This raises the fascinating speculation as to how far the very definition of such a composer's style may depend upon the foreground suppression of certain specific influences, even as its background is enriched by their appropriation. On the face of it, Britten had little time for the great originator of the 'luscious tutti effect' he so disliked in orchestral scoring – lampooning *Tristan und Isolde* directly in *Albert Herring* (1947) and, as Keller argues, *Die Meistersinger* unconsciously, too. Yet musical parallels and complements turn up too frequently to be coincidental. How curiously, for instance, the contour and deployment of the falling figure that runs through the scene of Mrs. Grose's revelation of the past history of Bly in Act I of *The Turn of the Screw* parallels that of Wotan's 'dejection motiv' in *Die Walküre*, Act II. How pervasively Wagner's ubiquitous association of the interval of a perfect fourth (especially in *Die Meistersinger* and *Siegfried*) with extrovert qualities of joy in nature, health and rough humour complements Britten's recurrent 'internal' association of the interval, not only with faith – in both the justified and deluded sense, as in *The Burning Fiery Furnace* (1966) – but also with obsession, corruption and evil: Claggart's broodings in *Billy Budd*, Miles's 'bad fourths' in *The Turn of the Screw*, the pedal fourth that underpins Aschenbach's festering passion in the Act II prelude of *Death in Venice*.

Such connections are bound to raise one's suspicions over Britten's expressed rejection of a composer such as Brahms, whom he appear to have anxiously replayed every so often to make certain he disliked the music as much as ever. Any composer's belief in the integrity of his own style depends on keeping worryingly 'other' manners at arm's length, of course, and intimations of Brahmsian tubbiness could hardly be allowed to muffle the acute sonority of Britten's scoring. But one should not be surprised if future commentators start turning up Brahmsian processes in the background of, say, the outer movements in the Sonata in C for 'Cello and Piano (1960). And what of the composers absent from the rather precise lists of likes and dislikes Britten made known from time to time, yet palpably present in certain of his works? Possibly such lists were more deliberately selected to channel listeners' responses to his music than might beseem so private and anti-journalistic a composer – and possibly they succeeded. It is certainly surprising that even

Keller, whose respect for Gershwin almost matches that for Britten, has failed (as far as one can discover) to comment upon the degree to which *Peter Grimes* is audibly steeped in *Porgy and Bess* (1935) – and not so much the tunesmith side of Gershwin either, but his much-criticized methods of transition, recitative and scene structure.

'I try to clarify, to refine, to sensitize,' Britten once remarked.[6] In view of the variety of techniques and influences, of dramatic concerns and extra-musical implications in circuit round his naïve, stable musical centre, Britten's urge to clarify has to be seen not merely as an aesthetic predilection but as a prerequisite for communication – one has only to compare the degree to which a composer such as Hans Werner Henze blurs and compromises his message through an indiscriminate indulgence in musical means. Yet to the extent that even Britten's simplest notes on the page often prove as teeming in musical interrelationships as they sound sensitized to all manner of atmospheric and psychological nuances, the task facing the analyst seeking to establish the exact nature (beyond simple description, that is) of Britten's primary compositional processes is one of the subtlest in contemporary music. In this respect, first impressions of Peter Evans's long-awaited *The Music of Benjamin Britten* (1979) were a little disappointing, with its rigid format of genre-by-genre description and occasional tendency to trust to the evidence of the score-reading eye rather than the analytic ear.[7]

But closer study suggests that most of the clues to Britten's musical personality, often finely delineated, are to be found scattered through the pages of what proves to be a deeply perceptive commentary, and one hopes that Professor Evans will bring them closer together in some future revision. His complementary discussion of the extent to which the librettos and song texts range and ramify beyond the themes of 'innocence betrayed' and 'compassion for the outsider' under which they are so often lumped, comprises an additional demonstration of Britten's artistic integration. It doubtless remains, though, for Britten's official biographer, Donald Mitchell, with the Britten archives and, not least, early diaries before him, to investigate how far the composer's fraught steadfastness of outlook, both public and private, and his 'darkly bright' musical personality alike may have depended in turn upon areas of nascent feeling of the kind coincidentally evoked ('wrong notes' and all) in a school memory by Dylan Thomas that concludes: 'And when they were bad, they sat alone in the empty classroom, hearing from above them, the distant, terrible, sad sound of the late piano lesson.'[8]

NOTES

Source: This article originally appeared as a review of David Herbert's *The Operas of Benjamin Britten* in *The Times Literary Supplement*, 15 February 1980, p. 182.

1   William McNaught, 'The Promenade Concerts', *The Musical Times*, September 1938.
2   *The Operas of Benjamin Britten*, ed. David Herbert, London, Hamish Hamilton, 1979.
3   Robin Mayhead, 'The Cult of Benjamin Britten', *Scrutiny*, Vol. 19, No. 3, Spring 1953.
4   Theodor W. Adorno, *Philosophy of Modern Music*, tr. Anne G. Mitchell and Wesley V. Bloomster, London, Sheed & Ward, 1973, p. 7.
5   See especially: Christopher Wintle, 'Theory and Analysis', *All the Gods: Benjamin Britten's* Night Piece *in Context*, London, Plumbago, 2006, pp. 57-75.
6   Murray Schafer, *British Composers in Interview*, London, Faber, 1963, p. 118.
7   Peter Evans, *The Music of Benjamin Britten*, London, Dent, 1979.
8   'Return Journey' (autobiographical radio script, 1947) in: *The Dylan Thomas Omnibus*, London, Phoenix Books, 1995, p. 323.

11   Stravinsky's Britten

It is a curious story. First there was the coincidence of the 'Lyke Wake Dirge', that dark fifteenth-century litany that Britten set so frighteningly in his *Serenade* for tenor, horn and strings in 1943, and Stravinsky ran like a refrain through his *Cantata* of 1952. Or was it a coincidence?[1] In 1957, Britten turned to another late-medieval source, the Chester Miracle cycle, for the libretto of *Noye's Fludde* and, five years on, chunks of the same text duly reappeared in Stravinsky's 1962 television commission, *The Flood*. Moreover, the master's very next work, completed in 1963, proved to be the sacred ballad *Abraham and Isaac* – the same narrative as Britten had tackled 11 years before in his *Canticle II*. Then, in an interview conducted in December 1966, two months after the first performance of his *Requiem Canticles*, Stravinsky conceded that "my working title was actually *Sinfonia da Requiem*, and I did not use it only because I have already borrowed so much from Mr. Britten in the matter of titles and subjects". But if so, invoking the by-then equally Brittenesque genre of canticle was surely arch, to say the least? And in any case, why should a master who had already attained a supreme standing in modern music with the première of *The Rite of Spring* in 1913, the very year of Britten's birth, apparently seek to haunt a composer 31 years his junior? How, indeed, could Stravinsky eventually allow himself to publish – at least in America – an attack on the reception of the *War Requiem* (1961) that struck the score itself some more than glancing blows? Was it a continuing desire to show that anything the younger composer could do, he could do better? Was it mere envy at Britten's greater popular success? Even to attempt an answer, one has to go back some six decades.

"So *you* are the little boy who likes Stravinsky!"[2] In fact, it is unlikely that 14-year-old E. B. Britten minor had heard any when he first arrived at Gresham's School, Holt, in September 1928, to be greeted so grudgingly by its Director of Music. Yet the remark was prophetic enough. Over the next decade, no living composer – not Ravel, Schoenberg, Bartók, the young Shostakovich, or even Berg – was to excite Britten so consistently as Stravinsky. Nor was it the glamorous early Russian ballets that preoccupied him – though scores and records of *The Firebird*, *Petrushka* and *The Rite* were eagerly sought and studied – but the more recent and far less favourably reviewed novelties of Stravinsky's so-called neo-Classical period.

Indeed, their sniffy reception by the British musical establishment may well have inflamed the young Britten's partisanship for, years later, he recalled being taken in January 1932 to an early performance of the *Symphony of Psalms* (1930) by his revered teacher, Frank Bridge, "and when everyone around was appalled and saying how sad about Stravinsky, Bridge was insisting that it was a masterpiece."[3] Soon enough Britten's own letter and diaries were invoking the work as 'marvellous', 'great' and 'an incredible masterpiece' too. Even before this, as a 17-year-old, he had evidently been struck by a broadcast of the string-orchestral ballet *Apollon musagète* (1928). Then, in February 1936, for almost the only time in his life, he found himself reluctantly fulfilling the role of music critic at a performance of Stravinsky's *Oedipus Rex* (1927). But there was nothing reluctant about his private response: 'a most moving & exciting work of a real inspired genius. Hats off, gentlemen.'[4]

And these three scores in particular seem to have exerted a lasting fascination. The pan-diatonic clarity and resonance of *Apollo*, for example, audibly informed Britten's writing for string orchestra well into the 1940s, while hints of Stravinsky's bold way with the setting of Latin in *Oedipus Rex* can still be heard in the *Cantata misericordium* of 1963. But the post-war score it is most difficult to imagine emerging in its distinctive way without the influence of Stravinsky on its formalistic structure, its stripped-down instrumentation, its obsessive melodic permutations of a few narrow intervals, is *The Rape of Lucretia* (1946) – and not just in such obvious derivations as the rocking timpani in the 'Goodnight' ensemble, straight out of the *Symphony of Psalms*. How ironic, then, that the one musical conversation Britten and Stravinsky are known to have shared should have thrown up an ominous misunderstanding over precisely this opera.

It was not quite their first encounter, for Britten's diary records on 19 October 1937:

> I go with Lennox [Berkeley] to Queen's Hall Courtauld Sargent concert to hear second English performance of Jeux [sic] de Cartes of Stravinsky (who I meet afterwards). It is a charming and delightful work – worthy of the master. His conducting is excellent too.

After Britten's temporary, and Stravinsky's permanent removal to the United States in 1939, the only point at which they might have met for more than a moment, but did not, was during Britten's visit to Hollywood in September 1941. Then, at the end of 1945, Stravinsky signed a contract with Boosey & Hawkes, bringing him into a company that now regarded Britten as its white hope – while his own reputation continued to languish. Nevertheless, reading through the vocal score of *Peter Grimes* (1944-45) may have confirmed Stravinsky in his intention to write an English opera of his own. And in June 1947 – a month after viewing Hogarth's engravings of *The Rake's Progress* and deciding they offered a suitable subject – he attended a Los Angeles production of *The Rape of Lucretia*.

It was a Britten-Pears recital tour of America in late 1949 that ultimately brought about the fraught meeting. As Stravinsky rather naughtily wrote to his friend, Nicolas Nabokov:

All week here I've listened to Aunt Britten and Uncle Pears, but we will discuss that later. Britten himself makes quite a favourable impression, and he is very popular with the public. He undoubtedly has talent as a performer, especially at the piano.[5]

Towards the end of November, Stravinsky attended a couple of Britten's recitals and, in early December, a local performance of *Albert Herring* (1947). Meanwhile, on either 24 or 30 November (the sources conflict) he received Britten in his home. According to Lord Harewood, Britten asked Stravinsky when he was going to write a full-length opera:

> "I have one in progress even now," said the old master. "But opera, not music drama is my interest – and I shall write it in closed forms." "Just as I did in *Lucretia*," said Britten. "Not at all," said Stravinsky. "My opera will have a *secco* recitative accompanied only by piano, not by orchestra!" Britten was dumbfounded. Had he not done exactly that in *Lucretia*, which Stravinsky claimed to have heard? Either the master was a liar, or a fool.[6]

It might be questioned whether Stravinsky would have talked in the future tense of an opera that was already half completed, or Britten would have gone on referring to Stravinsky as a master had he seriously doubted his probity or intelligence. Harewood was not actually present, but only recounts what he was subsequently told. Yet the misunderstanding itself remains instructive: for, in a sense, both composers were right. *Lucretia* does, of course, use closed forms and piano recitative, but without a hint of period reference, which is the whole point of Stravinsky's usage. Believing that true number opera had completed its historical evolution by the early nineteenth century, Stravinsky was seeking to open up the genre to new feeling by working through its old conventions. Britten's alternative attempt to free such devices from historical convention and to combine them in new ways according to the specific requirements of plot and character would undoubtedly have struck Stravinsky as tending towards music drama. Whether this, in turn, is enough to explain Britten's subsequent hostility to *The Rake* – his disappointment 'that easily the greatest composer alive should have so irresponsible and perverse a view of opera,' as he complained to Harewood in 1951 – may be doubted. From his correspondence of the time, one gets a strong impression that Britten did not *want* to understand; that, as an established composer with his own operatic agenda, he was now concerned to cast off the musical influence of Stravinsky in the same way as he had already rejected the literary influence of the librettist of *The Rake*, W. H. Auden. In any case, Britten's disapproval evidently became an item of cultural gossip. For, according to the diary of Stravinsky's young amanuensis, Robert Craft, on 20 August 1951, 'Conversation turning to *The Rake*, Wystan repeats his story about Benjamin Britten liking the opera very much, "everything but the music" (a story I. S. did not find very amusing).'[7]

And that, one might have thought, was surely that: Britten going his own way and Stravinsky, offended, losing any further interest in his progress. There were, indeed, to be no subsequent meetings and the only surviving correspondence comprises a joint Auden-Stravinsky telegram of best wishes for the first night of *Billy Budd* (1951), and a card from Stravinsky thanking Britten for eightieth birthday greetings in 1962. Yet all the evidence suggests that, far from getting shot of Stravinsky, Britten felt more and more bothered about him. The echoes of *Apollo* both in the trumpet tune of the noble prince and the strutting strings of the bad princess in *The Prince of the Pagodas*, completed in 1956, could almost be heard as a token of his divided feelings. Though Britten would continue in his public utterances to name Stravinsky with respect, he also, quite exceptionally, allowed himself to protest at Hull University in 1962 that 'one of the greatest artistic figures of our time has said some very misleading things … His judgements of other men's music often seem to me arrogant and ignorant, and they are always changing …'.[8]

In private, he could be fiercer still. Malcolm Williamson recalled a walk in the mid-1950s during which Britten suddenly exploded, "The trouble with Stravinsky is that he surrounds himself with sycophants!"[9] And to a letter from E. M. Forster in 1964 complaining about an encounter with Craft, he commiserated, 'You are quite right, "shit" is the only word … Having wrecked one great man (admittedly the weakest of Great men) he now tries to harm another great man by cheap pin-pricks.'[10] Britten was not the only musician in the 1950s and '60s to suspect Craft (less than fairly) of luring Stravinsky into avant-garde trendiness. Yet the dazzling novelty of a score such as *Agon*, completed in 1957, was more difficult to dismiss. Not only did it demonstrate the 75-year-old Stravinsky's continuing powers of self-renewal, when he might have been expected to wind down after *The Rake*, but also an idiosyncratic mastery of serial technique, which Britten still felt so ambivalent about – alternately tinkering with it in such works as *The Turn of the Screw* (1954), then deciding, "I can see it taking no part in the music-lover's music-making".[11] But the most startling evidence of Stravinsky's continuing, if by now unwelcome, hold over Britten's creative imagination comes in a diary entry of Peter Pears concerning a visit to Shostakovich in 1966. 'Ben tells of his recent dream of Stravinsky as a monumental hunchback pointing with quivering finger at a passage in the 'Cello Symphony: "How dare you write that?"'[12]

And Stravinsky? Considering his 'elephant's memory for slights', as someone once put it, the Britten defection over *The Rake* seems to have caused surprisingly little damage. In part, this may be explained by Stravinsky's admiration for the artistry of Pears, with whom he made a memorable recording of *Oedipus*

Rex in 1951. But he also continued, at least intermittently, to request Britten's latest scores from Boosey & Hawkes: thanking Leslie Boosey in September 1953 'for the beautiful edition of *Gloriana* … Now, I wish to have a chance to hear it because I find the music very interesting.'[13] Since the score of *Agon*, upon which he was about to embark, also contains stylized early-seventeenth-century courtly dances, it may be that he found the Britten a suggestive parallel. And he was still interested enough to ask for miniature scores of *A Midsummer Night's Dream* (1960) and the *War Requiem* in 1963. But the ecstatic reception of the latter was evidently beginning to get to him. It is worth remembering that, while Britten had had to put up with some pretty patronizing criticism in his earlier career, Stravinsky, even in his final apotheosis of Sacred Monster, was still as liable to dismissive reviews as he had been ever since the 1920s. In a letter of as late as December 1964, ruefully reporting the verdict of the New York press on *Abraham and Isaac* as 'monotonous and minor', Stravinsky wrote, 'And I really tried! Well, what can you do, not everybody can have Benjamin Britten's success with the critics.'[14]

But it was not just the fawning British press he attacked in the notorious comments on the *War Requiem* in *Themes and Episodes* – the fifth American volume of his so-called conversation books with Robert Craft, published in 1966.[15] 'A Honegger-type cinemascope epic in idiom derived in part from Boulanger-period Stravinsky', he described the work itself, featuring 'patterns rather than inventions … an absence of true counterpoint' and 'a bounteous presence of literalisms ("the drums of Time," sings the baritone, and "boom, boom, boom" go the obedient timpani)', so that 'the composer laureate's certified masterpiece has turned out, for this well-disposed listener, at least, to be a rather soft bomb.' The Nadia Boulanger reference would have particularly riled Britten, since he had always considered her pedagogy inhibiting and blamed her for encouraging what he heard as the increasing mannerism of Stravinsky's own post-1930 music. But did he ever see these comments? Did Stravinsky even think better of them? All that can be said for certain is that, by the time they achieved their belated publication in Britain a year after Stravinsky's death, they had been conspicuously shortened and mollified.[16]

Yet it could be that Stravinsky was still not entirely cynical in describing his attitude to Britten as 'well-disposed'. A strict believer who held that true religious music should confine itself to praise, penitence and fulfilling the canonic forms of the Church, he was bound to deplore the *War Requiem* as falling into the category of what he called 'secular religious music … inspired by humanity in general, by art, by *Übermensch*, by goodness, and by goodness knows what.'[17] But, as Stravinsky also often suggested, the most positive criticism is to show how it could be done differently, and it may well be that his retaining of a Brittenesque nuance in the title of his devout and numinous *Requiem Canticles* was intended to signal exactly that. One notes that Stravinsky's earlier 'borrowings' from Britten are all religious too, but that his responses are also strikingly complementary. Where Britten drew out the nightmare drama of the 'Lyke Wake Dirge' in his *Serenade* setting, Stravinsky's placid modal treatment in his *Cantata* reaffirms its ritualistic form. Again, while *Noye's Fludde* might be described as a comforting ceremony of innocence for children of all ages, Stravinsky's biblical strip cartoon for adults, *The Flood*, warns of the eternal catastrophe: 'The Flood is also the Bomb.'[18] Of the two versions of *Abraham and Isaac*, Britten's sweetly Medieval canticle is as redolent in spirit of the New Testament as Stravinsky's knotty Hebrew cantillation is of the Old. And if the *War Requiem* rages against the sacrifice of youth, *Requiem Canticles* responds with the visionary calm of an old age Britten never attained. Admittedly, Craft's agency in encouraging, and selecting the texts for many of Stravinsky's late projects is a complicating issue. Yet the fact remains that Stravinsky shadowed no other composer in quite this way. Did he, despite everything, sense a special relationship?

They were, of course, very different artists: Stravinsky cleaving to 'the idea of universality – of a character of expression not necessarily popular but compelling to the highest imagination of a decade or two beyond its time,'[19] whereas Britten believed in the local, in occasional music, in 'roots, in associations, in backgrounds, in personal relationships';[20] Stravinsky's music as he grew older taking on more and more of a factured, 'made' character, whereas Britten aspired, if often self-doubtingly, to a Schubertian directness and spontaneity; and so on. Yet their art certainly shared a commitment to service before self-expression – even if Stravinsky's work tended to serve God and other music, whereas Britten's served communal values and words. And something more: of course Britten owed a vast amount to Purcell and Mahler, and much has been made more recently of his affinity with Shostakovich and the East. But maybe the time has come to reopen the question as to whether – in its sharpness of articulation and economy of means, its habits of scoring and chord-spacing, its handling of harmonic false relation, tone centre and modality – Britten's musical language did not owe most to Stravinsky.

And, if so, did that master feel that, having given so much, he could occasionally avail himself of the teacher's traditional right to borrow, even to pinch, a pupil's bright ideas? After all: 'It is the composer's heritage to take what he wants from whom he wants – and to write music.'[21] And the beauty of those words is that they were written, not by the old Igor Stravinsky, but by the young Benjamin Britten.

NOTES

Source: 'The Fine Art of Borrowing', *Aldeburgh Festival Programme Book*, June 1994, pp. 14-19. The author was indebted to Philip Reed of the Britten-Pears Library for help over extracts from the unpublished and still-copyrighted letters and diaries of Benjamin Britten and Peter Pears.

1   In the series, *Conversations with Craft*, recorded with Stephen Walsh and broadcast by BBC Radio 3 in 1997, Robert Craft revealed he had drawn Britten's *Serenade* (1943) to Stravinsky's attention when he was composing *The Rake's Progress* (1948-51) as a model for setting English.

2   Humphrey Carpenter, *Benjamin Britten: A Biography*, London, Faber, 1992, p. 27.

3   'Britten Looking Back' (interview in *The Sunday Telegraph*, 17 November 1963) in: *Aldeburgh Festival Programme Book*, 1994.

4   Donald Mitchell, 'Britten on *Oedipus Rex* and *Lady Macbeth*', *Tempo*, No. 120, 1977, pp. 10-12.

5   *Stravinsky: Selected Correspondence*, ed. Robert Craft, Vol. 2, London, Faber, 1984, p. 376.

6   George, Earl of Harewood, *The Tongs and the Bones*, London, Weidenfeld & Nicholson, 1981, pp. 132-33.

7   Robert Craft, *Stravinsky: Chronicle of a Friendship*, rev. ed., Nashville, Vanderbilt UP, 1994, p. 58.

8   Christopher Headington, *Britten*, London, Eyre Methuen, 1981, pp. 95-6.

9   Malcolm Williamson in conversation with the author, c. 1993.

10   *E. M. Forster: Commonplace Book*, ed. Philip Gardner, Aldershot, Wildwood House, 1988, pp. 249 and 359 (note).

11   Murray Schafer, *British Composers in Interview*, London, Faber, 1963, p. 120.

12   Peter Pears, *Moscow Christmas: A Diary*, quoted in: Elizabeth Wilson, *Shostakovich: A Life Remembered*, London, Faber, 1994, p. 402.

13   *Stravinsky: Selected Correspondence*, ed. Robert Craft, Vol. 3, London, Faber, 1985, p. 376.

14   Ibid., pp. 450-51.

15   Igor Stravinsky and Robert Craft, *Themes and Episodes*, New York, Knopf, 1966, p. 13-14.

16   Igor Stravinsky, *Themes and Conclusions*, London, Faber, 1972, pp. 26-7.

17   Igor Stravinsky and Robert Craft, *Conversations with Igor Stravinsky*, London, Faber, 1959, p. 124.

18   Igor Stravinsky and Robert Craft, *Expositions and Developments*, London, Faber, 1962, p. 127.

19   Stravinsky and Craft, *Themes and Conclusions*, 1972, p. 124.

20   Benjamin Britten, 'On Receiving the First Aspen Award' (1964) in: *Britten on Music*, ed. Paul Kildea, Oxford, OUP, 2003, p. 262.

21   Mitchell, *Tempo*, 1977, p. 120.

12   Carter's Relativity Rag

During a public discussion chaired by the author at the Huddersfield Festival of Contemporary Music in November 1983, someone told Elliott Carter that his new *Triple Duo* (1982) sounded relatively 'free' compared with the elaborate constructions of his previous works. "Oh, no!" he replied. "It has just as strict an underlying scheme … only, at a certain point, this began to get boring, so I curtailed it." Instantly the faces of his predominantly student audience brightened: "If even the great Carter can break his own rules, then perhaps we needn't feel so inhibited," was evidently the unvoiced collective thought. It implied much, not only about Carter's reputation but also about certain notions of composition and musical analysis widely assumed today.

   Much, too, about the dilemmas David Schiff must have faced in planning the first full study of this formidable composer – little though one might suspect their existence from the confident and readable surface of his prose.[1] Admittedly, he undertook to explain Carter's work and only incidentally to criticize it – understandably, since he studied with Carter in the mid-1970s and has kept in close touch with him since. At least this enabled him to relay many an enlivening personal comment of Carter's in a study not ostensibly biographical.

   In fact, we get a tantalizingly brief account of Carter's life to start with. It is well known that he grew up in the 1920s during a radical phase of New York's musical history, when the scandalous latest from Arnold Schoenberg, Igor Stravinsky, Edgard Varèse, Carl Ruggles and others was all to be heard. And he had the good fortune, while still a schoolboy, to attract the attention of Charles Ives, who encouraged him in his composing. It is less well known that his parents expected him to go into the family lace-importing business and actively opposed his musical aspirations, cutting down his student allowance when he stuck to his plans and refusing, ever, to attend his performances. We are left to speculate how far the pugnacity of his mature music reflects his early experience of Modernism and how far a more personal rebellion.

   Schiff's most remarkable revelation, however, is that Carter destroyed the bulk of his output up to the age of 30 – including a piano sonata, a symphony, two or three string quartets, a comic opera and possibly a ballet collaboration with James Agee entitled *Bombs in the Icebox*. Clearly he took a long view of his musical development from fairly early on. In a way, necessity forced him to. Though his indiscriminate avant-garde ardours had begun to cool before he went to Paris to study with Nadia Boulanger between 1932 and 1935, the exactitudes of Boulanger's neo-Classical regime must still have come as a challenge. And when he returned to the America of the Depression, he found that neither the avant-garderie of Schoenberg or Varèse nor the neo-

Classicism of the followers of Stravinsky cut much ice; what was wanted was a mildly leftish populism after the example of Aaron Copland.

For the next few years Carter tried to synthesize these disparate approaches in an accessible idiom while variously earning his living as musical director of a ballet company, critic for *Modern Music*, teacher of mathematics and Greek at a liberal arts college, and, bizarrely, as an employee of the War Information Office in 1944-45 – where he found himself orchestrating national anthems ever more desperately as more and more countries came over to the Allies. Schiff does not mention the national anthems, but he confirms that around this time Carter came to the conclusion that synthesis of neo-Classical and populist modes was not the way forward and that what was needed was a fundamental reappraisal of the elements of musical discourse. There followed his first attempts to compose music out of the very characteristics of the instruments themselves. The Piano Sonata (1945-46) derives its harmony from idiosyncratic overtones of the concert grand, and the Sonata for Violoncello and Piano (1948) exploits the differences between the two instruments dialectically. His extra-creative work was henceforth to centre mainly on the teaching of composition itself.

Before embarking upon a chronological survey of all of Carter's published works, Schiff cogently summarizes his main technical innovations from this period on in a pair of chapters concerned with musical time and space. He discusses Carter's development of so-called 'metrical modulation': how, by taking such traditional rhythmic devices as hemiola – two-against-three – and shifting the beat from the two to the three, Carter was able to evolve methods of precisely gearing and even superimposing constantly fluctuating tempi, so that whole movements could be constructed free from a single unifying pulse. Schiff also describes Carter's parallel attempts to free himself from traditional harmonic procedures by evolving from such formulations as the 'all-interval tetrachord', the 'all-triad hexachord' and arrays of twelve-note verticals, systematic methods for blocking out the harmonic backgrounds of entire pieces. But throughout the survey, Schiff scrupulously relates such procedures to wider aesthetic and historical issues. Carter's advance towards an ideal of 'emancipated dissonance' in the late nineteen-forties and 'fifties, Schiff argues, was not an isolated development but was closely related to contemporary endeavours of such composers as Varèse and Wolpe, to the later poetics of Wallace Stevens and to the New York Abstract Expressionist painters, all of whom were (in Schiff's words) 'attempting to rediscover the basic elements of [their] arts free of familiar associations'.

This is doubtless true. Carter has always discouraged purely technical analysis of his music, analysis divorced from its expressive character, while his interest in the other arts has been deep and lifelong. Accordingly, even the most labyrinthine of the masterworks that slowly emerged during the next two decades – the First String Quartet (1951), the Variations for Orchestra (1953-55), the Second String Quartet (1959), the Double Concerto (1961), the Piano Concerto (1965) and the culminating Concerto for Orchestra (1969) – were either partly inspired by, or subsequently furnished with, visual, literary or other extra-musical analogies that help the listener get into them. Technically, for instance – as Schiff explained – the opening of the Concerto for Orchestra comprises a twelve-note chord that is then split into the segments that are to generate the work's contrasting textural layers. But this, in turn, was touched off by Saint-John Perse's vision of America as swept by great winds of change in his long poem *Vents*. It is as a sonorous image that Carter's opening pages prove so memorable: the music seems to approach from the distance as a numinous whirring and then to burst about one's ears.

Schiff's main problem in writing about these middle-period works was that, their technical and expressive preoccupations had already been set forth by the composer himself in interviews, record liner-notes and more formal articles, but were not yet so well known as to be taken for granted. There is fresher interest in the author's observations on the less familiar early music up to the Piano Sonata. Schiff also had much to reveal about the then more recent works from the Third Quartet (1971) to *Night Fantasies* for Piano (1980) – though the increasing spontaneity with which Carter has since exploited his accumulated resources means that a spate of further works have appeared since Schiff's original cut-off point. These, at least up to 1997, have been duly surveyed in Schiff's later edition, which retains Carter's own listing of all the possible three- to six-note chords that have provided him with the basic harmonies for his work, while the bibliography and discography have been much extended. The use of music examples throughout is also exceptionally lavish.

Schiff was always clear about his intentions. He was not concerned to 'place' Carter among his contemporaries; nor at any point did he promise the kind of full-scale analysis that would have impossibly increased the book's length. The book was intended as a guide for listeners, performers and composers and as such the first edition was widely welcomed. But not quite unanimously. Among certain students of Carter in Britain and, one gathers, certain American reviewers too, there was some disappointment that Schiff failed to raise a question about the apparent disparity between the clarity of procedures suggested in Carter's published descriptions and charts, and their sometimes less than obvious realization in the flux of the actual music.

In part, such complaints may simply reflect a surprisingly common confusion between compositional means and analytical ends. A composer such as Carter, who is not really interested in systems for their own sake, may still invoke some pre-compositional scheme of pitch, rhythm or structure as a way to 'get going' or as a psychological subterfuge for distracting consciousness so that unconscious fantasy can be drawn upon more readily. Moreover, once such a scheme is clearly articulated, it can be treated freely – interrupted, displaced, blurred – and brought into dialectic with other schemes. Not for nothing are Carter's scores scattered with directions like *drammatico, leggerissimo, fantastico*. To grasp the music and recreate it as the composer conceived it, the analyst, no less than the listener, must be capable of comparable imaginative leaps. As Schiff remarks: 'To see the music only as an illustration of tempo modulation, for instance, would be as misguided as to see *Tristan* only as example of chromatic tonality …'

Except that it would hardly have occurred to Wagner actually to publish a scheme of his harmonic practice for *Tristan* in the first place. It is true that composers since time immemorial have issued instruction manuals, aesthetic discussions, manifestos and whatnot. But only in the twentieth century and, in particular, after the Second World War, did the idea gain ground that a legitimate, even necessary aspect of a composer's activity is the setting forth of his specific techniques and pre-compositional plans. Here we ought to distinguish between, say, the scientist-messianic monomania of Karlheinz Stockhausen's series of *Texte* (1963-69) and the more covertly personal prescriptive historicism of Pierre Boulez's *Penser la musique aujourd'hui* (1964), between Milton Babbitt's systematic serial theorizing and Peter Maxwell Davies's classroom discussion of his 'magic square' practice.

To be fair, Carter long remained reluctant to reveal his hand in this way (perhaps recalling Schoenberg's well-founded forebodings about going public with the twelve-tone method). And he has always striven to link his disclosures to larger issues. So the pitch charts for the Double Concerto and Piano Concerto appeared in a discussion of the economics of concert-giving and the chart for the Concerto for Orchestra in a meditation on the nature of Time.[2] What nevertheless links all these statements – what leaves one regretting that Schiff did not, for all its difficulties, attempt a chapter 'placing' Carter among his contemporaries – is the Modernist assumption that vital composition is inseparable from a continuing reinvention of the musical language itself.

The sources of this assumption, of course, predate the Modern movement at least as far back as Wagner's foreshadowing (apropos *Tristan*) of the idea of music as 'the art of transition' and Brahms's technique (that Schoenberg was to call 'developing variation') of deriving almost everything in a work – theme, accompaniment, transition and development – from short basic motives. The ultimate supplanting of the discrete, easily recognizable motive itself by serialism – that is, by permutating a chosen ordering of the basic elements of pitch, rhythm or both to generate the entire fabric of a piece – simply completed the trend towards a total relativity of the musical elements. (Schoenberg's own habit of deriving tone-rows from primary melodic ideas was, arguably, a symptom of his conservatism.) This concept of relativity, in which a continuously shifting play of the elements casts up ever-new, passing shapes and musical gestures, has been seen both as a reversal (Stockhausen) and as a replacement (Boulez) of the Classical contrast of theme and development. Though the methods of generation and ordering in Carter's mature music are not explicitly serial, he would appear to regard such relativity, not merely as reversal or replacement of Classical procedure but also as an expansion of possibilities.

Not that his main impulse is ever likely to have been a desire to 'fulfil history'. Composers, even the greatest, commonly develop through an effort to remedy, or compensate for, some incompleteness in basic gifts (it is the all-round prodigies who often fail to grow). The thematic material of Carter's early, more traditionally constructed works is always well formed but it is rarely their most distinctive aspect. Possibly it was a growing awareness of this as early as the *Holiday Overture* of 1944 that led him to consider that:

> The traditional categories, like 'theme and accompaniment', or 'subject and counter-subject', really didn't deal with what began to seem to me

the vast spectrum of kinds of relationship that contributory vertical elements in the musical continuity can have with each other in respect of the past and future of the piece.[3]

Those, then, who would censure Carter for choosing at a certain point in his career to play what Virgil Thomson might have called 'the complexity gambit' to compensate for a lack of 'simple gifts' could well be right, yet beside the point; what matters is the uses to which Carter has put that complexity.

In fact, themes continued to play a part in his music up to the Variations for Orchestra. Only in the Second String Quartet were they superseded altogether by investing each of the instruments with its own repertoire of characteristic intervals and rhythms from which a continuing stream of new formulations could be derived – a procedure that Schiff calls 'epiphanic development'. Indeed, the ensuing Double Concerto generates its entire form from assembling such repertoires of rhythms and intervals from sound-atoms into more meaningful continuities – and spectacularly dissolving them back into atoms at the end. These advances served to fulfil Carter's aim, extending back a couple of decades, to express our multiple experience of time itself, in which a dozen independent happenings may be perceived with varying degrees of attention, proceeding at their own rate at any particular moment. The extent of his success in such scores as the Concerto for Orchestra can be measured by the fact that, virtually alone among composers who have progressed to a relativistic position, and without using the leverage of regular rhythm, he has written music that conveys a true dynamic sense of movement. Boulez himself was quoted on the jacket of the first edition of Schiff's book as praising Carter's handling of time, 'that elusive component of all music'.

Yet the suspicion lingers that new musical languages should not need the props of technical explanation such as even Carter, let alone Boulez, Stockhausen and others have seemingly felt compelled to provide. And this suspicion, by implication at least, appears to complement the perception of many a listener uncorrupted, on the one hand, by the critical and academic hard-selling of Modernism, or, on the other, by the commercial hard-selling of cross-over, film-music and classic-lite kitsch of more recent years. While the coruscating surfaces of a Carter, Boulez or Maxwell Davies score may be welcomed as the most exhilarating, dazzling or disturbing expressions of transformation, *what* is being transformed is by no means so obvious – and this is ultimately felt as an absence, or lack.

Of course, the difficulty of new music has often been ascribed to its lack of the familiar rather than to its innovations as such. Lack of melody, lack of structure, lack of tonality are charges with a history before the twentieth century, too. But in so far as the crisis of communication exacerbated by the Modern Movement of almost a century ago shows little sign of resolving itself for a great number of listeners, many of them highly musical, this suggests the existence of a more fundamental problem, to which these various lacks only contribute: the absence, or at any rate crisis, of identifiable musical *statement* – whether conceived as idea, theme, musical object, gestalt, or whatever. It is not so much a matter of missing the 'tune' but rather of finding any principle of stability against which the varying instabilities of the continuous process of change, development and transformation can be measured satisfactorily. In the relativistic play of Boulez or Carter, much that is expressively new has been won for the domain of music: we may think of the glittering mirror-sonorities of music becoming 'the object of its own reflection' in the one, or of the infinitely varied 'poetry of change' in the other. But the question remains whether their quasi-thematic passing formulations can ever achieve a full identity distinct from the interacting processes that throw them up.

This is not to suggest that the epigones of post-Modernism are somehow righter than Boulez and his confrères in relativity, whose evolution, after all, has its roots in the authentic Romanticism of the nineteenth century. Still less is it to pose an attack upon Carter. On the contrary, in the kaleidoscopic flux of his music, no other advanced composer has come as remotely close to convincing this enthusiast that the question of what is being transformed could still be irrelevant.

NOTES

Source: 'Fascinatin' Modulation' (review of David Schiff's *The Music of Elliott Carter*), *The New York Review of Books*, 31 May 1984, pp. 18-20; rev. 2008.

1   David Schiff, *The Music of Elliott Carter*, New York, Da Capo/London, Eulenburg Books, 1983; new, expanded and updated ed. London, Faber, 1998.
2   See in particular: Elliott Carter, 'The Orchestral Composer's Point of View' and 'Music and the Time Screen' in: *Elliott Carter: Collected Essays and Lectures, 1937-95*, ed. Jonathan Barnard, New York, University of Rochester Press, 1997, pp. 235-50 and 262-80.
3   See: Allen Edwards, *Flawed Words and Stubborn Sounds: A Conversation with Elliott Carter*, New York, Norton, 1971, p. 100.

[Ed. The author had also addressed the 'relativistic dilemma' in a long and prescient review of Boulez on *Music Today* (1971) in: 'Boulez's Theory of Composition', *Music and Musicians*, Vol. 20, No. 4, December 1971, pp. 32-6. In 'Notes on Copland', *The Musical Times*, Vol. 121, No. 1653, November 1980, pp. 686-89, he briefly discussed Copland's alternative approach to rhythm to Carter's, citing the Copland's remark that 'before long [Nadia Boulanger and I] were exploring polymetric devices together – their cross-pulsation, their notation and especially their difficulty of execution intrigued her.']

13   The 'Found Sounds' of Judith Weir

There is a question most contemporary composers dread but almost all get asked sooner or later: do you write more for your audience or for yourself? Confronted some years back by just such an enquiry, Judith Weir answered: "I have to say that I'm very interested in audiences' reactions. But I don't really think you can start off by taking that into account. It's funny, because often people say that my music is accessible – and I think they mean it as a compliment..."[1]

She went on to explain that, during the tour of her first full-length stage piece, *A Night at the Chinese Opera* (1987), she had been amazed at the difference in reaction between venues. "You'd go to one town which seemed to be a nice, gracious place, full of well-educated *Guardian* readers, and they wouldn't grasp the piece at all. And you'd go to another place which seemed like a bit of a dump, and have a great evening. If I didn't know it before, I know it now, and I don't think I would dare to start predicting what an audience would like." It is an answer that broadcasters, arts boards and funding authorities who so confidently prescribe their own notions of accessibility, relevance and all the rest of it to their supplicants would do well to ponder. For, after all, since *A Night at the Chinese Opera* first brought her name to a wider public, this is a composer who has gathered a considerable following both at home and abroad. And, even before that, Weir had been increasingly regarded by the small publics she reached, by the musicians she wrote for and, not least, by her fellow composers, as someone rather special.

Special for what? In the first instance, for her stark simplicity of means and modesty of aims, in the context of the tumultuous musical world of the early 1970s during which she came of age. Her first teacher, John Tavener, was elaborating trendy sacred blockbusters such as his *Celtic Requiem* (1969) and being hailed as 'Underground Classical' by the Beatles, while her second teacher, Robin Holloway, was striving to reassert Romantic sentiment against Modernist constructivism in scores heaving with notes. Yet Weir would typically take a tiny decorative figure or broken-off phrase of melody, tease out whatever permutational and structural possibilities it seemed to encapsulate, and, when these had been neatly worked through, simply stop. Like as not, she would then attach an amusingly paradoxical title: *Several Concertos* (1980) is actually a trio in which each of the instruments is treated soloistically in turn, while in *Music for 247 Strings* (1981), 243 of those strings turn out to be in the accompanying piano. If the resulting pieces intrigued by their terse, bright oddity, they also risked dismissal as merely lightweight or cute. How could one take entirely seriously a composer who offered in *King Harald's Saga* (1979) a grand opera in three acts featuring eight solo roles and chorus … scored for single unaccompanied soprano and running just 10 minutes?

Yet behind such apparent quirks there was already to be detected a more purposeful strategy in Weir's almost defiant obliqueness – marginality even – of stance. Most of the procedures of 'mainstream' European compositional tradition seemed to be elided in her earlier music, if not excluded altogether. One could scarcely find searching introductory passages, romantically evolving melodies, discursive transitions, dramatic development sections, clinching climaxes or imposing perorations – or, if more surging continuities and grandiose rhetoric threatened to emerge, these would be instantly subverted. Mostly she seemed to rely upon more ostensibly 'primitive' formal methods: patches of varied repetition, abruptly cross cut or superimposed to create balanced sequences of short paragraphs. But what such paragraphs also constituted were grids within which to lodge an ever widening range of musical citations, nuances and 'found sounds' from the cultures and places that have attracted her.

Most commonly she has drawn upon the melodic shapes, performing styles and basic structures of a variety of folk traditions – from her native Scotland, from Spain, Eastern Europe and Northern Africa – and evocations of the often remote landscapes from which they come. But more recently she has seemed to treat the great Classical traditions of China, India and even of Europe itself as if they, too, were vernacular, folkloristic sources. So the three tiny movements of *The Bagpiper's String Trio* (1988), with their Scotch-snap rhythms and Pibroch inflections, comprise a particularly sprightly and heart-felt sample of her native heritage; while in the piano quintet *I Broke off a Golden Branch* (1991), a Croatian folk tune is recomposed as if by Schubert; indeed, the concise Piano Concerto (1997) could be heard as a take on how a Mozartian structure might be revamped by a folk musician. Meanwhile, the interest in Chinese music and culture inaugurated by the enchanting stylization of her concert-drama, *The Consolations of Scholarship* (1985), has deepened, while her involvement with India that inspired her jubilant orchestral work, *The Welcome Arrival of Rain* (2003), subsequently took her in 2004 on a music and story-telling tour across the Sub-continent itself.

In some ways, Weir's determination to fashion a mini-language for each of her works out of the characteristics and limits of her chosen, often humble, vernacular material resembles the stance of Stravinsky's most intensively Russian period in the years immediately following *The Rite of Spring*, or Janáček's laconic late manner drawn from the folklore and speech intonations of his native Moravia, or even the more Hungarian-inflected movements of Haydn. And if, as one increasingly glimpses, she is slowly assembling a kind of personal world-mosaic of individual pieces derived from different musical cultures, then her enterprise could also be compared with the teaching and practice of Messiaen – if not with his theological intent and gigantism of conception. What it emphatically does not resemble is the kind of easy-mix that too-often passes for 'World Music' – that mélange of Afro-Celtic fusions and sitar with disco-beat so insistently thrust upon us by half-baked broadcasters and the recording industry. On the contrary, one senses behind Weir's stance the concerns and ethics of an ecologist: a desire to preserve the local, the idiosyncratic, the little-explored, not only for their unique human and cultural potential, but also as charms against the ever more destructive, not to say repressive, forces of mass consumer 'culture'.

That her lapidary structures somehow harbour this sense of responsibility is precisely due to the residual austerity that she has maintained from the start: an austerity that enables her to handle even the most potentially kitschy material with a saving discrimination, as in the tinselly innocence of her Emily Dickinson setting *Moon and Star* (1995). And behind this, as behind few other living composers, it is sometimes possible to sense something deeper: not in the sense of personal expression, which, in more recent centuries at least, has been the central preoccupation of Western music, but something more collective and ancient.

Ethnomusicologists and philosophers of music seeking to lay bare the common fundamentals underlying the world's vastly varied musics past and present – whether conveyed by African tribal ritual, the master-player traditions of the Orient or the vastly complex notated codes of the West – have suggested that music may have originated in the earliest societies as a mnemonic system for memory and survival, such as the 'songlines' of the Aborigines. Those of a more pessimistic turn of mind have speculated that some future universal catastrophe could well return it to such a residual function. In such a pass, the need or practicality of putting on a work remotely as sophisticated as, say, Boulez's *Répons* (1981-) would, of course, be quite inconceivable. But it is just possible to imagine some surviving descendant of Wordsworth's solitary Highland Lass drawing sustenance from the words and phrases, however garbled and simplified in the folk-memory, of *King Harald's Saga*.

NOTES

Source: Written to mark Judith Weir's 50th birthday on 11 May 2004, this appeared in a reduced form as: 'Judith Weir at 50', *The Independent*, 21 May 2004.

1   Remarks recorded at a Colloquium with Judith Weir at King's College London, 1994.

Part Four

William Glock, Milein Cosman

The States of Music

1 Earlier Than Thou

'Twas in the year of 'eighty-eight ... on Saturday 22 October 1988 on London's Southbank, the *Sounds in Time* festival, promoted by the Early Music Centre could be heard doing its bit for the then-inescapable Spanish Armada industry with an array of c. 1588 period music groups, ballad singers, clowns, an evening concert in the Queen Elizabeth Hall by the Dowland Consort and a final authentick knees-up led by the York Waits. Earlier that week, the festival celebrated the Glorious Revolution of 1688 with a Wigmore Hall programme of music from the time of William and Mary and seventeenth-century Anglo-Dutch pop, and on 23 October *Sounds in Time* culminated in a QEH concert by the Orchestra of the Age of Enlightenment of those supreme masterpieces of 1788, the last three symphonies of Mozart.

But Mozart as *Early* music? Up to only some 15 or 20 years before, his major works, to the ears of the ordinary music lover, were simply standard repertoire – music now – which successive generations had reckoned among the most beautiful ever written and continued to interpret in the manner they felt most natural. Then the historical performance movement got itself crossed with the recording industry and the damage – the word is not too strong – began.

The public was virtually told it had never *heard* Mozart until the launch of Christopher Hogwood's 'authentic' discs of the symphonies in 1980. Period instrument players developed a historicist dread of infringing some eighteenth-century treatise or other while modern instrumentalists began to wonder guiltily whether they should be tackling the pre-nineteenth-century repertoire at all. The 200-odd-year tradition of Mozart performance, with all its varying insights and shifts of taste, was effectively dismissed – and with a great deal of self-righteous one-upmanship – as a continual betrayal of the *composer's intentions*. These were, we learnt, the sole, selfless duty of the historically-conscious musician to fulfil.

This is an unbelievably suppositious objective. For a well-documented start, composers engrossed in the technical details of their pieces frequently have no clear idea themselves of their 'intentions' until they have heard a variety of performances; worse still, they may then embark on a potentially endless process of changing their minds. Stravinsky is considered one of the twentieth century's most clear-headed composers. Yet anyone attempting an 'authentic' *Rite of Spring* (1913) will have to face a nightmare choice between not only his several editions with their extensive revisions of speed, harmony and orchestration, but also the often contradictory further changes he made in rehearsal.

How much more problematic, then, would seem a figure such as Handel, who continuously recomposed his own music and plagiarized the music of others to meet the changing tastes of Hamburg, Rome, London and Dublin over a long career, and at a time when far less needed to be written down because the modern division of labour between composer and executant scarcely existed. The seventeenth- or eighteenth-century player took in the rudiments of composition – the rules of good part-writing, how to fill out an accompaniment tastefully, and so on – more or less as he learned his notes, whether or not he aspired to large-scale composition. How many period players today, approaching such music from the outside as an exercise in historical style, can claim either by training or intuition to capture the creative inner rapport the best of such playing must have embodied?

The irony is that the Early Music industry, as it has burgeoned over more recent decades, is now virtually bereft of exponents who are also creative in their own right. This was not always so. Before Early Music was hijacked by Authenticity, when it was still primarily concerned with the rediscovery and bringing to performance of old works for their musical substance, the composers were very much involved: Vincent d'Indy and Gian Francesco Malipiero, for instance, performing and editing Monteverdi; Britten and Tippett promoting Purcell. Their editions may now be out-of-date, but they regarded early music as a living source. The course of twentieth-century music would have been significantly different had Vaughan Williams never heard Tallis, nor Webern edited Isaac; had the old Stravinsky and the young Peter Maxwell Davies not become fascinated by the arcane techniques of the Renaissance and Middle Ages.

Nor was this just a symptom of an ageing culture. New bourgeois audiences in Mozart's day may have preferred the up-to-date, but the masters themselves always looked back – Brahms collecting manuscripts of Schütz, Mozart knocked sideways by his mid-career discovery of J. S. Bach, Bach himself studying Frescobaldi and the Antique Style of the sixteenth century. To a paradoxical degree the very evolution of Western music has been a process of recomposition. Robert Craft's Renaissance recordings of the 1950s may not have been the last word in authenticity, yet one hears instantly what got Stravinsky started on his *Canticum sacrum* (1955) and *Threni* (1957-58).

But it is difficult to imagine how any composer c. 1980 could have been similarly fired by Hogwood's Mozart. To the extent that at least the hardline authentics sought to limit compositional sense and significance to the strictly historical, their movement could be seen as profoundly anti-creative. In his contribution to the 1988 symposium *Authenticity and Early Music* edited by Nicholas Kenyon,[1] Robert P. Morgan went so far as to suggest that the rage for authenticity, not to say its popular and commercial success, represented a deep identity crisis in twentieth-century musical life: we cleave to the 'certainty' of historicism because we no longer feel confident that we have any performing (or composing) style of our own.

Actually, the editor and remaining five contributors to this scholarly stocktaking proved a lot more encouraging in their new-found scepticism (how one wishes more writing on contemporary music was anywhere near as lively and intelligent). Howard Mayer Brown provided a compact critical history of the period performance movement and Philip Brett elegantly winkled out the hidden assumptions in the editing of purportedly 'plain' texts. Kenyon himself, noting that a more expressive 'authenticity' was coming into vogue, suggested the hard line was simply an unavoidable phase, while the exuberant Richard Taruskin countered Professor Morgan by suggesting that the objective authenticity of the Hogwood era was precisely a modernist style after the manner of Stravinsky.

In fact the most convincing period performances – Norrington's fiery Beethoven symphonies for instance – do not sound much like Stravinsky. Yet Taruskin surely put his finger on a point so obvious, it has never been discussed in this context. However far the adopting of old instruments and so on may allow performers to feel they are re-capturing the Viennese style of 1800 or whenever, they are actually, irrefutably playing *now*. One might even begin to wonder whether the dash and transparency of Norrington's Beethoven might have arrived anyway as a natural reaction in taste to the more homogenized Karajan style without the prompting of any historical performance movement. Quite possibly – but then the record companies would have had to come up with a different selling line.

NOTES

Source: 'Earlier Than Thou', *The Independent*, 22 October 1988; rev. 2008.

    1   *Authenticity and Early Music*, ed. Nicholas Kenyon, Oxford, OUP, 1988.

2 *Style or Idea?*

Has the issue of 'period' performance become one of the great bores of music? When you hear the word 'authenticity' these days, do you instantly reach for some unregenerate old-timer such as Otto Klemperer or Wanda Landowska? Since the Early Music movement invaded the Baroque and Classical repertoire in the 1970s, no topic – except possibly 'controversial' opera production – has grabbed so much space in the musical press. But no longer; for it would seem that hard-line Authenticists have for some time constituted an endangered species.

Most performers and scholars in the field would now concede that claims of reconstructing exactly what eighteenth- or early nineteenth-century composers intended, or what their audiences actually heard, are not sustainable because – in the absence of comprehensive evidence and before the advent of recording – they simply cannot be tested. Many would agree that even if such literal re-creations were possible, we could not hear them with the ears of their contemporaries, innocent of all subsequent musical developments; and that, for the same reason, any attempt to approach the equivalent aesthetic or psychological effect of an original hearing must involve some compromise, whether conscious or not, with our own performing traditions.

Some, at least, would allow that the famous inadequacy and bafflement that marked first performances of many of the most hallowed masterpieces offer ambiguous evidence anyway; and that, for instance, given the desperate rate at which the piano had to evolve in the 1800s to keep up with the immoderate demands of a composer such as Beethoven, his 'intentions' might best be represented by instruments of a later date than the time he actually wrote. A few would even be prepared to admit that since masterpieces of their very nature tend to reveal their significance only bit by bit over many generations, the 'authentic' reconstruction of any stage of their performance history could claim equal validity – whether the much-maligned Victorian way with Handel or the variously idiosyncratic pacing of Beethoven by Mendelssohn, Wagner or Strauss.

But suppose one were to raise a naughty doubt as to how far, say, the live, bright sound of Roger Norrington's London Classical Players in early Beethoven reflects a genuine 'period' insight, and how far it is simply the perceptual result of transferring music long familiar in a large-scale orchestral context to a smaller, tighter one – a miniaturizing effect, ultimately no different psychologically from Mozart arranged for musical clock? This surely would be going a bit far for even the most open-minded Authenticists, not to speak of their large and enthusiastic following – for perhaps the most remarkable thing about the period performance movement as it advanced from the pre-Bach era into the standard repertoire was the sudden popularity it inspired.

Doubtless this was due in part to the influence of the record industry, always on the outlook for novel reasons to remake the popular classics – especially during the late 1970s, when it was investing so heavily in new technology. But part of the appeal of hard-line 'Authenticity' in the early 'eighties was surely the way in which its doctrinal principles, the Salvationist implications of the word itself, chimed in with fundamentalist tendencies in so many other arts, ideologies and creeds. To the extent that powerful reputations were made through the spreading of doubt, inhibition and guilt among performers who had hitherto played in blissful, natural ignorance, this musical fundamentalism proved as darkly ambiguous as any other kind.

What positive achievements has 'Authenticity' to set against such an indictment – not to mention the rather unprepossessing triumphalism of some of its practitioners about the extent to which the movement has supposedly seduced the public away from any lingering interest in new music? Well, the early instruments have been duly re-mastered; lost nuances and modes of articulation have been recovered and reapplied; certain areas of the classical repertoire – the Haydn piano trios, for instance – have proved to sound far better with a period balance of timbres, and some of these discoveries have worked through to our modern-instrument orchestras (though, as yet, to surprisingly few of our string quartets), helping to leaven the symphonic lump. The critic who hailed the earliest Authenticist to wow the mass public, Christopher Hogwood, for changing the way we hear music, may have had his point. But should the issue not have been the way we understand music?

Once upon a time – in fact between 1868 and 1935 – there lived and worked in Vienna a musical analyst called Heinrich Schenker who thought he had discovered the secret of how the great masterpieces of the tonal era from Bach to Brahms really worked. Starting from a perception shared by many ordinary music lovers, that beneath the teeming surface of a composition there lie longer-term changes of harmony which channel and unify the whole piece, Schenker gradually refined a method of analysing – foreground, middleground, background – down to the basic cadence he claimed underlay all tonal pieces.

This is not the place to go into the implications or limitations of Schenker's achievement, which still inflames academic controversy to this day. But two aspects of his work are striking. The first is that it was founded, not in nineteenth-century theory, which tended to systematize harmony into catalogues of chords, and musical forms into cut-and-dried shapes, but in such eighteenth-century practices as elaborating, 'composing-out' simple progressions of harmonies to create whole musical sections. The second is that between 1919 and 1935, Schenker was regularly consulted by the conductor many have come to regard as the profoundest of the twentieth century, Wilhelm Furtwängler.

It would be hard to imagine an interpreter further removed from 'Authentic' orthodoxy. Where Hogwood in his more doctrinaire days would apparently refuse to do anything to the music unsanctioned by some eighteenth-century treatise or manual, Furtwängler was notorious for phrasing and pacing the classics differently every time – the very apogee, it seemed, of German late-Romantic subjectivity. Yet far from going out of fashion, his recorded legacy has continued to gain adherents, not only for his unique communication of 'depth', but also precisely for his grasp of the deep structures in the composition that allowed him to take such life-giving liberties with the surface.

The question is irresistible: could it be that in his understanding of the musical substance of the classics, Furtwängler was more authentic than the Authenticists? Certain interestingly wayward later recordings by such an old Authentic hand as Nikolaus Harnoncourt suggest that the realization may be beginning to dawn: that the movement has hitherto tended to obsess itself with every 'period' factor – instruments, playing techniques, texts, acoustics – except the way the music was composed. The results of ignoring the latter have been palpable in even the most highly praised effects of Hogwood, John Eliot Gardiner or Norrington: a recurrent failure, beneath the severe, elegant or exciting surfaces, to give due weight and direction to bass lines or to placing and pacing the longer-term middle-ground events with the attention they require.

One is not suggesting that 'period' conductors and players should instantly take crash courses in Beethoven's sketchbooks or Schenker analysis, let alone Furtwängler's idiosyncrasies. But some involvement in the way eighteenth-century composers were trained (which in the early stages was the same way as players), some concern with deepening the movement's real gains, are surely overdue if authenticity is not in turn to be relegated to history by the next merely stylistic fad.

NOTES

Source: 'Digging out the Real Thing', *The Independent*, 30 June 1990; rev. 2008. This was written prior to a BBC 2 programme on the authenticity debate, 'The Real Thing?'.

3   *Down with Classical Music*

It all depends, of course, upon what one means by 'Classical'. Since the Latin word *classicus* – signifying a citizen, or, later, a writer of first rank – filtered through French into other European languages some 500 years ago, the terms classic, classical and classicism have acquired a bewildering variety of connotations.

Granted, they have often been used to point a continuing link with the Ancient World itself – if more saliently in literature and architecture than in the techniques of Western music. Yet the words are equally often invoked without any reference to Greece or Rome – as when the court traditions of Indian or Japanese music are labelled classical to distinguish them from their respective vernaculars. Nor is classicism necessarily synonymous with high culture. Light music, jazz and pop have all thrown up their own classics – though few of these would probably rate for qualities of balance, restraint and objectivity which constitute yet another notion of Classicism, in antithesis to the putative excess, wildness and subjectivity of Romanticism.

And while today's most common usage of the word Classical – as in the title of this article – may glance at the older meanings, it really signifies something different again. Only in our own century and under the influence of the record industry has it become a synonym for up-market. No doubt the advantages of lumping the entire repertoire of Western music under one classy sobriquet are obvious enough; at one moment it can be promoted as a luxury product for the upwardly mobile through the aura of a Karajan; at another, it can be lucratively brought down to 'the people' through the persona of a Pavarotti.

All the same, this appropriation of the term is something many musicians and music-lovers have come to loathe. To market 'Classical' as a consumer category like 'Hip-Hop', 'Rock', 'Easy Listening' and the rest, is to imply that it offers a relatively predictable and limited experience, whereas the actual range of Western repertoire is as diverse as the ideological, social, intellectual and demographic history of Europe itself over the last 15-odd centuries. Again, the commercial usage somehow suggests that Western tradition is complete, finished – that the classics are there to be endlessly reinterpreted and recorded rather than to inspire anything creatively new. Doubtless many would indeed rest content if no composer ever wrote another note. But it seems unlikely that those restless explorers, Haydn, Wagner or Stravinsky, would have felt happy about such a future.

And not least, the 'Classical' tag of the record industry has confused the issue with the specific historical meaning of the term that scholars and serious music-lovers have generally agreed about since the middle of the last century. There were evidently a variety of reasons why the era after the Renaissance

and Baroque and before the Romantics and the Moderns came to be called
the Classical Period – and not only to connect music with the classical
preoccupations of the other arts in the eighteenth century. There was the belief
that the Classical composers had laid the basis of a standard repertoire and
bequeathed a series of exemplary structures – symphony, concerto, sonata –
to perpetuity. Above all, the 'Classical Style' was considered to have attained a
coherence and autonomy, a fusion of feeling and form as never before in the
history of music.

    To the later nineteenth century, obsessed with notions of evolution and
organicism, the way in which the Classical Style had apparently grown out of
the decay of the Baroque to a glorious flowering towards 1800 before gradually
yielding to the more exotic growth of Romanticism must itself have seemed
classic. So the young Haydn could be envisaged gradually assembling from
disparate sources a new musical coherence which the still-younger Mozart
would then raise to the heights of perfection before Beethoven plumbed
the depths of profundity, finally exhausting its potential. Yet something like
this cyclic view persisted into the later twentieth century, conditioning the
attitudes of musicians, listeners and even critics to the Classical repertoire
and still permeating that most influential study of the period, *The Classical
Style* by Charles Rosen.[1] Only in 1991 was it seriously challenged in a book
accurately, if unsnappily, entitled, *Haydn's 'Farewell' Symphony and the Idea of
Classical Style* by the American musicologist, James Webster.[2]

    Haydn never actually called his Symphony No. 45 in F sharp minor the
'Farewell', but the nickname was already used in his lifetime and the work
remains famous for the extraordinary form of its finale, in which, after an
abrupt switch from a stormy *presto* to a wistful *adagio*, the players are
gradually required to drop out, leaving only a pair of violins at the end. But
right from the choice of initial key – the 'remoteness' of F sharp minor posed
tricky problems of intonations for eighteenth-century instruments – the first
three movements are quite as striking: a harsh, driving allegro in which the
development is largely displaced by an episode on unrelated material in an
unlikely key; a slow movement of hushed loneliness and a minuet of grating
uncertainty.

    Haydn was 40 when he produced the work in 1772 as a successful hint
to Prince Esterházy that his orchestra should be allowed to knock off for
its winter break. In traditional histories of the Classical Style, it is generally
assigned to Haydn's 'storm and stress' period – when he is heard as juxtaposing
the elements of the new manner with an increasing boldness, if falling short
as yet of the complete integration of the 'mature' Classicism to come. Yet,
in a colossal analysis, bringing to bear all the current academic techniques,
Professor Webster suggests that this most uncompromising of symphonies was
also as unified in its own terms as anything to come in subsequent 'Classical'

decades. And not only in thematic connections, key relationships, and so on, but in 'extra-musical' associations. For, in contradiction to nineteenth-century notions of Classicism as the supremely abstract or 'absolute' style, Webster contends that eighteenth-century listeners would have 'read' not only the finale but the entire 'Farewell' Symphony as an emblematic narrative.

In his final, and, to non-academic readers, most approachable chapter, Webster teases out the implications of his findings for the idea of Classicism itself – which, he reiterates, was essentially a late nineteenth-century construct: early nineteenth-century critics such as E. T. A. Hoffmann had thought of Haydn, Mozart and Beethoven as 'Romantics', while they would have called themselves 'Moderns'. In imagining them working towards a conscious stylistic ideal, Webster argues, we have seriously misconstrued and undervalued the earlier works, particularly of Haydn, in whose 'Farewell' Symphony are already to be found all the qualities traditionally attributed to Beethoven's Fifth. Not everybody will agree with Webster's submission that Haydn deserves recognition as Beethoven's equal, but his picture of the composers of the day simply making the best of the musical materials to hand and following their noses is surely more realistic than the older idea of a stylistic quest. If we must have a historical label, Webster half-seriously proposes 'First Viennese-European Modern Style' as an alternative for the period. Where this leaves the 'Classical' concept is another matter. Perhaps it will have to be abandoned to the record industry after all.

NOTES

Source: 'Hooked on Classicism', *The Independent*, 14 September 1991.

1   Charles Rosen, *The Classical Style: Haydn, Mozart, Beethoven*, London, Faber, 1971/72.
2   James Webster, *Haydn's 'Farewell' Symphony and the Idea of Classical Style*, Cambridge, CUP, 1991.

4   Behind Closed Doors

Arnold Schoenberg had his own line in Viennese jokes. But when he
told his baffled listeners "My music is not modern, it is just badly played,"
he was dead serious. Not only was he convinced that his tumultuous
compositional evolution from post-Wagnerian passion to twelve-tone
methodology represented an inevitable development of two centuries of
Austro-German tradition, but also that audiences would hear the continuity,
if only performances were clear and committed enough. In the summer of
1918, he put this belief to the test by offering a series of 10 open rehearsals
of his First Chamber Symphony (1906) working up to a pair of exemplary
performances. The response of the Viennese intelligentsia was positive
enough to prompt something more ambitious. Gathering about him his
closest pupils, Schoenberg proceeded to launch the most uncompromising
concert organization of the twentieth century.

According to the prospectus drafted by Alban Berg, the aim of the non-
profit making *Verein für musikalisches Privataufführungen* was to promote a
true understanding of modern music through the most thorough preparation
of significant works in an atmosphere removed from 'the corrupting influence
of publicity'. Where pieces required forces too large for the Society to afford,
performances were to be given in specially-made arrangements for chamber
ensemble or two pianos – with the Schoenbergian implication that this would
allow the compositional bare bones behind the orchestral fabric to come
through more directly. In order to neutralize prejudice, the programme of
each weekly concert was only to be revealed on the night, audience response
was discouraged and critics were banned. Though the statutes of the Society
accorded Schoenberg absolute authority, he characteristically refused to take
advantage, withholding his music entirely from its first 18 months of activity.

Yet the breadth of what he *did* choose strikingly undermines his posthumous
reputation as a narrow ideologue.[1] Stravinsky and Bartók were cordially
approached for their latest pieces – Schoenberg assuring the latter that 'your
piano music has given me extraordinary pleasure'. The profusion of items by
Mahler, Reger and Debussy might have been expected from Schoenberg's
background and known tastes – but not his inclusion of composers as varied
as Suk, Scriabin, Satie or Szymanowski. Nor was his choice exclusively
'progressive': time could equally be found for such a conservative contemporary
as Franz Schmidt. Most impressive was the certainty of Schoenberg's choice
among composers by no means well established at the time. Running through
the 200-odd works presented over the three years of the Society's existence, it
is difficult to find more than a dozen or so that have sunk without trace.

Maybe the emergence of the Society for Private Musical Performances
depended upon a unique conjunction of circumstances. In his mid-forties,

Schoenberg himself was poised between the Expressionism of his earlier maturity and the more Classical concerns of his serial future. The long Viennese tradition of private performance was meanwhile about to yield, as everywhere else, to a musical culture disseminated through radio and recording. Whether Schoenberg and his associates could have found the incredible lengths of time they were prepared to devote to coaching two-piano versions of Mahler symphonies for the Society once their careers picked up after the war might be doubted. And though it was galloping inflation that brought its operations to a halt in early December 1921, such pressures had already begun to nibble at the Society's ideals – necessitating several public fund-raising events, including a gala concert for which Schoenberg, Berg and Webern arranged Johann Strauss waltzes, played in their performances and then sold the manuscripts by auction.

Was the Society's impact, then, largely transitional? Not in the sphere of interpretation. By insisting that the performers should serve the work, rather than vice versa, Schoenberg powerfully contributed – through the subsequent careers of such Society participants as the young pianist Rudolf Serkin – to the 'New Objectivity' so many performers pursued between the wars. And the Society soon became a model for other such organisations as the International Society for Contemporary Music founded in Salzburg in 1922 or the League of Composers in New York – though these were soon enough to be overtaken by just the kind of cliquishness and public controversy Schoenberg had hoped to avoid.

Whether his conception of the Society had actually transcended such issues might itself be argued. While most of the performers and music-lovers in his ambit evidently found the concerts a uniquely enlightening experience, at least one young subscriber – Karl Popper – came to the conclusion that the Schoenbergians were dominated by fallacious notions of artistic 'progress', and he devoted much of his subsequent philosophical career to a campaign against Historicism.[2] More recently Charles Rosen has argued that Schoenberg's attempt to remove the experience of music from all taint of market forces only served to confirm how pervasive these had already become.[3] While Hans Keller, in other respects the deepest admirer of Schoenberg, went as far as to describe the Society as modern music's first 'progressive isolation ward'.[4] And if any would-be Schoenberg attempted to set up such an organization today, it would doubtless be dismissed as 'elitist'.

Yet the fact that the latter term is routinely chucked by way of insult at virtually anything these days attracting less than 10,000 listeners ought to give us pause. While the stance of the Society as a closed organization of advanced minds 'above the market' doubtless justified the criticism of Keller, Popper and Rosen, the fundamental impulse behind it seems to have been something rather different. In a famous passage on the nature of human culture, Arthur Schopenhauer once wrote:

Like an ethereal addition, a fragrant scent arising from fermentation, the intellectual life hovers over the worldly bustle, over the real life of the peoples which is led by the will; and alongside of the history of the world there goes, guiltless and unstained by blood, the history of philosophy, of science, and the arts.[5]

The idea that the ultimate function of art is not to stimulate or entertain but to foster understanding, to convey discoveries of the human consciousness that can be expressed in no other way, has a long history in Western music, from the cosmological metaphysics of the Renaissance with its Music of the Spheres, to the latter-day philosophy of culture Popper has called 'World 3'. Implicit in the idea is that such discoveries are self-validating: that if a Beethoven breaks through to an authentic new world of musical thought in his late quartets, it hardly matters if, initially, only a handful of listeners are able to follow him.

Some such ideal certainly seems to have hovered over Schoenberg and his friends as they strove with fanatical zeal to clarify the structures of the works they chose for their concerts. Maybe, in retrospect, the whole enterprise seems riven by the artistic, social and commercial conflicts of its time. But if Schoenberg's generation was wracked by aspirations to break through to new modes of expression without relinquishing all comprehensible links with the past, by the desire to change society without increasing the alienation of the artist, and by the need to live without compromising with the market – then how much more pressing have such conflicts become today.

NOTES

Source: 'Private Lives', *The Independent*, 23 November 1991.

1   A complete listing of all the programmes mounted by the *Verein* can be found in: Joan Allan Smith, *Schoenberg and his Circle: A Viennese Portrait*, New York, Schirmer Books, 1986, pp. 255-68.
2   For his experiences of the *Verein* and thoughts on the evolution of music, see: Karl Popper, *Unended Quest: An Intellectual Autobiography*, rev. ed., London, Flamingo, 1986.
3   Charles Rosen, *Schoenberg*, London, Fontana Books/Marion Boyars, 1975, pp. 72-8.
4   Hans Keller, *1975 (1984 minus 9)*, London, Dobson, 1977, p. 260.
5   Hans Keller, *Criticism*, ed. Julian Hogg, London, Faber, 1987, p. 81. The translation is Keller's.

5   Hollywood and Bust

Dmitri Mitropoulos, inspirational conductor of the New York Philharmonic from 1949 to 1958, was emphatic. 'All my life,' he wrote, 'I have searched for the perfect modern work. In this symphony I have found it.'

Surprisingly, the object of this accolade was neither one of the established masterpieces of Schoenberg or Stravinsky, nor some optimistic manifestation of Copland. Yet, when one listens to the only recording so far of the Symphony in F sharp major, Op. 40 (1950), by Erich Wolfgang Korngold, it is disarmingly obvious what Mitropoulos meant. The work opens in sub-Schoenbergian vein with a jagged clarinet theme over gritty rhythms, rises to an apostrophe blatantly plagiarised from the beginning of Stravinsky's *Symphony in Three Movements* (1945), calms into a flute and string passage suspiciously reminiscent of Copland's *Appalachian Spring* (1944) … and so on.

No doubt, it was Korngold's tragedy to be born a musician of talent, but a sponge of genius. Though quite personal touches are intermittently to be heard throughout his music, it was evidently his effortless absorption in his Viennese *Wunderkind* years of the entire sound-world of late Romanticism that so impressed Mahler and Strauss and sent his sumptuously decadent music-drama *Die tote Stadt* (1920) zooming around the opera houses of the world. Then came the rise of Hitler, and the rest – more or less ¬¬– was Hollywood. First arriving in 1934 to compose the score for Max Reinhardt's film of *A Midsummer Night's Dream* (1935), Korngold rapidly established himself alongside Max Steiner and Alfred Newman as a master of that lushest phase of Hollywood film music – which indeed, such revisionist musicians as the conductor John Mauceri have since tried to represent as the true centre of twentieth-century tradition. Granted, the composition of the Symphony after the war reflected Korngold's urge to return to the concert hall. But by then, his ever-open ear had been caught by some unexpected Los Angeles arrivals.

A three-part BBC 2 documentary, *City of Strangers* (1992), was specifically concerned with those European émigrés who became involved in the wartime Hollywood film industry itself.[1] Yet, with a little widening of scope, it could have posed the most pregnant cultural questions. By the late 1930s, not only Korngold and Reinhardt, but Schoenberg, Rachmaninov and Klemperer had moved to Los Angeles, soon to be followed by Stravinsky and Thomas Mann, Eisler and Brecht, Fritz Lang, Franz Werfel, Aldous Huxley, Christopher Isherwood, old aunt Alma Mahler and all. To many of these major European talents, uprooted from their social certainties and their supporting elites, thrown together in an alien subtropical environment under the sway of capitalism at its most populist, it must have felt as if their Old World civilization was itself on trial.

How, for instance, did that pair of paid-up Marxists, Eisler and Brecht, justify their collaboration with Lang on such a Hollywood vehicle as *Hangmen Also Die* in 1942? As the straightforward anti-Nazi propaganda it seems to be? As a more covert pact of German artists in a foreign culture? Or as a classic Marxist subterfuge of turning the weapons of bourgeois society against itself? Whatever the answer, it ultimately failed to save Eisler from getting chucked out of the United States in 1947 by the House Committee on Un-American Activities. But the most fascinating musical gloss on the period is provided by the intensely felt yet utterly resisted relationship between two of the greatest European masters of the modern century.

Schoenberg and Stravinsky had actually met just a few times in Berlin in 1913. Schoenberg had enjoyed *Petrushka* (1911) and Stravinsky was bowled over by the music, if not by what he heard as the *fin de siècle* aesthetic, of *Pierrot lunaire* (1912). But by the mid 1920s, Stravinsky's increasing recourse to techniques from the musical past had begun to irritate Schoenberg, who published a naughty canon satirizing 'Little Modernsky' for affecting a wig just like Papa Bach. Stravinsky responded with disdain for Schoenberg's futuristic stance and the apparent arbitrariness of the 12-tone method; their mutual misconceptions were fanned by camp-followers so that by the time Fate had cast them into the neighbourly proximity of Hollywood in the 1940s, it seemed impossible there should ever be a reunion. Their mutual friends, from the exiled Thomas Mann to the young Robert Craft – Stravinsky's assistant, but conductor also of Schoenberg – certainly felt the tension. But not till Schoenberg's death in 1951 had safely conveyed his music, too, into the past, did a kind of rapprochement emerge with Stravinsky's gradual appropriation of the 12-tone method.

On the quality of its production, European culture may doubtless be said to have come through its American exile with resilience. The period brought forth not only Eisler's beautiful *Hollywood Elegies* (1942) to song-texts of Brecht, but some of the very best of Schoenberg and Stravinsky – the concertos for violin (1936) and piano (1942) and the String Trio (1946) of the one; the Mass (1944-48), the *Orpheus* ballet (1947) and *The Rake's Progress* (1951) of the other. Yet it is significant that, though both Schoenberg and Stravinsky conducted the studio orchestras in their own and other music from time to time – which is doubtless where Korngold's magpie ear picked things up – neither achieved a single Hollywood film score. Schoenberg's relationship with the industry over such projects as *The Good Earth* proved a comedy of misunderstandings – his alleged reaction, for instance, to a particularly action-packed scene, was "With all that going on, why do you need music?" The ostensibly more business-like Stravinsky seemed to run into endless hitches, so that his sketches for such features as *Jane Eyre* and *The Song of Bernadette* ended up in his concert music. It took a third figure to link Schoenberg, Stravinsky and what he called 'the culture industry' in altogether the darkest polemical text to come out of the period.

Pupil of Berg and prime mover of the Marxist-Freudian Frankfurt School, Theodor Wiesengrund Adorno already loomed large as a social critic by the time he came to America. His most direct response was to collaborate with Eisler on a now-classic book, *Composing for the Films* (1947). But he was also Mann's musical adviser in the writing of *Doktor Faustus* (1947): that apocalyptic allegory of the collapse of Germany as seen through the life of a fictional 12-tone composer – a novel that understandably infuriated Schoenberg. Yet it was Schoenberg who Adorno defended in his *Philosophy of Modern Music*, published back in Europe in 1948.[2] According to this, the conditioning of society by forces of economic domination was already so powerful that authentic art was becoming impossible. A composer such as Schoenberg, trusting to unfettered subjectivity and its intrinsic methods of organization, might preserve his integrity, but only at the cost of alienation from his audiences; a composer such as Stravinsky, seeking objectively to manipulate accepted materials, could only come up with empty husks of the past.

It has often been argued that Adorno misunderstood Stravinsky and overstated his thesis, yet the questions focused by his American experience have not gone away. Indeed, some current thinkers in his tradition would now suggest matters have now gone far further: that the increasing grip of multinational capitalism and the promotion of minimalist-meditative modes of music designed to keep us in a state of diffused euphoria is no coincidence. Maybe. Yet *City of Strangers* proved well worth catching for its tantalizing clips of Schoenberg playing tennis with George Gershwin, Eisler defending himself before the House Committee,[3] and the apt choice of title music from the all-American scherzo of, yes, that Korngold symphony.

NOTES

Source: 'Hollywood and Bust', *The Independent*, 7 November 1992.

1   *City of Strangers* was televised on BBC 2 over three successive Sundays, 1, 8 and 15 November 1992.
2   Theodor W. Adorno, *Philosophy of Modern Music*, tr. Anne V. Mitchell and Wesley Bloomster, London, Sheed & Ward, 1973.
3   A transcription of Eisler's interrogation can be found in: Nicolas Slonimsky, *Music Since 1900*, fourth ed., London, Cassell, 1971, pp. 1394-1404.

6   Blueprints for an Expanding Universe

During the spring of 1949, a lanky Californian with a spiky haircut knocked on the door of a tiny apartment high above the Rue Beautreillis in Paris and introduced himself to its bouncy, not-yet-balding occupant. At 36, John Cage had already attracted a certain notoriety back in the United States as a musical maverick, whereas the 25-year-old Pierre Boulez was only just emerging from the avant-garde circle he had electrified with his intransigent early scores and articles. Yet, despite their utterly opposite backgrounds and personalities, they seem to have taken to each other at once. Over the next five years, some 40, often extended and densely argued letters were to pass between them. Of these, tantalising hints and snippets have occasionally surfaced since in the writings by, or studies of, one or the other composer, but only more recently has the whole sequence been gathered together. It emerges that Cage conducted some of the correspondence in passable French, while Boulez less often switched to a charmingly inept English. In the English edition, Robert Samuels has translated back the one without attempting to correct the other.

Intermittently risible on the Boulez side though they may be, the letters remain rather special in the annals of composers' correspondence. One can follow in detail down the centuries the struggles of their predecessors for decent professional conditions, from Monteverdi's querulous missives to his aristocratic employers, by way of outbursts from Bach, Beethoven and Berlioz, to Stravinsky's implacable demands for payment on the nail. One can learn a huge amount about the musical theatre from the letters with which Verdi and Richard Strauss endlessly harried their librettists. One can draw what musical insights one may from Mozart's scatological postscripts, Britten's prep-school lingo and Wagner's insatiable requests for luxuries from Paris. And from that intimate category of composers' correspondence with their muse – Brahms's letters to Clara Schumann, Tchaikovsky's to Nadezhda von Meck, Janáček's to Kamila Stösslova – one can divine something of the complex personal sources of artistic aspiration.

Boulez and Cage duly plotted ways of promoting one another's music and gossiped about the shortcomings of their peers – more generously on Cage's side than on that of the often-waspish Boulez. But their main concern was something rarer. Apart from discussions of key relationship and musical textures in a handful of letters between Mozart and his father, or the attempt to discover the true compositional path which runs through the correspondence of the young Brahms and the violinist and composer Joseph Joachim, it is difficult to think of a precedent for a pair of composers using their letters to sketch at length the theoretical and technical basis of what they hoped would prove an entirely new musical era.

To be sure, the historical and personal circumstances which brought them together were also exceptional. After the Second World War, and largely at the promptings of Boulez's polemics, the notion gained ground that the first generation Modern Masters – Schoenberg, Stravinsky, Bartók, Varèse, Berg – had failed to carry through the implications of their own most radical discoveries. Cage, meanwhile, who had never felt part of European tradition in the first place, evidently saw the determination of the post-war generation to push these discoveries further as a fertile field for his own alternative ideas. But just how alternative steadily emerged during the correspondence, and it seems probable that had the two composers met even five years later, the friendship could hardly have developed, so far had they moved apart.

The problem was that Cage ultimately turned out to be an anti-composer. Indeed, one of his pre-war teachers back in California – Schoenberg, no less – had already prophesied something of the sort when he noted the young American's inability to understand harmony. Nothing daunted, Cage had turned to percussive sounds for his materials – including his invention of that one-man percussion band, the prepared piano – and to rhythmic schemes for their organization. By the time he met Boulez he was already beginning to question the need for intentional schemes at all and to investigate various chance procedures for allowing sounds to be more 'themselves'. Meanwhile, Boulez, encouraged by *his* mentor, Messiaen, had developed in virtually the reverse direction. By accepting the serial principle from the start and extending it from pitch relationships into the domains of rhythm, tone colour and timing, the Frenchman believed he could progressively integrate all the most advanced developments – including the emerging technology of electronic sound generation – into a controlled yet ever-expanding universe of compositional possibilities.

The crossing of their contrary paths, however, seemed to throw up just enough in the way of shared concerns to prevent them from passing like ships in the night. The complex chimes and thuds Cage drew from the piano in his *Sonatas and Interludes* (1946-48) by inserting screws and bits of rubber between the strings evidently struck Boulez as analogous to the microtone aggregates he was attempting to organize by serial means. Conversely, the pages of mathematical formulations Boulez sent Cage were construed by the latter as comparable to the constructivist procedures he used to purge his own pieces of all personal expressiveness. In fact, the search for the impersonal seems to have been a shared ideal, though where Boulez doubtless viewed this as a process for discarding moribund tradition, Cage saw it more as a way of blurring the distinction between music and random environmental noise. The salient paradox is that, for a time at least, the very different approaches of the two composers seemed to throw up pieces which actually sounded, in their volatile gestures and abrupt silences, remarkably similar: the hyper-serial Second Piano Sonata (1948) of Boulez that Cage so admired, and the chance-generated *Music of Changes* (1951) of Cage that Boulez welcomed so warmly.

But in the end, the mutual misunderstanding that underlay their very amity was bound to tell, and by the late 1950s cultural politics had darkened the picture, with Cage invading Boulez's avant-garde citadel at Darmstadt, and for a time capturing his comrade-in-arms, Karlheinz Stockhausen. Battles long ago? In the longer run, neither Cage's hoped-for liberation of sound, nor Boulez's projected new musical languages, proved to inherit the earth. What did, at least for a time, was the hypnotic trundling of Minimalism, which Cage in his final years denounced as oppressive, and the bland simplicities of Holy Primitivism, which doubtless struck Boulez as irredeemably reactionary: styles devoted to the over-arching ideal of 'accessibility'.

From the standpoint of the new populism, the Boulez-Cage collaboration could only be construed as a hopeless old élitism. But however questionable some of their ideas eventually proved, what is strikingly absent from the letters, as the two composers excitedly urge each other on, is any sense that they are in the business for personal gain. To read the correspondence is to be reminded of something that current re-writers of musical history may prefer to forget: just how desirable, how necessary a radical renewal of the art felt in the immediate post-war period. Perhaps, also, it might set us wondering whether our present musical stupefaction, so profitable to the media corporations, could not now do with the sharp shock of a few uncompromising elitists as gifted and as idealistic as Cage and Boulez once were.

NOTES

Source: 'Blueprints for the Expanding Universe', *The Independent*, 30 October 1993.

1   *The Boulez-Cage Correspondence*, ed. Jean-Jacques Nattiez, tr. Robert Samuels, Cambridge, CUP, 1993.

7   Less Means Less

Of course, there were minimalists long before Minimalism – and not just Carl
Orff or Erik Satie. Composers have often reached stages in their evolutions
when it has seemed urgent to chuck out inherited techniques and begin
again from basics. At certain junctures, such chuckings-out have assumed
the force of major movements. When Monteverdi abandoned polyphony
for the enhanced expressiveness of the single singing line in the 1600s, when
the mid-eighteenth-century Mannheim symphonists jettisoned the melodic
and textural richness of the Baroque for a more dramatic exploitation of the
simplest tonal relationships, these developments were regarded by many in
their own day as woeful impoverishments of the musical language. Yet in the
longer term we can hear how a temporary concentration on single principles –
to see what could be got out of those *alone* – often led to surprising discoveries
which have ultimately enriched the possibilities of Western music as a whole.
By the mid-1770s symphonic thinking had evolved to such an extent that
Haydn and Mozart could bring the old Baroque techniques back into play
with new impetus.

Has Minimalism constituted such a movement? As a back-to-basics
phenomenon it could plausibly be heard as the most radical for centuries –
the more so in that its disciplines have derived partly from outside Western
tradition altogether: from Africa and the Orient. And while the earlier, more
rigorously minimal pieces by La Monte Young, Steve Reich and Philip Glass
were duly dismissed as empty by many a classical ear, Reich now fills concert
halls and Glass commands fees for new operas unheard of since Meyerbeer.
The question is really two-fold. Was the initial movement as it unfolded,
mostly in America, between the late Fifties and early Seventies, a coherent
response to historical forces? And does the music the minimalists are writing
now genuinely build upon their early discoveries: not only such large concert
pieces of the 1980s as Reich's *The Desert Music*, or Glass's widely-performed
operas, but also the music of younger American post- (or neo-?) Minimalists
such as John Adams and Michael Torke, the corresponding school of Dutch
systems composers around Louis Andriessen, even Britain's own dear Steve
Martland?

The two answers would seem to be, yes and no. The movement arose quite
simply as a collective reaction against the dominant serial avant-garde of
the 1950s, led in Europe by Boulez and in America by Milton Babbitt. Glass's
response to Boulez's Domaine Musical concerts in Paris has been much quoted:
"A wasteland, dominated by these maniacs, these creeps, who were trying to
make everyone write this crazy, creepy music."[1] But ironically, having all gone
through the serial-academic mill themselves, the early minimalists seem to

have felt inhibited from throwing in their lots with that ultimate American anarchist, John Cage. Instead, they brought their acquired discipline to bear upon the most primal musical materials.

Thus in Terry Riley's *In C* (1964) – the earliest minimalist piece to attract widespread enthusiasm – any number of players work their way through 53 tiny note-patterns, repeating and pausing at will, against a continuous fast pulse. The result is a kind of vast blurred canon sustaining a cycle of gentle chord progressions for upwards of an hour.[2] Meanwhile, Reich was investigating phase-patterns – the kind of aural Op Art effect one gets when a repeated rhythmic figure moves gradually out of step with itself. Glass's earliest minimal pieces that appeared slightly later concerned themselves, rather, with the long-term implications of adding tiny extensions to repeat figures.

What must have attracted many listeners to this music who cared nothing for the afflatus of pot and meditation it tended to come with, was the sheer relief it offered to the serialist grind. New composition, it seemed, need not involve 50 high-level decisions per second to qualify as relevant. With Riley to revive the old participatory joys of playing and Reich to show how the simplest rhythms and chords could be teased into freshness, it was easy enough to forget – at least temporarily – how one-dimensional such processes remained compared with even the 'simplest' structures of Western tradition – a Haydn minuet, say, or a Gershwin song. For some of Minimalism's earliest admirers, the doubts set in when Reich and Glass moved out of the New York lofts and art galleries into more conventional venues and the commercial big time. Had the style a potential, or its creators the artistry, to stand up to more direct competition with the standard repertoire? In blowing up his processes for full symphony orchestra, Reich relinquished – as he later admitted – the concentration of the tightly interactive group for something more ambiguous: a kind of vast, anti-individualistic machine music, which Cage even attacked as latently fascist.

Glass was able for a time to extend his appeal to the rock circuit and his operas up to *Akhnaten* (1984) retained at least a Satie-like mystery (if not brevity) through their austerity of musical means and appropriately ritualistic 'circular', non-narrative dramaturgy. But Doris Lessing's unaccountably sentimental libretto for *The Making of the Representative for Planet 8* (1988) is narrative, setting up the expectation for traditional numbers, dramatic leverage and so on. If one were ignorant of Glass's step-by-step effort to expand his style to meet the challenge, one might imagine oneself listening to a melodically short-winded conventional composer desperately trying to keep going on stodgy block harmony and hopeful figuration. John Adams's *Nixon in China* (1987) has an infinitely cleverer libretto and his own command of pacing is wider than Glass's steady chug. Yet the effect is much the same: an opera laid out in the usual lengths but filled with noodlings instead of 'real' music.

Though these pieces will doubtless continue to bring new audiences to the opera house for a time (whether or not they stay for *Figaro* or *Wozzeck* is another matter), they already leave the impression more of a falling between stools than of a fresh beginning about to revitalize the mainstream. Post-war avant-garderie arose out of the contention that the traditional language was moribund and needed to be re-invented; Minimalism out of the perception that the basics of avant-garderie were the wrong ones. Meanwhile the public has continued to flock to Brahms.

But this ought to be amazing. Brahms symphonies are some of the most complex and subtle examples of a unique tradition of musical thought and one of Western culture's greatest achievements. Yet thousands understand them instinctively – and if that is not living language, what is? In the long run, it may seem a shame that some of the liveliest musical minds of the last 50-odd years chose to pursue the sidetracks of 'new' languages, rather than addressing the musical question of the twentieth century: how the grammar and syntax that made for a Brahms could be furthered without lapsing into the merely neo-. The matter remains too important to be left to either the conservatives or a handful of opportunistic post-Minimal populists.[3]

NOTES

Source: 'Minimal Response', *The Independent*, 12 November 1988; rev. 2008. Philip Glass's opera, *The Making of the Representative for Planet 8*, was currently running at the London Coliseum.

1   As, for instance, in: Keith Potter, *Four Musical Minimalists*, Cambridge, CUP, 2000, p. 10.

2   Riley's original score contained no indication of a fast pulse. This seems to have arisen out of a suggestion of Reich, who took part in the first performance.

3   Although Glass, Reich and, especially, Adams have continued to fulfil high-profile commissions in the last 20 years, the author has not felt tempted to modify his diagnosis. Adams, in particular, has attempted to broaden his style by alluding to sources ranging from the Baroque and Prokofiev to Ives, Schoenberg and Nancarrow, to say nothing of various ethnic vernaculars and pop. But the persistence of his incessant old Minimalist habits has insured in almost every case that the results have sounded thinner, less characteristic, more diffuse than his models. Meanwhile, the influence of Minimalism upon younger composers has waned, even in the United States where the current vogue seems to be for a quasi-tonal orchestral lavishness verging on neo-Hollywood.

8   Reverberations of 1968

Was it really all so vital, so hopeful, so different from any other year? The English middle-class students copying their Paris comrades in college and art school protests against 'repressive tolerance' through the summer and autumn of 1968 would have liked to think so. But there was an air of instant mythologizing that seemed unconvincing even at the time. Whatever the bright novelties of Biba or the Beatles, the year's more serious events in the world at large could only induce a cumulative sense of déjà vu. As Martin Luther King was gunned down like President Kennedy before him, Nixon rose again from the political dead; it was Bloody Sunday once more in Grosvenor Square and Hungary 1956 in Prague. Meanwhile the horrors of post-colonial Africa and Far East dragged on; the shadow of the Bomb continued to loom and the avatars of the growing ecology movement were already warning of a Second Deluge. That anyone might still be around to celebrate the year a quarter of a century later would have seemed one of the unlikelier prophecies of 1968.

And to celebrate it how? Had radical protest carried the day, the obvious memento would be Hans Werner Henze's 'popular and military oratorio', *The Raft of the Medusa*. The scandal of the 1816 shipwreck from which the nobs had escaped in long-boats, abandoning 300 ordinary men, women and children to a raft, had not only inspired Géricault's famous painting but helped to ferment the revolution of 1848. By way of signalling his own new-found radicalism, Henze dedicated the score to the memory of Che Guevara and insinuated into his final chorus the 'Ho, Ho, Ho Chi-Minh' march rhythm of the anti-Vietnam war students. In the equivocal event, those same students proceeded to scupper the world premiere in Hamburg on 9 December 1968, raising the Red Flag, under which half the chorus refused to sing, and provoking a brutal incursion of police before a note had been heard. Henze was soon to admit his hope that a performance would lead straight to political discussion and action 'was a utopian and much too optimistic idea'.[1]

So, no doubt, was his dubbing as 'popular' a score largely composed in a fiercely post-Schoenbergian Expressionism – though the notion, dating back at least to the Russian revolutionary avant-garde, that advanced art and politics ought to go hand in hand still sustained some credence in 1968 (in the work, for instance, of Luigi Nono) as it hardly does today. Yet if *The Raft* comes up in its rare hearings as one of Henze's strongest scores, this is surely due less to its Marxist subtext than to an exceptional focus in his usually indulgent idiom and to the effectiveness of his dramatic scheme of a duel between Hope and Death, with chorus members actually passing across the stage as the survivors on the raft dwindle away. But it was apropos his

oratorio that Henze noted surely the dominant aesthetic development of the later 1960s when he remarked: 'I think the most important composer of this century is not Webern, but Mahler!'[2]

For almost a decade, the exclusive rigour of the post-Webernian avant-garde of the 1950s had been yielding to a renewed stylistic inclusiveness. How far the sudden, colossal cult of Mahler was cause, how far symptom, might be argued, but his vast collage-symphonies of 'found' materials – many of them indeed popular and military – evidently provided an irresistible stimulus. Compounded by the still wilder juxtapositions of the newly-discovered Charles Ives, the electronic montages of Karlheinz Stockhausen and the campaign of John Cage to break down the barriers between music and random environmental noise, the bias towards 'free-form' and the loosely pluralistic was to continue into the 1970s before the rise of Minimalism initiated a swing back to simpler, narrower styles. One cannot, however, resist the rider that where the rigours of the 1950s at least represented an aspiration towards the musically new, such latter-day anti-developments as Sacred Minimalism breathe an escapist nostalgia for the old.

Back in 1968, the problem for the composer who cleaved to a consistent, tightly defined style was rather how to gain a sympathetic appraisal at all. Luigi Dallapiccola's long-cogitated opera *Ulisse* (1960-68) was received with the respect due to a crowning opus at its Berlin world premiere on 29 September – the composer had, after all, written some nobly libertarian scores in the dark 1930s and 1940s – but without much enthusiasm. One can understand why. The opera is less a theatrical melodrama than a humanistic meditation and the austere constraints of Dallapiccola's late style simply have to be accepted if one is to perceive the often exquisite delicacy and bloom of its internal detail. Yet only a fortnight later, New York enjoyed the tumultuous first performance (if, as yet, minus its finale) of a score more spectacularly given over to the Mahlerian ideal of 'embracing everything' than almost any since Mahler himself. Luciano Berio's *Sinfonia* (1968-69) not only subsumed the serial technique that had sustained Dallapiccola into a musical 'deep structure' by analogy with the then-influential anthropology of Claude Lévi-Strauss, plus a Henze-like engagement in its second-movement lament for Martin Luther King; but it also took the entire scherzo of Mahler's Second Symphony (1895) as a container for a riot of other musical quotations topped up with the Swingle Singers babbling Samuel Beckett. Handled with less than Berio's intellectual energy and aural finesse, the concept might rapidly have confounded itself in modishness. Yet it survives as perhaps the most comprehensive expression of the collective agonies and ecstasies of its time.

Strictly limiting the survey to 1968, it might be questioned whether any American composer quite matched these large, not to say contradictory achievements of Dallapiccola, Henze and Berio – Elliott Carter was not to complete his surging Concerto for Orchestra (1969) until the following year. Back home, the motley temper of the time expressed itself less through solidarity with the students than a fascination with mixed media. Michael Tippett's opera-in-progress *The Knot Garden* (1966-69) was rumoured to have more to do with cinema and group therapy than traditional forms. Benjamin Britten's *The Prodigal Son* added to the vogue for music-theatre he had helped to inspire with *Curlew River* four years earlier. Harrison Birtwistle deafened Aldeburgh with his skirling *Punch and Judy* (1966-67); Peter Maxwell Davies was well advanced on his neo-Gothick period of screaming nuns; and Alexander Goehr pulled off an elegant fusion of Monteverdi, Noh theatre and cabaret in his *Naboth's Vineyard*. But there were also some surpassingly eclectic arrivals: 23-year-old John Tavener launching both himself and the London Sinfonietta with his Stravinskian-cum-pop cantata *The Whale* (the Beatles duly hailed him as 'underground classical') and 15-year-old Oliver Knussen stepping forth with a frighteningly competent and synoptic First Symphony.

On 12 August, democracy even reached the Proms, when William Glock invited the audience to vote on which of three new British offerings it would like to hear again. But the real issue of the period was what kind of democracy? 1968 has often been construed as the year when the failure of the starry-eyed Left opened the way to the long fight-back by the beady-eyed Right. Shortly after the premiere of *Ulisse*, Dallapiccola found himself having to plead against his more committed critics for the right of the individual artist to pursue difficult aesthetic, philosophical or spiritual ideas even in a collectivist age.[3] Today, when the idea of democracy has been virtually degraded to consumerism and the likes of David Mellor have been heard enthusiastically arguing against the recording of any further Henze if it helps to bring down the price of CDs,[4] Dallapiccola's eloquent words read more hauntingly than ever.

NOTES

Source: 'When Hope Fought Death', *The Independent*, 1 May 1993. The article heralded a short BBC Radio 3 season marking the 25th anniversary of the events of 1968.

1   Hans Werner Henze, 'Does Music Have to be Political?', *Music and Politics: Collected Writings 1953-81*, London, Faber, 1982, p. 168.
2   Ibid., p. 170.
3   Luigi Dallapiccola, *On Opera: Selected Writings, Vol. 1*, ed. and tr. Rudy Shackelford, London, Toccata Press, 1987, pp. 263-66.
4   David Mellor was formerly a Conservative MP for Putney and a cabinet minister; later he reviewed CDs on Classic FM.

9   Fear and Loathing of Modern Music

Prophecy in the arts is always a chancy business since, even if general trends can be more or less foreseen, the advent and impact of individual talent is far less predictable. Arnold Schoenberg may have thought of himself as the medium, even the victim, of ineluctable historical necessity, but it is likely that twentieth-century music would have modernized itself a lot more gradually without the goad of his driven genius.

Yet where more recent decades are concerned, one remarkable exception comes to mind. Back in 1967, the proponents of Serialism and Indeterminacy were still battling it out for the future of new music, and Minimalism was yet in its infancy (if it has ever left it), when Professor Leonard B. Meyer of Chicago University first published what has since proved an exceedingly prescient study under the sober title of *Music, the Arts, and Ideas*.[1] Some 25 years before 'the end of history' became an intellectual commonplace, Meyer singled out two trends that he predicted were increasingly likely to challenge the dominant notion of European culture more or less since the Renaissance, that the artist's primary function was 'to make it new'.

The first of these trends was a growing disbelief in the inevitability, or even desirability, of progress – a disbelief fomented as much by the ambiguous impact of modern science as by the public's increasing disinclination to keep up with the perpetual revolution of Modernism. The second, more specifically musical trend, was what Meyer called the increasing 'presence of the past', brought about not just by the piling up of the standard repertoire over the previous two or three centuries, but by the recovery and exploration of the music of the remoter past and of non-European traditions by scholar performers and ethnomusicologists.

Under the impact of these developments, Meyer suggested that the notion of cultural history as a linear succession of changes was about to lose itself in a 'cultural steady-state' more analogous to such relatively stable cultures as Ancient Egypt or China. 'As foreseen here,' he wrote, 'the future … will hold both a spectrum of styles and a plurality of audiences in each of the arts. There will be no convergence, no stylistic consensus. Nor will there be a single unified audience.' In such a relatively stable plurality, Meyer suggested, the pursuit of originality would come to matter less and the skill with which artists handled their chosen styles and materials more.

At the same time, it was likely to prove a 'fluctuating stasis' according to the relative fading in and out of fashion of the musical concerns that Meyer grouped under three broad headings: traditionalism, formalism and transcendentalism. By traditionalism, Meyer meant, obviously enough, composers seeking to extend the forms and techniques of the old European mainstream – Shostakovich and Britten being typical examples at the time he wrote. By formalists, he meant composers after the precedent of Boulez and Stockhausen, for whom composition was initially a medium for technical and aesthetic speculation; and by transcendentalists, those for whom music was but a stepping stone to some spiritual or metaphysical 'beyond', best exemplified in the 1960s by Cage's Zen-inspired mission to dissolve composition into pure contemplative sound.

For various reasons, Meyer thought that the formalists were likely to remain most prominent at least for the next few decades, and in this, time has proved him somewhat mistaken. Boulez and Stockhausen have remained presences, of course, and their successors, whether or not they accept the label of 'New Complexity', continue to pursue an aggressive modernism. Yet the formalist position currently feels a bit embattled, whereas Transcendentalism has reached the masses in the music of John Tavener, Arvo Pärt and Henryk Górecki, while traditionalist values have continued to renew themselves through the work of such composers as Alexander Goehr, Nicholas Maw, Robin Holloway and David Matthews. Yet Meyer's broader vision seems to be becoming truer every day.

Granted, the above is only a crude summary of a wide-ranging book that should never have been allowed to go out of print. Nor is it difficult to think of composers who fail to fit neatly into any one of Meyer's categories – indeed, one could argue that it was part of Schoenberg's unsettling impact that, at one time or another, and sometimes simultaneously, he contrived to be a traditionalist, formalist and transcendentalist. All the same, some of Meyer's scope and rigour could have been usefully taken to heart in one of the more recent symposiums to tackle the state of music: *Reviving the Muses: Essays on Music after Modernism*, edited by Peter Davison, artistic consultant to Manchester's Bridgewater Hall.[2] Since its publisher, the Claridge Press, has been one of the many enterprises run by Roger Scruton from his Wiltshire fastness, it is not unsurprising that all 11 of the chosen contributors tend towards traditionalist viewpoints.

This need not have mattered if the book genuinely fulfilled its aim to address 'the theoretical, philosophical and historical issues behind our current predicament' and to 'question the assumptions that currently govern the criticism, composition and promotion of new music'. Alas, it rapidly emerges that the editor has failed even to question the unsubstantiated assertions, dubious generalizations, non-sequiturs and factual errors that abound. The quality of argument is, at times, shockingly thin, with poor old Schoenberg, 50 years dead, arraigned yet again as the author of our current discontents. One excepts the contributions of Holloway and Matthews – decently written testaments of practising composers. One partially excepts Scruton's own comparison of Janáček and Schoenberg since, loaded against the latter though it may be, at least it gets down to the discussion of some actual music. But as for 'reviving the muse', all the book can come up with is a Jungian sermon from the editor, a burst of Blakean uplift from Sir Ernest Hall, and Scruton's wistful evocation, yet again, of the notion of organic community.

And yet, as Meyer partly predicted, these are interesting times for traditionalists. The relativity of the post-modern condition he sketched may be in the process of dissolving into a still more bemusing pick-and-mix stasis of all the world's musics. But this should at least serve to remind more thoughtful composers and listeners that each of the world's great musical traditions has enshrined its own unique features. Yet, of the contributors to *Reviving the Muse*, only Matthews touches on the special reflexivity of European tradition: the practice of simultaneously invoking and meaningfully contradicting familiar musical expectations to yield ever fresh significances.

Over the last century, this tradition of musical thought has faced some formidable challenges – indeed, the increasing 'anxiety of influence' induced by its ever-lengthening repertoire was one of the sparks that set off the Modernist explosion itself. Meanwhile, the advent of mechanical reproduction and the global commodification of pop have exerted all manner of unprecedented pressures upon the practices, aesthetics and economics that have sustained the European Classical tradition – pressures that some of the contributors to *Reviving the Muse* could have usefully investigated instead of wasting space working off grudges.

And yet, for all that, providing a composer can still summon up musical expectations familiar enough for his audience, large or small, to 'get' his meaningful contradictions, there is no good reason why this unique dynamic of European tradition should not go on evolving indefinitely. For traditionalists, this ought to be a cheering thought.

NOTES

Source: 'Schoenberg: Guilty as Charged?', *The Independent*, 2 March 2001.

1   Leonard B. Meyer, *Music, the Arts, and Ideas*, Chicago, Chicago UP, 1967.
2   *Reviving the Muse: Essays on Music after Modernism*, ed. Peter Davison, Wiltshire, The Claridge Press, 2001.

10   *Voices of the World, Unite!*

On 11 October 2003, a small group of robed men knelt in a semicircle upon the stage of the Purcell Room and launched into some two hours of what sounded curiously like plainsong to words strangely suggestive at once of Latin and Japanese. In fact, it *was* a sort of plainsong that the members of Orashio Kai were bringing to London – first conveyed to Japan by Portuguese missionaries 500 years ago, and secretly passed down by ear in an offshore island cult through all the subsequent centuries of anti-Christian persecution. So what had we here: East or West, 'Classical' or 'World' music, professional or amateur, art or ritual? Not least of the intentions, one suspects, behind the South Bank Centre's *WorldVoice* series planned by William Robson of which the Orashio Kai visit proved a highlight, was to question such categories. 'Singing in a group,' he wrote in the Programme Book, 'is an ancient activity which unites societies – a song's words contain the deepest beliefs of a society, and the occasions for singing are momentous: births, weddings, funerals and festivals. Choirs from all over the world have been invited to take part. Each of them has been chosen because it represents the very best in its tradition.'

Accordingly the fifteen events ranged from Russian Orthodox liturgical music by the Rossica Chamber Choir of St. Petersburg to shamanistic polyphony from the Malan Singers of Taiwan; from Zulu migrant songs by the Real Happy Singers of Durban to the virile dance-choruses of The Rustavi Choir of Georgia. The accomplished child-voices of the Tapiola Choir from Finland contrasted with a newly developed Sufi-orientated choral tradition by the Orfeon Chamber Choir from Turkey. The Jauna Muzika Choir surveyed Lithuanian music from the Renaissance to today while the BBC Singers offered a bill of contemporary pieces from four continents for voices and percussion. All the same, five of the events were squarely located in Western Christian tradition. Three of them comprised typical Evensong services in Westminster Abbey – the last of them bringing in the Choir of Westminster Cathedral as well for the annual ecumenical Festival Evensong in Honour of St. Edward the Confessor who lies in the Abbey he founded. The other two were a celebration of polychoral music from the Renaissance and Baroque by The Sixteen, and a survey of English church music from the early Medieval plainchant *Laudes Regie* to the twentieth century of Herbert Howells, Gerald Finzi and Gustav Holst, again by the Westminster Abbey Choir.

Those World Music ideologues who rail against Western cultural imperialism or who regard European Classical music as a cultural dead duck would doubtless see the usual bias here. But just possibly Robson's point was that the artistic, social, economic and religious issues that variously underlie the musics of the world – the sacred rituals, 'classical' court traditions, urban vernaculars, folk heritages, musical practices collective and solitary – can all be found working themselves out in Western tradition itself, hence its very richness. Take that fundamental source of so much in the last 1000 years of European tradition: plainsong. Today we tend to think of this as a more or less cut-and-dried repertory of melodies as notated in church music from the later Middle Ages onwards and standardized in such collections as the *Liber Usualis*. Yet, up to the time of Edward the Confessor's death in 1065, and for several centuries after, it more resembled a kind of sacred folksong, with chants being passed down by rote through generations of monks and varying in detail from one locality to another – a kind of vine-like proliferation of melody through the myriad services of the Church Year across Christendom.

On the other hand, the gradual emergence of the specifically Western concept of counterpoint and harmony, with the superimposition of new melodic lines on existent chants through the twelfth and thirteenth centuries, was very much the preserve of small elites of singing clerks who devised and read from music notation. So something of the dynamics of folk-vernacular versus art, amateur versus professional, status quo versus progress were already latent within the musical life of the still relatively unified Medieval Church. Once those methods of notation and composition had been carried over into development of more courtly and secular music, and once the Church itself had split between Catholic and Protestant with their divergent musical traditions, the stage was set for the incredible vitality and diversity of the Renaissance and Baroque. True, by the end of the eighteenth century, music was faced by another vast socio-economic and ideological upheaval, with the decline of Church and *ancien régime* patronage, the rise of the bourgeoisie and industrial working-classes and the emergence of the tension between the individual artist, the professional or amateur grouping and increasingly powerful commercial interests, that has driven musical life more or less ever since. Yet if liturgical music went into something of an eclipse, the urge to sing in groups simply reaffirmed itself in the great nineteenth-century oratorio culture that cut so remarkably across social divisions, from the middle-class choirs singing *Messiah* at the Crystal Palace to the great working class choruses belting out *Elijah* in the industrial North.

No doubt the vast conspectus of human belief, musical practice, aesthetic change, religious, political and economic turmoil, and so on, encoded into a thousand years of Western choral music, can be paralleled in the histories of the various long-established performance traditions that Robson chose to bring in from other parts of the world – and that was his point. The experience of a Thomas Tallis, obliged to live through three violent swings between Catholic and Protestant doctrine, or of Palestrina and his fellow composers threatened by the Council of Trent with exclusion from the liturgy because their marvellous counterpoint was held to obscure the Word, would seem familiar enough to the Chinese musician enduring Mao's successive cultural revolutions, or a contemporary Iranian folk group up against the puritanism of fundamentalist Islam. But such parallels only become clear through a respect for the integrity of these various traditions. By contrast, the current fashion for World Music 'fusions' favoured by well-meaning multiculturalists and puffed on the broadcast media in the name of relevance, accessibility and political correctness, can easily neutralize or obscure such understanding – which is presumably why these manifestations were broadly excluded from *WorldVoice*. What was reaffirmed was the incredible range of cultural and historical contrasts human ingenuity has thrown up in the common, rather primitive act of intoning words together.

There must be countless thousands, the present writer among them, who never developed any real competence on an instrument, but gained their essential, first-hand experience of performance through choral singing – whether holding their own course through the incredible, multilayered elaboration of a Bach Passion chorus or through the simple chords of a four-part hymn harmonization. The heightened sense of mutuality in shaping an individual line through an ever-shifting environment of difference that, nonetheless, all somehow fits together and makes sense, is doubtless common to concerted instrumental and choral music. But choral music has the additional complexity of a meaningful text, and of all the expressive, sensuous and semantic interrelations between word and tone. Sympathetic listeners in a live audience can doubtless intuit something of what it feels like to be actually 'inside' a performance; those increasing many whose musical experience comes exclusively from the passive consumption of recordings and broadcasts can have very little. Which was all the more reason to support such a wide-ranging and coherently planned series as this – or, better yet, to join a choir oneself.

NOTES

Source: 'Chorus of Approval', *The Independent*, 22 September 2003; rev. 2008. The Worldvoice series ran at London's South Bank Centre, at Westminster and on BBC Radio 3 from 26 September to 12 October 2003.

11   *Green and Prescient Land*

But for his sad demise a few weeks before, the Henry Wood Promenade Concert on 18 July 1992 would have resounded to the broad sway of that distinguished conductor Sir Charles Groves – an utterly English figure, it would have seemed, in an utterly English programme. Yet one had only to corner Sir Charles in the briefest conversation to suspect a fraught and searching sensibility behind the deceptively bluff, bearded persona. And what of the works that Vernon Handley duly conducted in his memory? Walton's comedy overture *Scapino* (1940) was actually inspired by a French artist's engraving of an Italian *commedia dell'arte* character and reveals a stylistic tendency perhaps closest to Prokofiev. Delius, who composed his Double Concerto in 1915, preferred to live in America, Germany, Scandinavia, France or anywhere rather than his native Bradford and cleaved to the philosophy of Nietzsche. As for *A Sea Symphony* (1903-09) by Vaughan Williams, this comprises settings of Walt Whitman by a composer who completed his musical studies with Max Bruch in Berlin and Ravel in Paris.

Granted, Walton came of age in the heyday of Diaghilev's Russian ballet and always inclined to the Italian south, while Delius was born of German stock in the first place. But surely no composer was more definitively Brtitish than Ralph Vaughan Williams? In his earliest years he certainly seems to have felt the need to counter the Germanic bias of his predecessors, Parry, Stanford and Elgar, with a more indigenous manner derived from Tudor polyphony and folk song. And in Grand Old Age, his influence was duly attacked by a new generation anxious to re-engage with the Continental avant-garde, for 'nationalism gone sentimental', as the fierce young Maxwell Davies put it.[1]

Yet mere insularity could hardly explain the extraordinary sweep of his development from the pleasantries of such early drawing-room songs as 'Linden Lea' of around 1900 to the fearsome force of the Fourth Symphony (1931-34) some 35 years later – nor the admiration of Ravel and Bartók, who praised respectively *On Wenlock Edge* (1909) and the Piano Concerto (1926-31); or Copland, who confessed his view of Vaughan Williams as an unexportable conservative was shattered by the Fourth Symphony itself. Neither could mere nationalism account for his scope. If, for instance, the spectral finale of his Sixth (1944-47) were to be spliced into one of the bleaker Shostakovich symphonies, one wonders how many unknowing listeners would notice any stylistic disparity. Still more saliently: were it not so well known, Debussy's prelude *La fille aux cheveaux de lin* (1910) could quite easily be passed off as School of Vaughan Williams. He is known to have loved *Pelléas et Mélisande* (1893-1902), yet Debussy's surely seminal influence upon his curvilinear melodism and modal, organum-like harmonies rarely seems to get discussed.

Has the received view of English music history served to obscure some of the most interesting affinities in his music?

The nub of this view is that though once – in the era of John Dunstable at the beginning of the fifteenth century – English music led Europe, it has languished ever since in an offshore condition, alternately resisting and embracing the influence of the Continental mainstream. Occasionally, that influence has proved almost overpowering, reducing our nineteenth-century talents, for instance, to pale imitations of Handel, Mendelssohn and Brahms. The resulting resistance of the Vaughan Williams generation had to swing to extremes, leading to an equally extreme embracing of the Schoenberg influence after the Second World War – and so on, and on. Inherent in this is the notion of the 'English time lag' in which we are supposed to show a certain knack for finding further possibilities in trends already exhausted on the Continent. So William Byrd is heard as belatedly synthesizing the entire Renaissance heritage, and Elgar as finding freshness in the idioms of Schumann, Brahms and Dvořák.

None of this is actually untrue. Indeed, it is occasionally truer than we know. It took the *echt* Austro-German ear of Hans Keller to discern that the Continentally-orientated Elgar was in fact more deeply – because less consciously – steeped in the typical pentatonic scales of English folk-song than many a committed subsequent folklorist.[2] All the same, the assumption that music history evolves as a kind of Darwinian process obscures the extent to which what we call tradition is often only a back-projection of individual synthesis. In retrospect, Haydn's central role in fathering the Classical style out of the ruins of the Baroque might seem obvious enough. Yet the disparities of his stylistic choices and his unpredictable development were arguably as idiosyncratic as the brilliantly empirical idiom which the apparently more peripheral Purcell threw together from French, Italian and English sources.

Maybe it is less realistic to seek the Englishness of English music in specific stylistic usages than in lasting biases to more general tensions such as have helped to define all European cultures since at least the ancient Greeks: such issues as sacred versus secular, town versus country, high art versus the vernacular, professional versus amateur. It has often been observed, for instance, that many of the most radical innovators of the modern movement – Schoenberg and Stravinsky in music, Ezra Pound and D. H. Lawrence in literature – tended, paradoxically, to reactionary politics, as if they needed the psychological insurance of authoritarianism against the uncertainties of artistic risk.

Admittedly, the right-wing leanings of such Englishmen as Elgar and Walton may have reflected more a simple discomfort over their humble class origins. But what has been striking ever since Parry used, apparently, to bemuse his aristocratic dinner guests with Blakean visions of socialism, is the leaning of most of our subsequent composers to the left – not always, perhaps, in active political engagement but in a firm commitment to music as a communal activity and to the sustaining of accessible styles through the incorporation of the musical vernacular. Holst and Vaughan Williams were directly inspired by the socialism of William Morris; Tippett and Britten took their stand from the Marxist and pacifist movements of the Thirties; Robert Simpson and Maxwell Davies, maybe, from the post-war Labour vision. But their cumulative tradition continues in the involvement of countless contemporary composers in school projects, 'outreach' work, amateur and non-establishment music-making.

No doubt from the standpoint of the Continental modern movement from Schoenberg to Boulez, primarily concerned with professional innovation, the English leaning towards the amateur has seemed artistically reactionary. How could a composer like Vaughan Williams produce a consonant, placid *Pastoral Symphony* in 1923 after the musical revolutions of Schoenberg and Stravinsky, and the apocalypse of the First World War? Yet even if we disregard the discovery that the piece is actually a covert requiem for the fallen, or its remarkable originality in sustaining a sonata structure without recourse to Austro-German dramatics, or the fact that Vaughan Williams's folklorism was part of a socially conscious search for a 'people's music'; even if we regard the work simply as the pleasant, provincial bit of landscape music it has too often been taken for, history may still have a surprise up its, literally, Green sleeve. For with the consciousness of environmental crisis, what Tippett has called 'the pastoral metaphor' looks set to take on an altogether more central significance.

NOTES

Source: 'Angles on Saxons', *The Independent*, 18 July 1992; rev. 2008.

1   Murray Schafer, *British Composers in Interview*, London, Faber, 1963, pp. 179-80.
2   See: Hans Keller, 'Elgar the Progressive' (1957), *Essays on Music*, ed. Christopher Wintle, Cambridge, CUP, 1994, pp. 63-7; and Hans Keller, 'Musical Self-contempt in Britain', *Music and Psychology*, ed. Christopher Wintle, London, Plumbago, 2003, pp. 197-209.

12   *Deteriorating Reception on the Third*

Out of a bottom drawer stuffed with decades of old music magazines and concert programmes it emerges in faded strawberry-pink covers: *The Third Programme Quarterly Plan*, Saturday 30 June to Friday 29 September 1962, 'sent post free to any applicant' and enabling them to plot a pattern of listening through the music broadcasts, plays, talks and poetry programmes of an entire three-month period.

What was on offer that distant summer when William Glock was in his third year as BBC Controller, Music? Between dramatizations of the *Dialogues of Plato* and Angus Wilson on *Evil in the English Novel,* one notes a particularly impressive repertoire of Russian music from the Edinburgh Festival, with recitals by Sviatoslav Richter and the Western premieres of Shostakovich's Fourth and Twelfth Symphonies. Elsewhere, there was plenty of Stravinsky in the wake of his eightieth birthday and no less than five works of Schoenberg, doubtless to make up for the extent to which Glock's predecessor, abetted by such music producers as Robert Simpson, had succeeded in keeping the Second Viennese School off the air throughout the 1950s. The similarly derided Elisabeth Lutyens was also evidently in the ascendant by 1962, together with such young toughies as Alexander Goehr, Hugh Wood, Peter Maxwell Davies and Richard Rodney Bennett. Yet the classical repertoire was by no means sidelined – highlights included Pears and Britten in Schubert's *Winterreise* and Haydn piano sonatas played by Glock himself – and there was a fair smattering of earlier music, including Dietrich Fischer-Dieskau in Schütz and selections from the *Eton Choirbook.*

The range of this music looks the more remarkable when it is remembered that speech-based programmes took up a substantially larger proportion of the time than they do in today's Radio 3. Moreover, the Third Programme was still suffering from the grievous cutback of 1957 and broadcasting most days only from 8 to 11 in the evenings – though this was partly offset by a greater give-and-take with the Home Service, which often carried the first half from the Proms, including 1962's most memorable new commission, *Scenes and Arias* by Nicholas Maw. Where Glock's influence is most evident in the *Quarterly Plan* is in the often bold juxtaposition of early and contemporary music, of standard and neglected classics, as initiated by his Thursday Invitation Concerts – or Irritation Concerts, as the old guard dubbed them. One Prom, on 13 September, otherwise comprising familiar Bach, Haydn and Mozart, included Vaughan Williams's Sixth and the latest from Maxwell Davies – a then-startling confrontation that has proved unexpectedly prophetic, for in more recent years Sir Peter has actually taken to conducting Vaughan Williams himself.

Yet the Quarterly Plan also divulges something else: scattered through the programmes are chamber works by Edmund Rubbra, a string quartet by Bernard Stevens, two of them by Robert Simpson, a Sinfonia by Arnold Cooke, a choral work by Anthony Milner, no less than five pieces, including a Proms commission, by Lennox Berkeley – just the kind of conservative English composers whom Glock's latter-day detractors, such as the journalist Edward Pearce, are always telling us his regime so ruthlessly suppressed. Surely it is time these complainants sought to balance the handful of composers' hard-luck stories upon which their case is based with an honest survey of the Proms and broadcast programmes that Glock and his successors Robert Ponsonby and John Drummond actually presided over – not forgetting that the pendulum of musical taste does swing from time to time and that, for instance, curiosity about Stockhausen, whether justified or not, really was widespread enough around 1970 to fill the Royal Albert Hall.

For this critic, in any case, what the disinterred *Quarterly Plan* brings home is just how intensely so many of that summer's broadcasts lodged in his then 22-year-old ears – though not particularly the Rubbra, Stevens and so on, of whom quite a lot had already been heard in the 1950s. Too young to remember the founding of the Third Programme in 1946, he reads with fascination of its high ideals and occasionally risible practices in Humphrey Carpenter's anniversary canter through its history, *The Envy of the World: Fifty Years of the BBC Third Programme and Radio 3*.[1] But from a dimly recalled relay of the premiere of Britten's *Gloriana* in 1953 onwards, so much proved seminal. Still vivid from the 1950s are how strange Stravinsky's first serial pieces then sounded, how illuminating were the music talks of Deryck Cooke, how naughty the Hilda Tablet plays of Henry Reed, with their avant-garde parodies by Donald Swann (Elisabeth Lutyens nearly sued). There was the evening in September 1957 when Hans Keller first introduced his concept of 'functional analysis' with a commentary in music composed by himself on Mozart's D minor String Quartet, K. 421 (Carpenter, incidentally, gets both the work and the date wrong), and six months later one heard a none-too-secure BBC Symphony Orchestra under Sir Adrian Boult famously break down in the premiere of Tippett's vibrant Second Symphony.

All the same, the earlier years of the Glock regime from 1959 came to this young listener as a liberation. Not only was the range of contemporary, early, and indeed Baroque to Romantic music on offer suddenly so much broader, but linked so richly with the network's presentation of literature, drama and the history of ideas. In retrospect, one realizes that the programmes of the early 1960s represented the culmination of the ideals upon which the Third had originally been founded: the belief in the absolute value of high culture and in the duty to convey the ideas and works that had engaged the best minds of the past to the most intelligent and creative minds of the present, irrespective of the actual size of the audience. Of course, the increasing competition of television in the 1950s had already raised the dread spectre of ratings that led to the truncation of the Third in 1957. And this was only the first in a periodic sequence of assaults on the network's integrity: since then, there has been the debacle over *Broadcasting in the Seventies* that resulted in a more continuously music-based service re-titled Radio 3, the attempt to disband the BBC orchestras which provoked the Musicians' Union strike of 1981, and, some would argue, the response of a more recent Controller, Nicholas Kenyon, to the challenge of Classic FM – that portent of a culture entirely commodified and manipulated by media capitalism.

But if the basis of our culture has shifted so radically over the past 60 years, and the history of the Third itself has proved so fraught with ideological in-fighting and managerial change, how is one to account for the paradoxical fact that, on the basis of Carpenter's figures, its modest audience has remained so relatively constant? Must one conclude that this represents an unchanging proportion of the professional and lay public for whom high culture remains a serious matter, a kind of natural elite whose numbers are unlikely to be much affected either by the expansion of higher education on the one hand or by gestures towards 'accessibility' on the other? Does the continuing propensity of Radio 3 to engross and provoke even depend upon John Drummond's acerbic contention that it broadcasts to 'about 30 minorities, each of which is characterized by its intense dislike of the other 29'?[2] Either way, given the BBC's increasingly uncertain status, it looks as if the survival of the network in anything like its present, let alone past, form is likely to depend upon an intensifying battle between the principles of value for money, and value for values.

NOTES

Source: 'Into the Third Dimension?', *The Independent* (Section Two, Friday), 27 September 1996; rev. 2008.

1   Humphrey Carpenter, *The Envy of the World: Fifty Years of the BBC Third Programme and Radio 3*, London, Weidenfeld and Nicolson, 1996.
2   Ibid., pp. 335-36.

13   *It's a Cultural Revolution*

It was around 1960 that Benjamin Britten told a sympathetic interviewer: "I remember at a tennis party at Lowestoft once, about the time I was leaving school, I was asked what career I intended to choose. I told them I intended to be a composer. They were amazed! 'Yes, but what else?'" Even at the height of his success and influence, Britten evidently continued to regard this provincial response as typical of an inveterate British philistinism: "The average Briton thought, and still thinks, of the Arts as suspect and expensive luxuries."[1]

Two years later, he went on to develop this theme in what was to remain his only formal statement of his position as a composer in his much-reprinted lecture, *On Receiving the First Aspen Award*. True musical communication, he argued, only occurred within the 'holy triangle' of composer, performer and listener if each was actively involved in the experience. The composer's part in this, Britten thought, was to serve the needs and aspirations of performers and listeners – and through them, the larger community – with the utmost adaptability, skill and artistry he or she could command, limited only by the promptings of his or her artistic, social or personal conscience. Admittedly, listeners' powers of focussed attention were increasingly menaced by the proliferation of canned background music; admittedly, composers could all too easily be deflected from their natural gifts by 'pressure groups which demand true proletarian music; snobs who demand the latest avant-garde tricks; critics who are already trying to document today for tomorrow.' Nonetheless, Britten was firm in demanding what he felt to be the genuinely involved composer's due in the 'semi-socialist Britain' of his day: that his art should be accepted as an essential part of human activity and consequently of value to the community, and that, in return, he should be adequately paid – 'we must at least be treated as civil servants'.[2]

The quaintness, as one might now think, of the latter formulation, is doubtless an index of how much seems to have changed since then. Or has it? In the Royal Philharmonic Society Annual Lecture for 2002, *Public Culture, Private Passions*, the composer, broadcaster and festival director Michael Berkeley – Britten's godson, no less – could be heard lamenting that most of his British contemporaries were still compelled to buy their own composing time out of some other occupation. Not only were commercial publishing and Performing Rights falling away, but public funding bodies, translating their residual utilitarian suspicion of artists into ever more strident demands for 'accountability' and 'accessibility' seemed ever less willing to subsidize risky work. For instance, Berkeley continued, the Arts Council grant he received to commission pieces for the Cheltenham Festival was now less than a third of that of seven years before when he first became artistic director – and this at a time when, building on the achievements of Britten and Tippett, this country currently fielded an array of compositional talent that compared favourably with any other in the world. How was it, he asked, that, not just the general public conditioned by the short attention spans of mass entertainment but also an intelligentsia that still tried to keep up with the latest in books, films and fine arts seemed so indifferent to our serious composers, compared with equivalent publics on the Continent? And how could this be reversed save by ever more enlightened education of the young?[3]

In so saying, Berkeley was of course recapitulating an ideal not just of Britten and Tippett, but also of Holst and Vaughan Williams before them, running back to William Morris's famous declaration: 'I do not want art for a few any more than I want freedom for a few or education for a few …'[4] It was in this spirit that such publicly funded institutions as the BBC and the Arts Council spread their cultural bounty in those hugely productive decades of semi-socialist consensus after the Second World War. What Britten died too early to detect, and Berkeley failed quite to focus, was the ferocity with which this very ideal has latterly come under attack. It was Alexander Goehr, in yet another diagnostic lecture entitled *The Songs We Love to Sing* delivered at the 1998 Aldeburgh Festival, who asserted that, over the last decade or so we have been living through the turmoil of nothing less than an ongoing cultural revolution.[5]

The most obvious symptom, he claimed, has been the denunciation of precisely those ideals and institutions of high culture bequeathed by the post-war consensus as elitist, paternalistic, often extravagantly mismanaged and irrelevant to the concerns of young people or an increasingly multi-cultural Britain. But behind all this, Goehr discerned a more fundamental confrontation 'between a high culture, demanding an actively participating listener, and a commodity-producing music industry with all the modern means of selling its products.' The latter, he suggested, reflects the drive towards 'a new commercial utopia – a controlled environment in which nothing unsaleable or disagreeable is to be seen,' or, presumably, to be heard. Accordingly, genuinely participatory musical experience epitomized by Britten's 'holy triangle' has increasingly been subverted or replaced by the passive stimulation of pleasing background music, or foreground music – Philip Glass, Michael Nyman, John Adams – composed out of the same bland clichés. 'If, as it seems, the industry must win, then the Cultural Revolution will have been accomplished,' concluded Goehr. Except that, 'I have the impression that, if anything, a greater number of our young grow up deeply committed to music, playing, listening and even composing it.' Just as in the past the Western classical tradition often seems to have attained its most intense and meaningful expression under conditions of privation, warfare or political repression, so, it seems, there will always be those musicians and music lovers, however small a proportion of the total population, who wish to perpetuate the heritage as an alternative, or irritant, to whatever consumerist utopia might seem to threaten.

Admittedly, given the genuinely diversifying society of this country, it seems improbable that the surviving directors and institutions of our post-war high culture will ever regain quite the centrality and influence they once exercised. The support that composers can expect from that quarter, therefore, will doubtless remain restricted. But then the likeliest immediate development seems more along a third path that Berkeley did touch on, when he noted the increasing tendency of funding bodies to direct what music subsidies they still have less into commissions than into 'outreach' programmes – sending composers and performers into schools, prisons and whatnot to try to raise the interest of the young and the marginalized in creativity and new music. At best, such activities doubtless achieve positive results and may indeed seem to fulfil Britten's ideal of being musically useful to the community. But in the last resort, they tend to depend more upon the abilities of a composer as an animateur, even a social worker, than upon his or her creative individuality. For those who continue to believe in the Western ideal of composition, at best, as a means of revealing aspects of human thought and feeling that can be grasped and articulated in no other way, this third path could well prove the least rewarding of all. All the more ruefully one remembers Stravinsky's injunction, that composers ultimately 'have a duty toward music, namely, to invent it.'[6]

NOTES

Source: 'It's a Cultural Revolution', *The Independent*, 1 November 2002.

1   Murray Schafer, *British Composers in Interview*, London, Faber, 1963, p. 124.
2   Benjamin Britten, 'On Receiving the First Aspen Award' (London, Faber, 1964) in: *Britten On Music*, ed. Paul Kildea, Oxford, OUP, 2003, pp. 255-63.
3   Delivered at the Royal Academy of Music, 26 October 2002.
4   Quoted in Imogen Holst, *Holst*, London, Faber, 1974, p. 21.
5   Alexander Goehr, *The Songs We Love to Sing: The Prince of Hesse Memorial Lecture 1998*, Aldeburgh, Britten Pears-Library, 1998.
6   Igor Stravinsky, *Poetics of Music*, tr. Arthur Knodel and Ingolf Dahl, New York, Random House, 1947, p. 54.

14   Last Waltz?

Whatever happened to the waltz? The question is current because we are all supposed to be living in an increasingly post-modern paradise in which composers, listeners – and dancers for that matter – now feel free to mix classical and pop, ethnic and electronic, austerity and kitsch, as the spirit takes them. And in recent centuries, no genre of Western music has crossed barriers of class, taste, wealth or custom so completely as the waltz itself. Though initially disguised under a variety of names such as German Dance or Ländler as it emerged in central Europe in the mid-eighteenth century, the waltz has always exploited triple time – three beats in the bar – whether as a slowish glide or a fastish dash, and has always involved clasped partners whirling one another around. The latter development soon moved moralists to denounce the lascivious waltz as the downfall of civilisation, but to no avail – not least because composers of the calibre of Mozart, Beethoven and Schubert realized that they could turn a penny on the side by scribbling sets of waltzes for court occasions or for the bourgeois music trade. In the 1790s, the waltz was already a popular craze – by 1819, it was aspiring to the highest flights of Art.

That year, the Viennese publisher Anton Diabelli sent a modest little waltz of his own making to some 50 composers, including Schubert and the very young Liszt, requesting a variation from each to put out in a collected volume. Yet what he got back from Beethoven some three years later was a set of no less than 33 variations comprising one of the profoundest masterpieces in the history of piano music. Meanwhile, Weber published a rondo for piano comprising a chain of waltzes enclosed between a more poetic introduction and epilogue. Subsequently orchestrated by Berlioz under the title, *L'invitation à la valse* (1841), this was to become a model for the waltz sequences developed by such dance band leaders as Joseph Lanner and Johann Strauss the Elder in the 1830s and '40s, and brought to perfection in such masterpieces of Strauss's most famous son as the so-called *'Blue Danube' Waltz*, Op. 314 (1867). By now, the introductions were symphonic elaborations, magical summonses to the couples at an Imperial ball to drift dreamily on to the floor before moving as one into the great circle of the opening waltz itself.

In fact, Berlioz had long since introduced the waltz into the symphony proper with his *Symphonie fantastique* of 1830, while Chopin and Liszt had developed the piano waltz into a vehicle for the subtlest nuances or the most diabolical display. By the mid-nineteenth-century, the waltz seemed ubiquitous, infusing the symphonies of Tchaikovsky as audibly as his ballets, and insinuating its way into the most private piano pieces of Brahms. When the young Richard Strauss (no relation) sought to evoke the 'dance song' of the Nietzschian Superman in his tone-poem *Also Sprach Zarathustra* (1896), he moved without the slightest inhibition into a Viennese waltz. Nor was this pervasiveness confined to ballroom or concert hall. The chorus of Hebrew slaves in Verdi's early opera *Nabucco* (1842) was already a kind of slow waltz; Gounod contrived to slip the flightiest French valse into *Faust* (1859); and even Wagner ultimately succumbed, evoking the flower maidens in *Parsifal* (1882) in what he called an 'American waltz' – by which he can only have meant the slow genre known at the time as the Boston.

Then in the 1900s, as if the pre-eminence of the waltz had raised it to a kind of early-warning system of the zeitgeist, something happened. Suddenly the waltz passages in Mahler's Fifth Symphony (1902) turned self-conscious and satirical; suddenly, in the run-up to the First World War, there appeared a whole clutch of scores – Ravel's *Valses nobles et sentimentales* for piano (1911), Debussy's ballet *Jeux* (1913), Berg's 'Reigen' from his Three Orchestral Pieces (1915) – in which waltz structures seem to dissolve, leaving mere drifts of feeling. Meanwhile, Stravinsky was siphoning off the feeling, leaving the mechanics in such dry little numbers as the waltz from *L'histoire du soldat* (1918), though it fell, once more, to Ravel to deliver what some have heard as the symphonic deathblow with his vision of Imperial Vienna whirling itself to oblivion in *La valse* (1920). True, the cult of the waltz lingered longer among composers of genteel light music and in the domains of the musical and the film score (Ivor Novello, Richard Rogers, *Murder on the Orient Express*), but as little more than nostalgic pastiche. As for waltzing itself, this now seems mainly confined to the ever more stylized world of ballroom dancing.

Well, doubtless the most popular forms have their day, and if we no longer write or dance waltzes, neither do we minuets or jigs. But there is something else here. Any survey of dance music since it began to be written down in quantity during the Renaissance will quickly reveal how the dominant dances at particular periods have tended to divide rather evenly between those in duple time – two or four beats in the bar – and those in triple time. This complementary relationship even held in the nineteenth century when the waltz, at its zenith, was almost rivalled by the duple-time polka.

It is at this point that one comes across a historical anomaly in twentieth-century dance music – indeed, in popular music as a whole – so pervasive it is rarely remarked upon. If one surveys the commercialization of the popular, from the emergence of ragtime, jazz and such dances as the tango before the mid-twentieth century and the evolution of rock, pop, disco and so on since, one finds that the music has been overwhelmingly cast in duple time. Of course, exceptions spring to mind, from the odd ragtime waltz by Scott Joplin to the slow triple-time ballads that have emerged occasionally in the charts over more recent decades. But the bias remains striking. Nor is it any longer confined to popular genres. Admittedly, the history of rhythm in twentieth-century music has been complicated by a sustained effort of several generations of 'advanced' composers to get away from any sense of regular pulse whatever – to achieve a perpetual irregularity of rhythm in keeping with the perpetual turnover of pitches freed from traditional tonality. Yet in the widespread retreat from such avant-garde aims over the last two or three decades, attempts to restore tonality, particularly in the more trundling modes of Minimalism, have brought corresponding obsessions with duple time. It is almost as unlikely to find Philip Glass coming out with a triple-time number as it is Oasis.

In this supposedly pluralistic era, we are therefore confronted by the singular and possibly sinister paradox that the casting of the vast bulk of the most marketable music in one of the two basic metres in Western tradition threatens the marginalization of the other. No doubt it would take the aesthetic, economic, psychological and philosophical insights of a latter-day Adorno to tease out the implications. For instance, if we accept the old association of duple time – the rhythm of marching, hammering and so on – with masculinity, and of triple time with femininity, what does the dominance of the duple really tell us about the status of women? And, as the disco beats boom through the shopping malls, do we begin to sense the grip of social control behind the glittering consumer choices? Duple time, or its double, quadruple time, is after all the beat of machinery, of military parades. It has to be rigid to work; if the second beat of a 2/4 bar is lengthened, treated as an up-beat, the metre immediately turns into triple time. Triple time itself, by contrast, can be treated with the utmost flexibility and still remain recognizable, as in the Viennese tradition of performance in which the second beat of the bar is minutely anticipated and the up-beat third can be prolonged as much as desired. Which is just one of the reasons why composers seeking to do something fresh and spontaneous, that flies free of the relentless beats that now oppress our sound environment, could do worse than reconsider the resources of rhythm and phrasing still latent in that old, old Straussian waltz.

NOTES

Source: 'Last Waltz', *The Independent (Eye on Friday)*, 1 May 1998. Johann Strauss II was the upcoming composer of the week on BBC Radio 3, from noon on Monday, 4 May 1998.

Envoi

Igor Stravinsky, Milein Cosman

In Search of an Ending

1 In Search of an Ending

'Great is the art of beginning, but greater the art is of ending,' wrote Edward Elgar in July 1900 on the revised score of his *Enigma Variations*. Although the triumphant first performance in June 1899 had proved the greatest breakthrough in his career, opinion had reached him that the ending seemed too abrupt. At first he had baulked at extending it: 'Now look here, the movement was designed to be concise,' he told his trusted editor at Novello, August ('Nimrod') Jaeger, 'I *could* go on with those themes for half a day but the *key* G is exhausted …'. However, he soon found a way – throwing in the organ as an extra option – to create the more grandiose ending usually played today. Some have subsequently felt it is too grandiose for the rest of the work. Yet the original ending, which Sir Frederick Ashton revived for his Royal Ballet choreography, does remain curiously truncated. So we have the paradox of one of the defining masterpieces of the late-Romantic repertoire with two endings, neither of which convinces everyone.

Not that the work is by any means alone in this. Wagner supplied an alternative concert-ending for the Prelude to *Tristan und Isolde* (1857-59) encompassing a snip from Act II and the final bars of Act III, though this is little heard today. Stravinsky added an alternative concert ending to his 1947 revision of *Petrushka* (1911), an oddly perfunctory one compared with the wonderful ending of the ballet itself. Bartók offered alternative codas to his Second Violin Concerto (1938) and Concerto for Orchestra (1943/45); Walton to his 'Cello Concerto (1956). Then there are those works which have contrasting endings built into their very structure: Shostakovich's Fourth Symphony (1936) culminates in what sounds like an absolutely final rampage, only to give way to a coda of utterly opposite remoteness and stasis; the epilogues of Vaughan Williams's 'London' and Sixth Symphonies (1913 and 1947) offer comparable instances. Sometimes this kind of double ending can mislead the unknowing. Audiences occasionally burst into applause where the stressful finale of Tchaikovsky's Fifth Symphony (1888) momentarily grinds to a halt on the dominant – only to hear the music start up again with the final march-like apotheosis of the work's motto theme.

More bemusing still are those pieces, like the perpetual canons of Bach or the minimalist noodles of Philip Glass, which one feels could continue going round and round without ever ending. Yet perhaps most disturbing are the pieces where the end seems utterly arbitrary, such as Malcolm Arnold's Fifth Symphony (1961) in which, just before the completion of the clinching Big Tune, the music suddenly vanishes into an eerie void. Are endings ever as immutable and final as they pretend to be, one wonders? Does a length of music have to have a defined ending to constitute a 'work'? Or is it ultimately true, as the saying goes, that works of art are never completed, only abandoned?

Even to attempt answers depends in the first place, of course, upon what we mean by an ending. At it most localized, this may simply comprise the rounding off of a phrase, a final unison or a harmonic cadence, whether on the end of a 16-bar dance, a 40-minute symphony or a three-hour opera. But most longer or more elaborate structures are likely to have quite lengthy last sections, perorations or codas to signal that the end is coming. In multi-movement structures such as symphonies, in which each movement has its own ending, but which are conceived to hang together in some larger unity, the matter may be more complicated still. It has, after all, long been an ideal of Western tradition that the course of a piece, including its ending, should already be somehow latent in its initial material. 'My end is my beginning, and my beginning is my end,' wrote the great fourteenth-century poet-composer Guillaume de Machaut, centuries before anyone thought of symphonies – setting his words to a melody accompanied by itself backwards. And there is plenty of evidence of later composers conceiving or sketching the endings of larger pieces quite early in the creative process as something to aim at or work towards.

Admittedly, it took some time for the ending of the finale to become crucial in symphonic thought. Early symphonies, including most of Haydn's, tended to concentrate their structural centre of gravity in their opening movements, with slow movement, minuet and finale following as almost suite-like extras. It was Mozart who first shifted the centre of gravity to the finale in his 'Jupiter' Symphony (1788). This concept arguably reached its apogee in Beethoven's Fifth (1808), in which not just the finale's coda but its entire triumphant C major course is felt as the fulfilment and resolution of everything set in train by those fateful C minor poundings half an hour before. But then Beethoven was composing at a time in which musicians still agreed that the essential function of an ending was to complete a structure, to achieve a sense of closure by reaffirming the home key. A whole range of harmonic, rhythmic, gestural and textural conventions lay at hand to reinforce this sense. True, an exceptionally witty composer like Haydn might disrupt such conventions for a tease; true, they might be suspended for exceptional dramatic or pictorial reasons – a mad scene, say, or a representation of chaos. But not till the nineteenth century did these conventions come under strain, partly because old patterns of patronage, with their built-in expectations and tastes, were beginning to break down and composers found themselves in the market place competing ever more keenly in the pursuit of musical novelty.

One could, indeed, cite the conclusion of Tchaikovsky's Fifth as a typical symptom of such strains: a finale in which the ending of the movement and the ending of the whole symphony no longer coincide. One could cite, too, the so-called 'finale problem' in which composers were often felt to have failed to devise symphonic finales that genuinely topped all that had gone before. Bruckner's last movements were regularly criticized on this basis, though it is possible he was trying to do something quite different. The situation was also complicated by the tendency of Romantic symphonists to place the structural centre of gravity not in the opening or closing movements but in their intervening slow movements. The logical conclusion of this development was to turn the slow movement *into* the finale, as Tchaikovsky did in his 'Pathétique' Symphony (1893), thus opening up an alternative tradition of finales for symphonists who no longer wanted to attempt the older style Beethovenian triumphalism

Which is not to say that nineteenth-century composers abandoned the older tradition of unambiguous cadential closure; on the contrary, they came up with two new procedures to reinforce such endings. One was to bring back a work's initial idea at its very end, as Brahms does so beautifully in the finale of his Third Symphony (1883), where the ardent first-movement motto returns, as it were, 'in calm of mind, all passion spent' – a nuance emulated as late as Stravinsky's Symphony in C (1940). This principle of clinching reprises was intensified in the triumphant finale coda of Bruckner's Eighth Symphony (1890), where the main themes of all four movements are cited in counterpoint; and it was formalized in the 'cyclic' methods of Liszt and César Franck, in which themes that have appeared in various transformations throughout a work fly home to roost at the end. The other, still bolder (if rarer) new procedure was to round off a work with a complete statement of an entirely new theme. Mendelssohn seems to have invented this in his 'Scottish' Symphony (1842), but Tippett was still doing it in his Concerto for Double String Orchestra (1939). Yet, as the decades passed, such endings tended to sound increasingly contrived, more in the nature of special cases.

For the twentieth century not only ushered in an ever more radical questioning of musical tradition – including the very concept of defined endings – but a new environment for composers and listeners alike. With the advent of recording and broadcasting, music was increasingly experienced as a more or less endless background, or as something randomly switched on and off in mid-flow. In response, more progressive composers have tried

three ways of keeping ahead in the end game. The first has been to set up the
strong expectation of a conventional ending gesture or cadence, and then to
subvert or withhold it, so that listeners have to complete it in their mind's ear.
The ending proper of *Petrushka* is a lovely example of subversion: the music
tiptoes to a stop on the keynote, only to be thrown into total doubt after a
pause by just one subsequent note a tritone lower. The apparently arbitrary
end of Arnold's Fifth is really also of this kind, since, although the big tune
is indeed deprived of its final cadence, we have already heard it complete
earlier on.

The second way of getting round the ending problem has been to suggest
that the music, though it might move beyond audibility, is essentially endless.
This was already implied in the lingering fade-outs of a number of late-
Romantic works, such as Mahler's *Das Lied von der Erde* (1909/1911), but
achieved its definitive form with the alternating chords receding to infinity
at the end of Holst's 'Neptune' in *The Planets* (1916) – endlessly imitated since,
not only in 'serious' music, but ad nauseam in pop. The third way of ending is
simply to cut off without warning. Already back in the 1830s, Schumann was
approaching such an idea in songs and piano pieces deliberately composed
to sound like incomplete fragments. In the 1910s, Erik Satie and Stravinsky
made a feature of mechanistic little pieces that suddenly just stopped, and this
has remained a composer's resource: for example, in the way that the collage-
like cross-cuttings and superimpositions of material in all three movements of
Tippett's Concerto for Orchestra (1963) are snipped off, seemingly at random.

The trouble is, there is a limit to how variously one can use, subvert or
withhold traditional conventions of ending in a meaningful way. For that
matter, the second category – the eternal fade-out – has already been done
to death; and even the third category of randomly stopping dead begins to
lose its surprise value with over-use and to become just another convention.
So what now? Are there, in fact, *any* other ways of ending a work? Haydn,
of course, was quite capable of putting what sounds like an ending at the
beginning of a piece, as in the perfect cadence that opens the first movement
of his String Quartet Op. 33, No. 5 (1782); or of fragmenting the final statement
of the main theme of his finale, as in Op. 33, No. 2 (1782), so perversely, that
we are still caught out when it starts up yet again – only to stop. One might
wonder how far such antics might be taken before a composition ceased to
be apprehensible as a work: with its opening planted as an insert into the
previous work in the programme, perhaps, or its ending postponed until the
audience has left and then performed to an empty concert hall?

But one suspects the work-concept is not so easily subverted. After all, in
that ultimate anti-work of John Cage, in which the performer or group sit
down and do not play for four minutes, thirty three seconds (1952), while the
audience listens to whatever random environmental noises happen to occur,

the moment the player(s) rise to signal the end of the allotted time cannot help but come over with a strong sense of an ending.

NOTES

Source: 'In Search of an Ending', *BBC Music Magazine*, November 2004; rev. 2008.

2   *It Tolls for Thee*

The scene: Ludgate Hill one Sunday in June 1914 with the bells of St. Paul's in full swing. A passing taxi suddenly pulls to a halt. Inside, the young Igor Stravinsky – visitor to London for his new opera *The Nightingale* (1908-14) – is listening intently and scribbling notes on a scrap of paper. He turns to his companion, the critic Edwin Evans, and exclaims: "That is really the ideal way of making music. A man pulls a rope … the bells do all the rest. The music is not in him; it lives in the bells …"[1]

Evidently, the business of bell-ringing appealed to Stravinsky, not only as a Russian, but also as an anti-romantic, dedicated to suppressing Wagnerian subjectivity through a renewal of the ritualistic. But his remark is also historically suggestive. For something like 800 years, composers fascinated by bell sounds have been trying to absorb them into the fabric of Western music, yet somehow, the bells have always resisted the process. The most obvious reason for this is the sheer weight and size of genuine church bells. 'Great Paul', the tenor, or lowest bell of the scale of 12 Stravinsky was listening to, has a fundamental tone no deeper than D sharp below middle C, but it weighs 16,003 kilogrammes. A few theatres, such as the Bolshoi, have a set of church bells for operatic effects; dragging them on to the concert platform, however, is another matter.

Of course, musicians have used smaller sets of chimes and hand-bells since the Middle Ages, but no one ever pretended they remotely approached the sonority of the real thing. For the church bells in the satanic finale of his *Symphonie fantastique* (1830), Berlioz was obliged to prescribe an alternative of pianos and gongs, and a variety of contraptions with piano wires and what-not have been tried over the years for the deep bells of Montsalvat in Wagner's *Parsifal* (1882) – while tubular bells, apparently first used in Arthur Sullivan's oratorio *The Golden Legend* in 1886, remain lightweight substitutes. These days, it is possible to use a recording of bells or to link up a live performance electronically with a belfry miles away for passages such as the end of Gustav Mahler's 'Resurrection' Symphony (1894), which demand a surpassing clamour. But it is still not quite the real thing.

Then again, even a tuned church bell is a complex sound. In addition to its fundamental tone, one may hear a so-called hum note an octave below and a fainter scale-like array of higher resonances known as upper partials and usually dominated by the minor third immediately above the fundamental. These are all clearly audible in Jonathan Harvey's remarkable tape piece, *Mortuos Plango, Vivos Voco* (1980), based upon an electronic analysis of the great tenor bell of Winchester Cathedral. If a bell remains untuned or has suffered a fault in casting, its resonances are likely to compound a more complex character still – as we all know from the baleful boomings of Big Ben.

Because a set, or 'ring', of bells is usually tuned in a major scale, the minor-sounding upper partials impart a continuous tingle of dissonances – technically known as false relations – when they are rung in a melodic sequence. When several bells are heard simultaneously, as in the harmonized tunes of seventeenth-century Dutch carillons, it can sound very weird indeed. And, not least, bell-ringing developed long ago into an entire craft on its own. On the Continent, it has been traditional to allow each bell to swing at a rate governed by its own weight, thus setting up continuous cross-pulsations between them – an effect echoed by Busoni in the prelude to his opera *Doktor Faust* (1916-23). But seventeenth-century England saw the emergence of an intricate practice of varying chimes by methods of permutation known as change-ringing. One could argue that a complete cycle of, say Stedman Doubles – named after the greatest campanologist of the day – pre-empts the Minimalism of Steve Reich by three centuries.

No doubt the unwieldiness of church bells, the problems of matching their resonances with traditional harmonies and textures and, maybe, the mystique of bell-ringing, have inhibited all but the boldest composers from attempting any sustained fusion. But the vocal, instrumental and orchestral music of the West is, by comparison, full of sounds and patterns suggested by bells. Already, in a fourteenth-century anonymous English motet, *Campanis cum cymbalis*, one hears the lower voices chiming like bells. William Byrd captures the sounds of change-ringing in his hypnotic keyboard tour-de-force, *The Bells*, from around 1600. J. S. Bach could rarely resist plucked chords and pinging woodwind patterns where his cantata texts referred to bells – most graphically in a recitative of No. 198, the *Trauerode* (1727), which symbolizes all the funeral bells in Saxony lamenting its dead Electress.

The Viennese Classical composers, manipulating perhaps the most integrated and self-referential language music has ever known, seem to have been the least interested in bells. But their sounds soon reappear amidst the picturesque paraphernalia of Romanticism – for instance, the tolling trombones at the climax of the fourth movement of Schumann's 'Rhenish' (Third) Symphony (1851), inspired by a visit to Cologne Cathedral. Most preoccupied, of course, were the Russians, inspired by their own layered tradition of bell-ringing; one thinks of Rimsky-Korsakov's tintinnabulating *Russian Easter Festival* overture (1888), or Rakhmaninov's birth-to-death choral symphony, *Kolokola* (1913) setting Edgar Allan Poe's poem 'The Bells'. Even here, it was Mussorgsky, the composer least beholden to musical tradition, who drew bell sounds most convincingly into his continuities – as in the awesome grandeur of the coronation scene of *Boris Godunov* (1874) or the serene prelude to *Khovanshchina* (1872-80). And of French composers, it was those influenced by the Russians – Debussy, Ravel and Messiaen – who evoked the most vivid bell sounds, though often touched by intimations of that wholly other source of bell-like sonorities, the far-Eastern gamelan.

Among other twentieth-century figures, Manuel de Falla had an especially fine ear for the overtones of the Spanish bells in his background, and bell-registrations also mark the piano writing of Poulenc. Meanwhile, the English have drawn strikingly from their own tradition. Britten's 'Sunday Morning' Interlude in *Peter Grimes* (1945) climaxes in one of the most cunning of all re-creations in orchestral terms of a deep bell sound; Tippett ran a familiar pattern of change-ringing through the brilliant Intrada of his *Birthday Suite for Prince Charles* (1948); and Gordon Crosse's *Changes* (1966), an entire choral work founded on bell texts and sounds, deserves far more frequent performance. But of all the moderns, Stravinsky remains the most bell-obsessed, from the 'Infernal Carillon' in *The Firebird* (1910) by way of the cracked wind-band chimings of the *Symphonies of Wind Instruments* (1920) to the hieratic resonances of his culminating masterpiece, the *Requiem Canticles* (1966).

And never more so than in the aftermath of that moment of exaltation on Ludgate Hill. Transcribing his jottings of the St. Paul's Bells into a sketchbook, Stravinsky recorded what had really moved him: 'Astonishingly beautiful counterpoint such as I have never heard before in my life.'[2] That same month in London, he conceived his cantata on Russian wedding customs, *Les noces*, which was finally to emerge in 1923 for soloists, chorus and an unprecedented accompaniment of four pianos and extensive percussion. At the end of its 25 minutes of joyous chanting and stamping, the voices fall silent and we are left with the spacious resonances of bells, as though some long-term cycle of permutations was coming round to its conclusion. It is a totally original ending, yet one that sounds as if it had always been waiting to be written: an ending, as it were, both before and after music.

NOTES

Source: 'It Tolls For Thee', *The Independent*, 22 December, 1990.

1   Quoted in: Eric Walter White, *Stravinsky: The Composer and His Works*, 2nd ed., London, Faber, 1979, p. 564.
2   Vera Stravinsky and Robert Craft, *Stravinsky in Pictures and Documents*, London, Hutchinson, 1979, pp. 126-27.

3   *Echoes from Selborne*

He tested the hearing of bees by hallooing at them through a speaking trumpet and listened in still weather for the boom of the evening gun from Portsmouth, some 20 miles away. He sought the most curious comparisons to convey the different songs of birds and wondered whether all owls hooted in the key of B flat. To 'fine music' itself, he confessed an almost dangerous susceptibility: 'I am haunted with passages therefrom night and day; and especially at first waking, which, by their importunity give me more uneasiness than pleasure...' No doubt the very rarity of the experience actually heightened his responsiveness, since he cannot have heard larger-scale pieces more than a few times a year, on trips back to his old university, Oxford, or up to London. But we read Gilbert White now for what he heard – almost as much as for what he saw – in the tiny Hampshire village where he spent most of his life and died in 1793.

'In a district so diversified as this, so full of hollow vales, and hanging woods, it is no wonder that echoes should abound,' he wrote to the Honourable Daines Barrington in Letter 38 of the second half of *The Natural History of Selborne* (1789). Barrington, lawyer and polymath, must have pricked up his ears, for he had published one of the earliest treatises on birdsong and, nine years before receiving White's letter, a celebrated investigation of the youthful Mozart's musical prowess. White duly proffered an account of how he had discovered the focal point and measured the length of many local echoes by shouting Latin verses, sounding a hunting horn, or a 'tunable ring of bells'; how the response seemed to vary according to the time of day or the 'elasticity' of the air; even how a gentleman of fortune might build an echo in his park by strategic placing of banks and walls – complete with quotations from Virgil, Ovid and Lucretius concerning the myths and superstitions the Ancient World attached to the phenomenon.

As a pioneering field worker before the parcelling-out and professionalizing of the sciences had much advanced, White was bound to take an interest in the acoustic properties of his environment along with everything else. As an Oxford Fellow he could scarcely resist disporting his classical learning in allusions to Echo as 'this loquacious nymph'. Yet had he been touched with the more speculative spirit of his enlightened contemporaries, the French Encyclopaedists, he would surely have gone on to consider the possible relevance of echoes to the origins of music itself. For while sounds of winds, waves and torrents might have been held up as sources of sonorous texture, and the songs of certain birds as models of decorative melody, it could be argued that echoes, alone among natural phenomena, suggest an actual polyphonic structure: that of a round or canon. Whether Western counterpoint actually arose this way – from the echoing, say, of plainchant in great cathedrals – or perhaps, more likely, from the very failure of people in groups to sing in unison, will presumably never be established. Nonetheless echo effects, simulated or evoked for their own acoustic delight, as a compositional resource or as a carrier of picturesque, literary or emblematic implications, have run through music at least since the revival of ancient learning and the growth of scientific enquiry in the Renaissance.

The most obvious way of imitating an echo was to pass the music between two or more groups placed at varying distances. Though doubtless practiced intermittently far earlier, this was first systematically developed in the instrumental canzonas Andrea and Giovanni Gabrieli bounced around St. Mark's Venice in the later sixteenth century. And, without ever quite becoming a tradition, such spatial arrangements have recurred often enough since – from Mozart's elaborate if bland *Notturno* for four orchestras, к. 286 (1777), to Karlheinz Stockhausen's ricocheting *Gruppen* (1957) for three. Yet already by the 1580s madrigal composers – such as Lassus in his popular part-song, *O la, o che bon eccho* (1581) – had begun to explore the other obvious echo-equivalent of simply repeating a texture or phrase at a lesser volume. From the antiphony of diapason and echo in a Sweelinck organ fantasia to the loud and soft repetitions of a Vivaldi concerto ritornello, the device was to become one of the clichés of the Baroque – doubtless partly because it enabled composers to fill out twice as many bars from the same patch of composition.

But it is Monteverdi we tend to think of as the first composer to explore the more expressive or iconographic correspondences of echoes. The flamboyant tenor duet, with one singer echoing the other, that crowns the *Gloria* of his Vespers of 1610 comes over not just as an embodiment of cathedral acoustics, but an emblem of the heavenly vault itself. Richer still is Act 5 of *Orfeo* (1607), where the hero's lament on losing Eurydice for the second time is punctuated by the dying falls of a male-voice Echo. Maybe Monteverdi was consciously emulating a tradition initiated by the double echoes in Jacopo Peri's Florentine *intermedio, Aron and the Dolphin* (1589) and the echo-duet between the Soul and Heaven in Cavalieri's *Rappresentazione di anima e di corpo* (1600) – reminding us that one composer's borrowing from another can also be construed as an echo. In context, the Monteverdi not only seems to conjure up the desolate plain of Thrace in which the scene takes place, but, for contemporary audiences, would surely have insinuated an ironic twist to the classical myth of Narcissus and Echo.

Associations of echoes with pathos or remoteness were to run through Baroque music from Carissimi's *Jephte* (before 1650) to Purcell's *Dido and Aeneas* (1689) before re-emerging after a lull rather differently in nineteenth-century Romanticism. Now, with the enhanced technology of stage and orchestra, the effort was towards greater realism – the echoes of the chase in Berlioz's 'Royal Hunt and Storm' from *The Trojans* (1856-58), Wagner's reverberating fjords in *The Flying Dutchman* (1843) – yet, on the other hand towards the weaving of echo imagery into the very fabric of symphonic discourse. The landscape-like spaciousness of Bruckner, Mahler or Sibelius surely owes as much to their continual deployment of reverberant fanfares and dying horn calls as to any vastness of form or forces. And with Debussy, for whom resonances became the very stuff of music, the motivic argument itself seems to dissolve into receding echoes of initial statements that, often enough, he seems to have withheld.

One could go on with Copland's prairie echoes and Tippett's antiphonal trumpets. The point is that, reconstituted or stylized, echoes seem to have touched off all manner of musical procedures; to have been heard, through a kind of pathetic fallacy, as expressive of all kinds of human emotion; to have symbolized innumerable dualities – from body and spirit to event and memory. For Gilbert White, pacing his hollow vales of a calm summer evening in the depths of a countryside undisturbed as yet by flight paths, bird scarers and distant trains, there would have been still another, ultimate duality as the echoes of his hunting horn faded away: awareness of a silence more profound than many of us will ever know.

On a June day of 1968, this author – in an earlier incarnation as English lecturer at a south coast college of education – found himself in White's garden watching his students wander earnestly around with their sheaves of extracts from *The Natural History*. So intense was the noonday heat, so drowsy the hum of bees, there could be little thought of testing the reverberations from the slopes of the nearby Hanger. Far away, in London and Paris, Chicago and Prague, other students would be raising their clamour all that momentous summer. Yet no tumult of the time has continued to echo in this pair of ears like the resonant stillness of Selborne.

NOTES

Source: 'Now You Hear It, Now You Don't', *The Independent*, 26 June 1993; rev. 2008. The article commemorated the bi-centenary of the death of Gilbert White on 26 June 1793.

4   The Rest is Silence

If only … but it is not just the roar of the traffic, the rattle of passing trains, the jumbo-jets droning overhead. Down the shopping malls twinkle the up-tempo ditties; Vivaldi vibrates through the take-aways, Heavy Metal booms from the boutiques. No doubt we are wise enough to all this by now: stimulation, conditioning are the names of the game – to put a spring in the step, not to worry, to spend … But what about the student next door tapping out his essays to endless Country and Western; the gent with the personal stereo in the tube-seat opposite reading the *Financial Times* to – can it be? – *Götterdämmerung*; the car full of kids yelling at one another over the throbbing disco track, which gets switched off indifferently in mid-sequence as they tumble out of the doors? A placebo, a drug, something only noticed when it stops? The mania of the Victorians for cramming every façade, fabric, mantelpiece, wallpaper with decorative detail has been put down to a deep cultural *horror vacui*. Has the fear of emptiness simply transferred itself in our own time from the visual to the auditory?

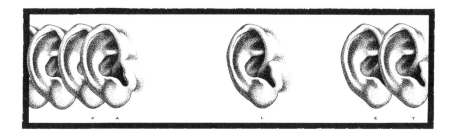

In any case, it has deeply affected recent music. It is one of the ironies of Minimalism that it has so singularly failed to exploit that most minimal quality of all – silence itself. Once the opening phase pattern of a Steve Reich piece begins its interactions, we know we are in for a span of absolutely unbroken incessantness for the next twenty minutes, forty minutes, hour and a half … Or take pop: once Kate Bush or whoever begins to permutate her ululations over an alternating pair of synthesizer chords, we know she may build to a climax but that in the final fade out, the same unresolved chords will still be alternating to eternity. Whatever became of the song as a memorable closed structure of balanced phrases? Whatever became of musical form as a sequence of contrasts clearly demarcated by pauses, silences?

∿

For a dramatic demonstration of the power of such silences, one has only to think of the opening bars of Beethoven's Fifth Symphony (1808) – and then to imagine their loss of tension if the long notes were sustained across the pauses. The Fifth struck its early listeners as the wildest, most unbridled music they had ever heard. Yet the seven minutes of its opening movement are articulated by no less than forty sudden silences of varying lengths. For Beethoven, as for Stravinsky, an exactly measured silence was equivalent to an exactly measured sound; the interaction of the two was part of what constituted rhythm. But then who gives the pauses in Beethoven, or any other Baroque, Classical or Romantic score, their full, true value any more? Among the starriest conductors and soloists, traditionalists and authenticks alike, it seems ever the thing to press forward, to create excitement – or to evade silence? – by continually shortening the written rests and pauses. And such is our habituation to incessantness, that almost no one notices or complains.

~

'Like a long-legged fly upon the stream/His mind moves upon silence,' wrote W. B. Yeats. An urban, social composer such as Mozart may shape his music through the most subtle play of phrases and pauses, but one never ceases to sense the ambience, the silken rustlings and appreciative sighs as it were, of a listening audience in its background. Yet certain composers have the power to convey an intense silence behind their very notes. The hushed, wandering lines of a Haydn middle-period symphonic slow movement or the nocturnal *frissons* of a Bartók string quartet can sound as if heard against an emptiness like the great Hungarian plains themselves – as remote as an ethnomusicologist's recording of a Japanese shakuhachi keening from some mountain shrine.

~

Structurally, silences generally point backwards. The mind's ear has a natural propensity to go on revolving a sound just heard through an ensuing silence until interrupted by another sound. No composer has ever exploited this more powerfully than Anton Bruckner in the gigantic pauses that punctuate his symphonies. As an organist used to resonant spaces, he evidently conceived such pauses as filled with receding echoes of the preceding music; moments for the sound to settle and clear. Yet even in such dead-sounding acoustics as the (pre-improved) Royal Festival Hall, where the resonance lingers only in the imagination, there persists at such moments a sense of structural grounding and weight: the pauses are, in effect, the pillars that support the glorious musical vaulting.

∽

Yet a silence can be just as anticipatory, as Wagner demonstrates in the aching, up-beat pauses at the opening of the Prelude to *Tristan und Isolde* (1857-59). Admittedly, compared with many composers, Wagner can often seem poor in silences; unwilling to arrest for a moment the wave-like surge of his musico-dramatic continuities. In the tumultuous peroration to *Götterdämmerung* (1869-74), where the Rhine bursts its banks and Valhalla goes up in flames, it has become customary, almost universal, for conductors to insert a short up-beat silence (or '*Luftpause*') just before the final reminiscence of the 'Redemption through Love' motif of the last few bars. One has heard performances in which the entire meaning of the four nights of the Ring has seemed to hang on that pause. Yet Wagner barely hints at anything of the sort in his score.

∽

The sound of silence? In choosing Keats's *Ode to a Grecian Urn* as text for the slow movement of his *First Choral Symphony* (1925), Holst faced the paradoxical problem of setting such lines as 'Thou foster-child of silence and slow time' and 'Heard melodies are sweet, but those unheard/Are sweeter ...'. One solution might have been to insert long pauses, actual silences, between the setting of each few words. Instead, to evoke a music that speaks 'not to the sensual ear' but 'to the spirit ditties of no tone', Holst lodges his setting in a hushed, unchanging and expressionless harmonic structure of bare fifths – suggestively offering the quality of stasis as an emblem of, an equivalent to, silence.

∽

And the silence of sound? Into the already irregular rhythms towards the end of his Variations for Piano (1937), Anton Webern inserted an empty bar of three beats with an instruction to continue an *accelerando* on from the previous bar. But, unless the pianist is observed beating the speed-up to himself or is heard muttering "Eins, zwei, drei", as, according to Peter Stadlen, Webern himself did when coaching him for the work's first performance, how could one possibly hear a silent acceleration?[1] It is an especially tricky question here, since the music resumes at a slower speed than when it left off. The theorists are still haggling about this one.

~

At Harvard in 1951, John Cage stood in an anechoic chamber and realized that there could be no such thing as total silence, at least for the human ear; one would always hear the fizz of one's nervous system and the rumble of one's bloodstream.[2] He accordingly conceived *4'33" for Any Instruments* (1952) with instructions *not* to play for precisely that length of time. From such 'performances', Cage finally concluded that the mundane joys of the sound-world about us are so absorbing that one might as well abandon art altogether. But not every one took it that way. Wicked old Stravinsky expressed the hope that silent pieces might catch on and that soon there would be entire contemporary music festivals devoted to them: 'I hope, moreover, that they turn out to be works of Nibelungen length.'

~

But of course, it is not just the nature of human perception that precludes absolute silence. There is the matter of the musical mind itself, haunted by all manner of favourite passages, echoing with melodies, rhythmic gestures or harmonic progressions from who knows where. For composers, that 'who knows where' is quite likely to prove the inception of invention of their own; indeed, one gains the strong impression from the biographies of such figures as Sibelius or Shostakovich that the primary function of dashing their thoughts down on paper was the sheer release of ridding the mind of its musical obsessions. Gilbert White's complaint, on waking, that music-on-the-brain could give more uneasiness than pleasure reminds us that lay-listeners may be similarly affected – without the composer's means of relief. Either way, the reliving of music in the memory can seem almost as intense as hearing the real thing. Waking in the deep silence of the night, your mind is suddenly invaded by the development section of the first movement of Beethoven's *Pastoral Symphony* …

NOTES

Source: 'The Sound of Silence', *The Independent*, 21 December 1990; rev. 2008.

1   Peter Stadlen, 'Serialism Reconsidered', *The Score*, No. 22, February 1958, pp. 12-27.
2   John Cage, *A Year from Monday*, London, Calder and Boyars, 1968, p. 134.
3   Igor Stravinsky, *Themes and Conclusions*, London, Faber, 1972, pp. 30-31.

Bibliographical Note and Index

Harrison Birtwistle, Milein Cosman

Bibliographical Note

Bayan Northcott (b. 1940) took a BA in English at Oxford in 1962, followed by a Dip. Ed. in 1964. After teaching English for several years (1964-70), he gained a (postgraduate) BMus at the University of Southampton in 1971. Thereafter he became a self-employed writer on music for various publications and, from 1978, a periodic composer. This note shows the principal sources of his writings on music and his main compositions up to the end of 2008, including the essays reprinted in this book. Each section is arranged chronologically.

1 Regular or Semi-regular Contributions to Magazines and Newspapers

MUSIC AND MUSICIANS (April 1969-April 1974): long features on Peter Maxwell Davies (April 1969), Alexander Goehr (October 1969), Copland (November 1969), Composers of the 'Sixties (January 1970), Fauré (April 1970), Nicholas Maw (May 1970), Tippett (November 1970), Cheltenham Diary (September 1971), Pierre Boulez (December 1971), Elliott Carter (August 1972) and Jonathan Harvey (March 1973); 71 other articles and reviews.

THE NEW STATESMAN (January 1973-August 1976): 109 music articles, book and record reviews; a short obituary on Shostakovich (15 August 1975).

THE SUNDAY TELEGRAPH (July 1976-June 1986): 420 weekly review columns; 95 monthly record reviews; leader page articles on Britten (5 December 1976), *The New Grove Dictionary* (22 February 1981) and Elgar (26 February 1984); a feature on Handel (24 February 1985).

THE INDEPENDENT (from October 1986 to the present): 301 Arts Page lead music articles – weekly (10 Sept 1988-31 August 1991), fortnightly (17 August 1991-8 October 1994) and thereafter approximately monthly (4 November 1994-21 May 2004); 71 'Music on the Air/Radio Round-up/Music on Radio' columns, approximately monthly (14 July 1995-11 May 2001); some 530 shorter articles, obituaries and reviews.

BBC MUSIC MAGAZINE (from August 1992 to the present): composer features on Copland (November 1995), Poulenc (December 1998), Holst (August 1999), Britten (November 2001), Wagner (November 2004) and Elliott Carter (December 2005); a brief column on 'The Classic Book' (August 1992-August 2002); and 31 'Bayan Northcott Reviews...' monthly book-page columns (August 2002-January 2005); some 40 shorter articles, book and record reviews.

2   Intermittent Contributions to Magazines and Periodicals

THE LISTENER: eight instalments of 'Last Week's Broadcast Music' (August 1971-September 1972); articles on Alexander Goehr (21 January 1971 and 25 November 1971), Music of 1956 (18 March 1971), Tippett (11 November 1971), Alexander Goehr and Dominic Muldowney (21 July 1983), Colin Matthews (6 September 1884), Wolpe (3 July 1986) and Gordon Crosse (3 December 1987); 4 shorter articles.

THE MUSICAL TIMES: articles on Robin Holloway (August 1974), Anthony Payne (January 1975), Elliott Carter (December 1978), Oliver Knussen (September 1979), Copland (November 1980), Walton (March 1982), Arthur Berger (May 1982), Alexander Goehr (August 1982), American Music (July 1983), Nicholas Maw (August 1987), Elliott Carter (December 1988) and 'Auden and Music' (January-February 1993); 8 shorter reviews.

TEMPO: articles on Richard Rodney Bennett (December 1975), Robin Holloway (June 1976), Ligeti (December 1976), Weill (April 1977), Alexander Goehr (April 1978/July 1978), Finnish Music (February 1979), Robin Holloway (September 1979), Robert Simpson (January 1981), Gordon Crosse (July 1981), Schmidt (March 1985) and Wolpe (September 1985); 15 shorter reviews.

DANSK MUSIKTIDSSKRIFT: feature reviews of Per Norgaard's Symphony No. 3 (June 1977 and May 1978) and Berg's *Lulu* (May 1979 and May 1980); feature-surveys, 'Brev fra London' ['Letter from London'] 1-7, (November 1978-May 1981).

3   Dictionary Entries and Articles in Books

Entries on Elliott Carter, Alexander Goehr, Nicholas Maw, Jonathan Harvey, Robin Holloway and Oliver Knussen in *The New Grove Dictionary of Music and Musicians*, ed. Stanley Sadie, London, Macmillan, 1980; Carter entry revision in *The New Grove Dictionary of American Music*, ed. H. Wiley Hitchcock and Stanley Sadie, London, Macmillan, 1986; entries on Robin Holloway and Oliver Knussen in *The New Grove Dictionary of Opera*, ed. Stanley Sadie, London Macmillan, 1992; entry on Julian Anderson in *The New Grove Dictionary*, 2nd ed., London 2001.

'The Recent Music' (revision of *Tempo* articles of April and July 1978) in: *The Music of Alexander Goehr: Interviews and Articles*, ed. Bayan Northcott, London, Schott, 1980, pp. 88-103.

'That was 1985-86 – An Attempted Survey' in: *New Music 87*, ed. Michael Finnissy and Roger Wright, Oxford, OUP, 1987, pp. 1-9.

'Bayan Northcott in *The New Statesman*, 22 June 1973' (reprint of review of the premiere of Britten's *Death in Venice*, with 'Afterthought, 1985') in: *Benjamin Britten: Death in Venice*, ed. Donald Mitchell, Cambridge, CUP, 1987, pp. 200-04.

'Twaalf ensemblevisies' ('Twelve Ways with Ensembles') in: *Ssst! Nieuwe Ensembles Voor Nieuwe Muziek* [Holland Festival 1996], Amsterdam, International Theatre & Film Books, 1996, pp. 70-103.

'A Not-So-Little Music: Goehr's Op. 16 as paradigm' in: *Sing, Ariel: Essays and Thoughts for Alexander Goehr's Seventieth Birthday*, ed. Alison Latham, Aldershot, Ashgate, 2003, pp. 159-70.

'Preface' in: Hugh Wood, *Staking Out the Territory and Other Writings on Music*, ed. Christopher Wintle, London, Plumbago, 2007, pp. ix-xii.

4   *Longer Articles in Periodicals, Programme Books and Booklets*

'The Story of Vasco' [Gordon Crosse], *Opera*, Vol. 25, No. 3, March 1974, pp. 188-93.

'Since *Grimes*: A Concise Survey of the British Musical Stage', *Musical Newsletter*, Vol. 4, No. 2, New York, Spring 1974, New York, pp. 7-11 and 21-22.

'Opening up: British Concert Music since the War', *Musical Newsletter*, Vol. 5, No. 3, New York, Summer 1975, pp. 3-9.

'Carter the Progressive' in: *Elliott Carter, a 70th Birthday Tribute*, London, Schirmer, 1978, pp. 4-11.

'The Search for Simplicity' [Benjamin Britten] in: *Times Literary Supplement*, 15 February 1980, p. 182.

'Fascinatin' Modulation' [Elliott Carter] in: *New York Review of Books*, 31 May 1984, pp. 18-20.

'Alexander Goehr – ein Portrait' in: programme book for the premiere of *Die Wiedertaufer*, Deutsche Oper am Rhein, Duisburg, 19 April 1985.

'The Fine Art of Borrowing: Britten and Stravinsky' in: programme book for *The Forty-Seventh Aldeburgh Festival of Music and the Arts*, 10-26 June 1994, pp. 14-19.

'The Once and Future Tippett' in: programme book for the revival of *The Midsummer Marriage*, Covent Garden, November 2005, pp. 1-4.

5   *Radio Scripts, Miscellaneous, Programme Notes and Recording Notes*

Some 35 scripts for talks and programme presentation on BBC Radio 3, 1971-2001.

Two short runs of brief reviews: *Financial Times*, October-November 1972 and *The Daily Telegraph*, April 1975-July 1976; sundry one-off preview pieces, tributes, reviews, etc. in other publications.

Long programme notes on Tippett, Symphony No. 3 (Boston SO, 15 February 1974), Sibelius, *Kullervo* (BBC Proms, 29 August 1979), Sibelius, Symphony No. 1 (San Francisco SO, 29 April 1981), Copland, Symphony No. 3 (San Francisco SO, 29 February 1984), Britten, *Curlew River* (BBC Proms, July 2004) and Tippett, *The Knot Garden* (BBC SO, Barbican, May 2005); some 70 further programme notes and short composer profiles, mainly for the BBC Proms.

Substantial notes for recordings of works of Michael Tippett, Elliott Carter, Alexander Goehr, Nicholas Maw, Oliver Knussen and others on the Philips, Argo, Unicorn, Chandos, Virgin, Deutsche Gramophon and Bridge labels, and for recordings of Elisabeth Lutyens, Colin Matthews, Jane Manning and collections of orchestral music and song for the NMC label, of which the author has been a director since 1991.

6   *Published Compositions (Stainer & Bell)*

Sonata for Solo Oboe, Op. 1, 1978, 7'.

Six Japanese Lyrics, Op. 2, Japanese verse trans. Northcott, 1971/79,
    sop., cl., vn., 8'.

Fantasia for Guitar, Op. 3, 1982, 9'.

Hymn to Cybele, Op. 4, Catullus trans. Northcott, 1983,
    sop., ten., bar., chorus, 2 perc., db., 12'.

Sextet, Op. 5, 1984-85,
    fl./picc., cl./b. cl., pno., 1 perc., vn., vc., 12'.

Carillon (after Machaut), 1987,
    14 players, 5'.

Three English Lyrics, Op. 6, anon. 15th – 16th century texts, 1988,
    sop., cl., vla., db., 6'.

Of All the Instruments (after Purcell), 1994,
    fl., ob., cl., 1 perc., vn., vc., db., 2.30'.

Four Votive Antiphons, Op. 7, Medieval Latin texts, 1997/2003,
    mezzo, 3 ten., bar., or SATTB choir, 21'.

Concerto for Horn and Ensemble, Op. 8, 1990-98,
    solo horn + 10 players, 23'.

Fandango for Harpsichord, Op. 9, 2006, 7'.

Canticle: *The Doubting of Thomas*, St. John (Authorized Version), 2007,
    alto, ten., bar., optional ATB choir, organ, 5'.

Poet and Star, Thomas Hardy, 2008,
    sop., ten., pno., 2.30'.

Index

Adams, John, 166-67, 186; *Nixon in China*, 167

Adès, Thomas, 95, 97; *Brahms*, 97; Piano Quintet, 97

Adorno, T. W., 35, 82, 123, 161, 190

Aeschylus, 91

Anon: *Campanis cum cymbalis*, 199; *Laudes Regie*, 176

Aesop, 102

Agee, James, 134

Andreissen, Louis, 166

Apollinaire, Guillaume, 103

Arnold, Malcolm, 194, 196; Symphony No. 5, 194, 196

Ashton, Frederick, 193

Auden, W. H., 17, 51-3, 64, **65-74**, 92, 129-30; *The Composer*, 66, 74; *Delia*, 71-2; *The Dyer's Hand*, 66; *For the Time Being*, 65, 68; *The Sea and the Mirror*, 73; *Thank You, Fog*, 74

Babbitt, Milton, 114, 138, 166

Bach, C. P. E., 35, 79

Bach, J. S., 6, 10, 22-3, 30, 32, 35-6, 46, 65, 70, **79-83**, 88-9, 111, 148, 160, 163, 178, 182, 199; Mass in B minor, 82; *Passion According to St. Matthew*, 79-80; *Singet dem Herrn*, 79; Cantata No. 198 (*Trauerode*), 199; *The Well-tempered Clavier*, 80-1

Barber, Samuel, 115

Barrington, Daines, 201

Bartók, Béla, 13, 105, 112, 117, 127, 156, 164, 179, 193, 205; Concerto for Orchestra, 193; Violin Concerto No. 2, 193

Beckett, Samuel, 51-2, 171

Beecham, Thomas, 104

Beethoven, Ludwig van, 3, 5, 7, **10-12, 13-16**, 17-18, 22-3, 34-5, 40, 56, 79-80, 89, 91, 95-6, 101, 110, 117-19, 122-23, 149-150, 152, 154-55, 163, 188, 194, 205, 207; *Fidelio*, 34, 56; String Quartet, Op. 95, 118; Symphony No. 3 (*Eroica*), 40; Symphony No. 5,

10-12, 155, 194, 204; Symphony No. 6 (*Pastoral*), 3, 4, 207; Symphony No. 9, 13-16

Beethoven, Karl von, 15

Bellini, Vincenzo, 61, 63

Benda, Georg, 55; *Medea*, 55

Benjamin, George, 39; *On Silence*, 39

Bennett, Richard Rodney, 182; *Murder on the Orient Express Waltz*, 189

Bent, Ian, 11

Berg, Alban, 26-8, 56, 61, 91, 103, 105, 111, 127, 156-57, 161, 164, 189; Four Pieces for Clarinet and Piano, 27; *Lulu*, 61; Three Orchestral Pieces, 189; *Wozzeck*, 28, 56, 61, 91, 168

Berio, Luciano, 43, 56, 73, 171; *Circles*, 56; *Un re in ascolto*, 73; *Sinfonia*, 171

Berlioz, Hector, 29, 61, 70, 79, 90, 163, 188, 198; *Symphonie fantastique*, 29, 90, 198; 'Royal Hunt and Storm', *The Trojans*, 203

Bernac, Pierre, 99, 100

Berkeley, Lennox, 73, 128, 183; *Five Poems of W. H. Auden*, 73

Berkeley, Michael, 185-87

Bernstein, Leonard, 14, 73; Symphony No. 2 (*The Age of Anxiety*), 73

Birtwistle, Harrison, 13, 17-18, 60-1, 172; *Gawain*, 18, 60-1, 63; *Punch and Judy*, 172

Bizet, Georges, 31

Boosey, Leslie, 131

Bosch, Hieronymus, 37

Boulanger, Nadia, 131, 134,

Boulez, Pierre, 23-4, 28, 35-7, 43, 53, 57, 80, 100, 114, 138-40, 143, **163-65**, 166, 174, 181; *Le marteau sans maître*, 53; Piano Sonata No. 2, 165; *Répons*, 143

Boult, Adrian, 183

Bowles, Paul, 51

Brahms, Johannes, 7, 8, 10, 14, 34-5, 52, 65, 79, **95-7**, 101, 110, 114, 122-24, 138, 148, 163, 168, 180, 188, 195; Double Concerto, 97; *Fest- und Gedenksprüch*, 34; Symphony No. 1, 96; Symphony No. 3, 95, 122, 195;

Symphony No. 4, 95; *Variations on a Theme of Haydn*, 9; *Variations on a Theme of Handel*, 96
Brecht, Bertolt, 51, 65, 70, 72, 159-61
Brendel, Alfred, 97
Brett, Philip, 149
Bridge, Frank, 127
Britten, Benjamin, 34, 52-3, 55-6, 60-1, 63-9, 73, 80, 95, 97, 99, 100, 103, 108, 110-11, 114, 116-18, **121-25**, **127-32**, 148, 163, 172, 174, 181-83, 185-87, 200; *Ballad of Heroes*, 67; *Billy Budd*, 121, 130; *Cabaret Songs*, 67; *Cantata misericordium*, 128; *Canticle II*, 127, 132; *Coal Face*, 67; *Curlew River*, 172; *Death in Venice*, 122; *Gloriana*, 131, 183; *Hymn to St. Cecilia*, 67-8; *Les Illuminations*, 110; *A Midsummer Night's Dream*, 61, 131; *Night Mail*, 67; *Noye's Fludde*, 127, 132; *On This Island*, 67; *Our Hunting Fathers*, 67; *Owen Wingrave*, 122; *Peter Grimes*, 97, 121, 125, 128, 200; *Paul Bunyan*, 66-70; *The Prince of the Pagodas*, 130; *The Rescue*, 55; *The Rape of Lucretia*, 60, 128-29; *Serenade*, 52, 127, 132; *The Prodigal Son*, 172; *Sinfonia da Requiem*, 123, 127; Sonata for 'Cello and Piano, 97; *Spring Symphony*, 69; String Quartet No. 1, 110; String Quartet No. 3, 122; *The Turn of the Screw*, 56, 121-22, 130; *War Requiem*, 69, 121, 127, 131-32
Brown, Howard Mayer, 149
Bruch, Max, 179
Bruckner, Anton, 11, 13, 122, 195, 203, 205; Symphony No. 8, 195
Bryers, Gavin, 39
Buckland, Sydney, 100
Bush, Kate, 204
Busoni, Ferrucio, 199; *Doktor Faust*, 199
Byrd, William, 199; *The Bells*, 199
Byron, Lord, 56

Cage, John, 18, 42, **163-65**, 166, 171, 174, 197, 207; *4' 33", for Any Instruments*, 196, 207; *Music of Changes*, 165; *Sonatas and Interludes*, 164
Cahill, Thaddeus, 41
Campion, Thomas, 51-2
Carissimi, Giacomo, 202; *Jephte*, 202
Carpenter, Humphrey, 183-84

Carter, Elliott, 13, 17, 38, 95, 106-07, **134-40**, 171; Concerto for Orchestra, 136, 138-39, 172; *Double Concerto*, 38, 136, 138-39; *Holiday Overture*, 138; *Night Fantasies*, 137; Piano Concerto, 136; Piano Sonata, 135; Sonata for 'Cello and Piano, 135; String Quartet No. 1, 106, 136; String Quartet No. 2, 136; String Quartet No. 3, 137; *Triple Duo*, 134; Variations for Orchestra, 136
Casals, Pablo, 10, 72
Cavalieri, Emilio de, 202; *Rappresentazione di anima e di corpo*, 202
Chabrier, Emmanuel, 31, 101
Char, René, 53
Chitty, Alison, 61
Chopin, Frédéric, 34, 46, 79, 101, 103, 188
Cocteau, Jean, 100
Cooke, Arnold, 183
Cooke, Deryck, 46, 183
Cope, David, 45-7
Copland, Aaron, 7, 124, 135, 159, 179, 203; *Appalachian Spring*, 159
Corelli, Arcangelo, 32
Costello, Elvis, 39
Couperin, François, 80
Cowell, Henry, 105
Craft, Robert, 130-32, 148, 161
Crawford Seeger, Ruth, 104-07; *Diaphonic Suites*, 105, 107; *Music for Small Orchestra*, 105; *Rissolty, Rossolty*, 106; String Quartet, 105, 107; Suite No. 1, 105; *Three Chants*, 105, 107; *Three Songs of Carl Sandburg*, 105, 107
Cristofori, Bartolomeo, 42
Crosse, Gordon, 200; *Changes*, 200
Crotch, William, 88

Dahlhaus, Carl, 114
Dallapiccola, Luigi, 171-72; *Ulisse*, 171
Dante Alighieri, 93
Dargomizhsky, A. S., 63
Dart, Thurston, 38
Davies, Peter Maxwell, 28, 38, 138-39, 148, 172, 179, 181-82; *Taverner*, 38
Davies, Tansy, 39
Davison, Peter, 174
Debussy, Claude, 22, **29-31**, 61, 79, 93, 101, 156, 179, 189, 200, 203; *Études*, 31; *Gigues*, 31; *Ibéria*, 30; *Images*, 30-1; *Jeux*, 30-1, 189;

La fille aux cheveaux de lin, 179; *La mer*, 30-1; *Nocturnes*, 30; *Pelléas et Mélisande*, 61, 179; *Prélude à l'après-midi d'un faune*, 30-1; *Rondes de Printemps*, 31
Delibes, Léo, 23,
Delius, Frederic, 179
Del Tredici, David, 41; *Final Alice*, 41
Diabelli, Anton, 188
Diaghilev, Serge, 22, 74, 108, 179
Diana, Princess of Wales, 55
Dickinson, Emily, 143
Dolmetsch, Arnold, 37
Donizetti, Gaetano, 5
Donne, John, 66
Doone, Rupert, 67
Dove, Jonathan, 39
Dowland, John, 39, 66; *Lachrimae*, 39
Drummond, John, 183-84
Dun, Tan, 39
Duncan, Ronald, 60, 121
Dunstable, John, 180
Dürer, Albrecht, 80
Dvořák, Antonin, 180
Dylan, Bob, 51

Edward the Confessor, 176-77
Eisler, Hanns, 105, 159-62; *Hollywood Elegies*, 161
Elgar, Edward, 46, 95, 108-10, 114, 122, 179-80, 193; *Enigma Variations*, 193; Introduction and Allegro, 109; Symphony No. 3, 46
Eliot, T. S., 65
Eluard, Paul, 103
Eno, Brian, 45
Esterházy, Prince Nicolaus, 85, 154
Euripides, 74; *The Bacchae*, 74
Evans, Edwin, 198
Evans, Peter, 125
Ewart, Gavin, 64

Falla, Manuel de, 38, 101, 200; Harpsichord Concerto, 38
Fauré, Gabriel, 70,
Feldman, Morton, 52
Ferneyhough, Brian, 4
Finzi, Gerald, 176
Flaubert, Gustave, 92
Forster, E. M., 10, 65, 130
Foss, Lukas, 73; *Time Cycle*, 73

Franck, César, 195
Frescobaldi, Girolamo, 148
Freud, Sigmund, 92, 105
Furtwängler, Wilhelm, 14, 151-52

Gabrieli, Andrea and Giovanni, 202
Gardner, John, 72; *The Entertainment of the Senses*, 72
Gardiner, John Eliot, 82-3, 152
Géricault, Théodore, 169
Gershwin, George, 45, 125, 162, 167; *Porgy and Bess*, 125
Gesualdo, Carlo, 36
Giraud, Albert, 57
Glass, Philip, 4, 166-67, 186, 190, 194; *Akhnaten*, 167; *The Making of the Representative of Planet 8*, 167
Glinka, Mikhail, 31
Glock, William, 172, 182-83
Gluck, C. W., 63, 91, 101
Goehr, Alexander, 24, 28, 34, 39, 53, 172, 174, 182, 186-87; *The Deluge*, 28; *Naboth's Vineyard*, 172; *Sing Ariel*, 53
Goethe, J. W. (von), 51, 80, 93
Goldschmidt, Berthold, 46
Górecki, Henryk, 174
Graham, Colin, 121
Green, Kenneth, 121
Greenberg, Noah, 37, 73
Grieg, Edvard, 56
Groves, Charles, 179
Gounod, Charles, 61, 101, 189; *Faust*, 189
Guevara, Che, 169

Haba, Alois, 42
Hall, Ernest, 175
Handel, G. F., 32-3, 63, 66, 82, 96, 148, 150, 180; *Messiah*, 177, Mozart version, 33
Handley, Vernon, 179
Harewood, George (Lord), 129
Harnoncourt, Nikolaus, 37-8, 152
Harsent, David, 60-1,
Harvey, Jonathan, 6-8, 198; *Mortuos Plango, Vivos Voco*, 198
Hassall, Christopher, 113
Haydn, Joseph, 13, 35, **84-86**, 89, 94, 122, 142, 151, 153-55, 166-67, 180, 182, 194, 196, 205; Sonata in G minor, Hob. XVI, 84-6; Symphony No. 45 (*Farewell*), 154-55; String Quartets Op. 33, Nos. 2 and 5, 196

Henze, Hans Werner, 64, 72-4, 125, 169, 171-72; *The Bassarids*, 74; *Elegy for Young Lovers*, 73-4; *Moralities*, 72; *The Raft of the Medusa*, 169
Herbert, David, 121
Herz, Djane, 105
Hildegard of Bingen, 104
Hindemith, Paul, 28, 37-8, 110, 112, 117; *Kammermusik* No. 5, 110
Hitler, Adolf, 10, 90-1, 159,
Ho Chi-Minh, 169
Hoffmann, E. T. A., 155
Hofmannsthal, Hugo von, 61, 70, 73
Hofstadter, Douglas, 45-6
Hogarth, William, 71, 128
Hogwood, Christopher, 147-49, 151-52
Holloway, Robin, 33, 64, 73, 141, 174; *Boys and Girls Come out to Play*, 64; *Clarissa*, 64; *Domination of Black*, 33
Holst, Gustav, 116, 176, 181, 186, 196, 206; *First Choral Symphony*, 206; *Hymn of Jesus*, 116; *The Planets*, 196
Honegger, Arthur, 100, 131
Hopkins, Gerard Manley, 52
Housman, A. E., 51-2
Howells, Herbert, 176
Howes, Frank, 108
Huckbald, The One-Legged of Gröbhausen, 37
Huxley, Aldous, 159

Ibsen, Henrik, 92
Indy, Vincent d', 148
Isaac, Heinrich, 148
Isherwood, Christopher, 66-7, 159
Ives, Charles, 105, 134

Jacob, Max, 103
Jacquet de la Guerre, Elisabeth-Claude, 104
Jaeger, August, 193
Janáček, Leoš, 38, 63, 142, 163, 174
Joachim, Joseph, 10, 163
Joplin, Scott, 189

Kagel, Mauricio, 38, 82; *Music for Renaissance Instruments*, 38; *Passion According to St. Bach*, 83
Kallman, Chester, 70-4
Kandinsky, Wassily, 26-7
Karajan, Herbert von, 10, 149, 153

Keats, John, 52-3, 206
Keller, Hans, 4-5, 12, 20, 25, 57-8, 66-7, 74, 82, 95, 121-22, 124-25, 157, 180, 183
Kennedy, J. F. (President), 72, 169
Kennedy, Michael, 108, 114
Kenyon, Nicholas, 149, 184
Kermode, Frank, 53
King, Martin Luther, 169, 171
Kirkpatrick, Ralph, 38
Klemperer, Otto, 80, 150, 159
Knussen, Oliver, 73, 107, 172; *Requiem: Songs for Sue*, 73
Korngold, E. W., 159, 161-62; Symphony in F sharp major, 159; *Die tote Stadt*, 159

Lambert, Constant, 108
Landowska, Wanda, 37-8, 81, 101, 150
Lang, Fritz, 159-60
Lanner, Joseph, 188
Larkin, Philip, 53
Lassus, Orlando di, 202; *O la, o che bon echo*, 202
Lawrence, D. H., 180
Lean, David, 121
Lessing, Doris, 167
Lévi-Strauss, Claude, 171
Ligeti, György, 43, 56; *Aventures*, 56
Liszt, Franz, 33, 35, 70, 79, 90, 188, 195
Lowenberg, Alfred, 64
Lomax, John and Alan, 106
Lucretius (Titus Lucretius Carus), 201
Luther, Martin, 80
Lutyens, Elisabeth, 38, 73, 104, 182-83; *The Teares of Night*, 38

MacColl, Ewan, 106
Machaut, Guillaume de, 36, 194; 'My end is my beginning', 194
McNaught, William, 121, 123
Maelzel, Johan, 13-14
Maeterlinck, Maurice, 61
Mahler, Alma, 104, 159
Mahler, Gustav, 14, 27, 46, 79, 81, 104, 110, 123, 132, 156-57, 159, 171, 189, 196, 198, 203; *Das Lied von der Erde*, 110, 196; Symphony No. 2, 171, 198; Symphony No. 5, 189; Symphony No. 10, 46
Malipiero, G. F., 148
Mallarmé, Stéphane, 30
Mann, Thomas, 159-60

Manning, Jane, 57
Mao Zedong, 178
Marc, Franz, 26
Maria Theresa (Empress), 85
Martland, Steve, 166
Marx, Karl, 92,
Mason, Colin, 108
Massenet, Jules, 101
Matthews, Colin, 46
Matthews, David, 46, 174-75
Mauceri, John, 159
Maw, Nicholas, 73, 174, 182; *Nocturne*, 73;
    Scenes and Arias, 182
Meck, Nadezhda von, 163
Mellor, David, 172
Mendelssohn, Fanny (Hensel), 104
Mendelssohn, Felix, 34, 51, 56, 79-80, 88, 95,
    110, 150, 180, 195; *Elijah*, 177; Symphony
    No. 3 (*Scottish*), 195
Mengelberg, Willem, 80
Menotti, Gian Carlo, 61
Messiaen, Olivier, 17, 18, 42-3, 53, 100, 143,
    164, 200; *Turangalîla-symphonie*, 18
Metastasio, Pietro, 61
Meyerbeer, Giacomo, 37, 61, 166; *Les
    Huguenots*, 38
Milhaud, Darius, 100; *Études*, 100
Millington, Barry, 90
Milner, Anthony, 183
Mitchell, Donald, 67, 111, 125
Mitropoulos, Dmitri, 159
Monet, Claude, 30
Monteverdi, Claudio, 60, 94, 101, 148, 163,
    166, 172, 202; *L'Orfeo*, 60; Vespers of 1610,
    202
Morgan, Robert P., 149
Morley, Thomas, 122
Morris, R. O., 32
Morris, William, 181, 186
Mozart, W. A., 13, 23, 29, 33-5, **45-7**, 55, 61,
    64-5, 70, 72-3, 79-80, 85, **87-89**, 91, 94, 101,
    104, 114, 122-23, 142, 147, 150, 154-55, 163,
    166, 182-83, 188, 194, 202, 205; *Così fan
    tutte*, 29, 34, 91; *Die Entführung aus dem
    Serail*, 85; *Musikalisches Würfelspiel*, 87;
    Notturno for four orchestras, K. 286, 202;
    Le nozze di Figaro, 168; Piano Concerto
    in E flat, K. 271, 88; Piano Concerto in C,
    K. 467, 87; Requiem, 46; String Quartet
    in D minor, K. 421, 183; String Quintet

in G minor, K. 516; Symphony No. 41
    (*Jupiter*), 194; *Zaide*, 55
Munch, Edvard, 26
Munrow, David, 37-8
Murrill, Herbert, 66
Mustel, Victor, 42
Mussorgsky, Modest, 61, 91, 101, 111, 199;
    Boris Godunov, 91, 199 *Khovanshchina*,
    199

Nabokov, Nicolas, 74, 128; *Love's Labours
    Lost*, 74
Nancarrow, Conlon, 107
Newman, Alfred, 159
Nicholls, David, 106
Nietzsche, Friedrich, 70, 91, 93
Nixon, Richard, 169
Nono, Luigi, 169
Norrington, Roger, 10, 15, 149-50, 152
Novello, Ivor, 189
Nyman, Michael, 186

Offenbach, Jacques, 101
Ogny, Claude (Compte d'), 85
Oliver, Stephen, 60-1, 63,
Orff, Karl, 166
Osborne, Nigel, 39
Ottaway, Hugh, 109
Ovid (Publius Ovidius Naso), 201

Palestrina, G. P. de, 177
Parry, Hubert, 179-80
Pärt, Ärvo, 174
Pavarotti, Luciano, 153
Payne, Anthony, 46
Pearce, Edward, 183
Pears, Peter, 61, 68, 99, 100, 111, 119, 121,
    129-30, 182
Peele, George, 71
Pergolesi, Giovanni, 22
Peri, Jacopo, 202; *Arion and the Dolphin*,
    202
Perle, George, 57
Perse, Saint-John, 136
Pfitzner, Hans, 61
Picasso, Pablo, 26, 116
Piper, John, 121-22
Piper, Myfanwy, 122
Plomer, William, 121
Poe, Edgar Allan, 199

Polzelli, Luigia, 84
Ponsonby, Robert, 183
Popper, Karl, 157-58
Pound, Ezra, 65, 180
Poulenc, Francis, 34, 38, 51, 66, **99-103**, 200;
    Les animaux modèles, 102; *Aubade*, 102;
    Les biches, 102; *Concert champêtre*, 101;
    Concerto for Two Pianos, 99; *Dialogues
    des Carmelites*, 99; *Figure humaine*, 99;
    Gloria, 102; *Les mamelles de Tirésias*, 99;
    Rhapsodie Nègre, 100; *Sept répons des
    ténèbres*, 102; Sinfonietta, 101; Sonata
    for Two Clarinets, 100; Sonata for Two
    Pianos, 102; *Tel jour telle nuit*, 99
Prokofiev, Sergei, 34, 101, 109-10, 115, 123,
    179; Violin Concerto No. 1, 109-10
Purcell, Henry, 39, 52, 119, 121-22, 132, 148,
    180, 202; *Dido and Aeneas*, 202

Rachmaninov, Sergei, 159, 199: *Kolokola*
    (The Bells), 199
Ravel, Maurice, 19, 34, 95, 101-02, 111, 113,
    127, 179, 189, 200; *Boléro*, 19: *La valse*, 189;
    Valses nobles et sentimentales, 189
Ravenscroft, Thomas, 67
Reed, Henry, 183
Reger, Max, 95, 156
Reich, Steve, 4, 166-67, 199, 204; *The Desert
    Music*, 166
Reichardt, J. F., 51
Reinhardt, Max, 159
Richter, Hans, 80
Richter, Sviatoslav, 182
Riley, Terry, 167; *In C*, 167
Rimbaud, Artur, 66
Rimsky-Korsakov, Nicolas, 31, 199; *Russian
    Festival Overture*, 199
Robson, William, 176-77
Rogers, Richard, 189
Rorem, Ned, 73
Rosen, Charles, 4, 5, 11, 34, 82, 154, 157
Rossini, Gioacchino, 70, 123
Rousseau, Jean-Jacques, 55; *Pygmalion*, 55
Roussel, Albert, 110, 115; *Bacchus et
    Ariadne*, 110; Symphony No. 3, 110; *Suite
    en fa*, 110
Rubbra, Edmund, 95, 183
Ruders, Paul, 39
Ruggles, Carl, 105-07, 134

Sackville-West, Edward, 55
Saint-Saëns, Camille, 88
Salieri, Antonio, 46, 88
Samuels, Robert, 163
Satie, Erik, 101, 156, 166-67, 196
Sax, Adolphe, 42
Schenker, Heinrich, 151-52
Schiff, David, 134-39
Schiller, Friedrich, 15, 122
Schillinger, Joseph, 45
Schmidt, Franz, 156
Schoenberg, Arnold, 5, 19, 24-5, **26-8**, 35-6,
    52-3, 56-8, 80, 95-6, 103, 111, 122, 127, 134,
    138, 156-57, 159-62, 164, 173-74, 180-82;
    Erwartung, 19, 27; Five Orchestral
    Pieces, 27-8; *Die glückliche Hand*, 26;
    Gurrelieder, 56; *Kol Nidre*, 56; *Modern
    Psalm*, 56; *Moses und Aron*, 56-7; Piano
    Concerto, 161; *Pierrot lunaire*, 27, 53, 57-8,
    160; *A Survivor from Warsaw*, 56, 58;
    String Trio, 161; Three Pieces for Piano,
    Op. 11, 26; Variations for Orchestra,
    Op. 31, 5, 111; Violin Concerto, 161
Schopenhauer, Arthur, 93, 157-58
Schubert, Franz, 11, 34, 51-2, 56, 88-9, 101,
    123, 132, 142, 182, 188; *Abschied von der
    Erde*, 56; *Winterreise*, 182
Schumann, Clara, 95, 163
Schumann, Robert, 4, 14, 27, 33, 56, 95-6,
    101, 180, 196, 199; *Manfred*, 56; Symphony
    No. 3 (*Rhenish*), 199
Schütz, Heinrich, 34, 148, 182
Schweitzer, Albert, 81
Scriabin, A. N., 26, 105, 156
Scribe, Eugène, 61
Scruton, Roger, 174-75
Sculthorpe, Peter, 39
Searle, Humphrey, 55
Seeger, Charles, 105-06
Seeger, Peggy, 106
Seeger, Pete, 106
Sellars, Peter, 52
Serkin, Rudolf, 157
Shakespeare, William, 53, 55, 60, 63, 74, 93
Shaw, G. B., 104, 107
Shelley, P. B., 6
Shostakovich, Dmitri, 108, 110, 115, 123, 127,
    130, 132, 174, 179, 182, 193, 207; Symphony
    No. 4, 193

Sibelius, Jean, 6, 8, 11, 14, 42, 44, 51, 56, 65, 108-10, 203, 207; *Nightride and Sunrise*, 109; Symphony No. 5, 109; *Tapiola*, 109

Simpson, Robert, 11, 13, 34, 181-83

Sitwell, Edith, 53, 55

Sloboda, John A., 8

Smith, Bessie, 118

Smyth, Ethel, 104, 106; Mass in D, 104; Overture *Antony and Cleopatra*, 104

Spenser, Edmund, 53

Splod, Tatiana, 37

Stadlen, Peter, 14, 206

Stanford, C. V., 179

Steiner, Max, 159

Stevens, Bernard, 183

Stevens, Wallace, 136

Stiedry-Wagner, Erika, 57

Stockhausen, Karlheinz, 4, 13, 17, 19, 43, 137-38, 165, 171, 174, 183, 202; *Gesang der Junglinge*, 43; *Grüppen*, 202; *Momente*, 19

Stösslova, Kamila, 163

Straus, Joseph N., 106

Strauss, Johann, 157, 188; 'Blue Danube' Waltz, 188

Strauss, Johann (the elder), 188

Strauss, Richard, 13, 27, 29, 38, 56, 61, 63, 70, 150, 159, 163, 188; *Also Sprach Zarathustra*, 188; *Elektra*, 27; *Enoch Arden*, 56; *Der Rosenkavalier*, 29; *Salome*, 27, 61; *Symphonia domestica*, 38

Stravinsky, Igor, 8, 14, 17-20, **22-5**, 33-6, 43, 45, 51, 53, 57-8, 64-5, 69-72, 74, 80, 94, 96, 101-02, 108-13, 116, 123, **127-32**, 134, 142, 147, 149, 153, 156, 159-62, 163-64, 180, 182-83, 187, 189, 193, 195-96, 198, 200, 205, 207; *Abraham and Isaac*, 131-32; *Agon*, 21, 131; *Apollo* (*Apollon Musagète*), 23, 128, 130; *Cantata*, 127; *Canticum sacrum*, 102, 148; *Dumbarton Oaks* (Concerto in E flat), 23; *The Fairy's Kiss*, 23, 33; *The Firebird*, 22, 127, 200; *Fireworks*, 102; *The Flood*, 127, 132; *Jeu de Cartes*, 128; Mass, 23, 161; *Les noces*, 200; *Oedipus Rex*, 23, 128, 130-31; *Orpheus*, 23, 161; Piano Concerto, 23; Piano Sonata, 23, 34-5; *Petrushka*, 22, 127, 160, 193, 196; *Pulcinella*, 22, 102; *Ragtime*, 102; *The Rake's Progress*, 22, 69, 71, 73, 128-30, 161; *Requiem Canticles*, 127, 131-32, 200; *The Rite of Spring*, 22, 127, 142, 148;

Serenade in A, 102; *The Soldier's Tale*, 22; Symphony in C, 110, 195; *Symphony of Psalms*, 127-28; *Symphony in Three Movements*, 159; *Symphonies of Wind Instruments*, 21, 200; *Threni*, 148

Striggio, Alessandro, 60

Strindberg, August, 26

Stubbs, Annena, 121

Suk, Josef, 156

Sullivan, Arthur, 61, 198; *The Golden Legend*, 198

Süssmayr, F. X., 46

Sutherland, Graham, 121

Swann, Donald, 183

Sweelinck, J. P., 202

Szymanowski, Karol, 156

Tablet, Hilda, 183

Tallis, Thomas, 33, 148, 177

Taruskin, Richard, 149

Tavener, John, 141, 172, 174; *Celtic Requiem*, 141; *The Whale*, 172

Tchaikovsky, P. I., 8, 23, 33, 79, 95-6, 101, 163, 188, 193, 195; Symphony No. 5, 193, 195; Symphony No. 6 (*Pathétique*), 195

Telemann, G. P., 82

Tennyson, Alfred (Lord), 56

Theremin, Leon, 41

Thomas, Dylan, 121, 125

Thomson, Virgil, 139

Tick, Judith, 106

Tippett, Michael, 32, 34, 52, 61, 64, 66, 69, **116-20**, 148, 172, 181-82, 186, 195-96, 200, 203; *Boyhood's End*, 119; *A Child of Our Time*, 119-20; Concerto for Double String Orchestra, 32, 118, 120, 195; Concerto for Orchestra, 196; *Fantasia Concertante on a Theme of Corelli*, 32, 119-20; *Fantasia on a Theme of Handel*, 32; *The Heart's Assurance*, 119; *The Ice Break*, 119; *King Priam*, 116; *The Knot Garden*, 119-20, 172; *The Mask of Time*, 119; *The Midsummer Marriage*, 118-19; *New Year*, 118; Piano Concerto, 119; *The Rose Lake*, 116, 119; Sonata for Four Horns, 119; Symphony No. 1, 119; Symphony No. 2, 119, 183; *Suite for the Birthday of Prince Charles*, 200; *The Vision of St. Augustine*, 119; *The Windhover*, 52

Tomasini, Luigi, 84

Tovey, Donald Francis, 10-12
Trevis, Di, 61
Turner, J. M., 30

Varèse, Edgard, 41, 43, 105-07, 134, 136, 164; *Ecuatorial*, 41; *Déserts*, 43
Vaughan Williams, Ralph, 33, 80, 122, 179-82, 186, 193; *Fantasia on a Theme of Thomas Tallis*, 33; *A London Symphony*, 193; *On Wenlock Edge*, 179; *Pastoral Symphony*, 181; Piano Concerto, 179; *A Sea Symphony*, 179; Symphony No. 4, 179; Symphony No. 6, 179, 193
Verdi, Giuseppe, 13, 23, 56, 61, 63-5, 70, 92-3, 123-24, 163, 189; *Nabucco*, 189; *La traviata*, 56
Vernon, P. E., 52
Virgil (Publius Vergilius Maro), 201
Vivaldi, Antonio, 5, 80, 202, 204

Wagner, Cosima, 80
Wagner, Richard, 3, 7, 14, 22, 24, 29-30, 35, 61, 63-5, 70, 79-81, **90-4**, 95-6, 104, 114, 121, 123-24, 138, 150, 153, 163, 189, 193, 198, 203, 206; *Faust Overture*, 90; *Die Feen*, 90; *Der fliegende Holländer*, 92, 203; *Götterdämmerung*, 91, 92, 204, 206; *Der Liebesverbot*, 90; *Lohengrin*, 92-3; *Die Meistersinger*, 80, 90, 92-3; *Parsifal*, 92, 93, 96, 122, 189, 198; *Das Rheingold*, 81; *Rienzi*, 90-1; *The Ring*, 3, 91-3; *Siegfried*, 29, 91, 121; *Siegfried Idyll*, 91-2; *Tannhäuser*, 92; Symphony in C, 90; *Tristan und Isolde*, 65, 90-3, 137-38, 193, 206; *Die Walküre*, 81, 92; *Wesendonck Lieder*, 91
Walton, William, 34, 53, 56, 72, **108-15**, 179-80, 193; Bagatelles for Guitar, 113; *The Bear*, 111; *Belshazzar's Feast*, 109, 112; *Capriccio burlesco*, 113; 'Cello Concerto, 113, 193; *Crown Imperial*, 109; *Façade*, 53, 56, 108, 112; *The First Shoot*, 111; *Gloria*, 111; *Henry V*, 113; *Improvisations on an Impromptu of Benjamin Britten*, 113-14; Partita, 110, 112; *Portsmouth Point*, 108, 111; *The Quest*, 112-13; *Scapino*, 113, 179; *Siesta*, 108; Sinfonia Concertante, 109; Sonata for Strings, 113; String Quartet in A, 110, 113; Symphony No. 1, 108-09, 112-13; Symphony No. 2, 108, 113; *The Twelve*, 72; *Troilus and Cressida*, 108, 110, 113-14; *Variations on a Theme of Hindemith*, 111, 113-14; *Varii capricci*, 113; Viola Concerto, 109-10, 113; Violin Concerto, 108-10, 112-13; Violin Sonata, 110-11, 113
Weber, C. M. von, 56, 91, 93, 188; *Euryanthe*, 91; *L'invitation à la valse*, 188; *Der Freischütz*, 56
Webern, Anton, 26-8, 35, 103, 148, 157, 206; Variations for Piano, 206
Webster, James, 154-55
Weill, Kurt, 72
Weir, Judith, 104, **141-43**; *The Bagpiper's String Trio*, 142; *The Consolations of Scholarship*, 142; *I Broke off a Golden Branch*, 142; *King Harald's Saga*, 141, 143; *Moon and Star*, 143; *Music for 247 Strings*, 141; *A Night at the Chinese Opera*, 141; *Several Concertos*, 141; *The Welcome Arrival of Rain*, 142
Werfel, Franz, 159
Wesendonck, Mathilde, 90
West, Nathaniel, 64
Whistler, J. M., 30
White, Gilbert, **201-03**, 207
Whitman, Walt, 179
Williamson, Malcolm, 130
Wilson, Angus, 182
Wolf, Hugo, 70, 95
Wolpe, Stefan, 136
Wood, Henry, 179
Wood, Hugh, 114, 182
Wood, James, 42
Woolf, Virginia, 104
Woolrich, John, 39; *The Theatre Represents a Garden – Night*, 39

Yeats, W. B., 39, 51, 65, 205
Young, La Monte, 166

Zander, Benjamin, 15
Zehme, Albertine, 57
Zelter, C. F., 51